Educational Television – What Do People Want?

COMMUNICATION RESEARCH AND BROADCASTING
No. 12

A publication series of the
Internationales Zentralinstitut für das Jugend- und Bildungsfernsehen (IZI)

Other titles from this series:

No. 11
Educational Programmes on Television -
Deficiencies, Support, Chances
Contributions to an International Symposium
Edited by Manfred Meyer. 1993. 284 pages. Paperback.

No. 10
Aspects of School Television in Europe
A Documentation
Edited by Manfred Meyer. 1992. 596 pages. Paperback.

No. 9
Media Communication in Everyday Life
Interpretative Studies on Children's and Young People's Media Actions
Edited by Michael Charlton and Ben Bachmair. 1990. 224 pages.
Paperback.

No. 8
Television and Young People
A Bibliography of International Literature 1969-1989
Compiled by Kurt Aimiller, Paul Löhr and Manfred Meyer
1989. 225 pages. Paperback.

No. 7
Children and Families Watching Television
A Bibliography of Research on Viewing Processes
Compiled by Werner Müller and Manfred Meyer
1985. 159 pages. Paperback.

No. 6
Children and the Formal Features of Television
Approaches and Findings of Experimental and
Formative Research
Edited by Manfred Meyer
1983. 333 pages. Paperback.

(Available from the IZI)

Educational Television – What Do People Want?

Proceedings of a European conference

Edited by Manfred Meyer

UNIVERSITY
UP *of*
LUTON PRESS

A publication of the
Internationales Zentralinstitut für das
Jugend- und Bildungsfernsehen (IZI)
Munich 1997

British Library Cataloguing in Publication Data
A catalogue record for this book is available from the British Library

ISBN: 1 86020 528 3

This is No. 12 of
COMMUNICATION RESEARCH AND BROADCASTING
A publication series of the Internationales Zentralinstitut für das
Jugend- und Bildungsfernsehen (IZI)
Address: Bayerischer Rundfunk
              Internationales Zentralinstitut
              D – 80300 München
Telephone: +49 (0)89 5900 2140
Fax: +49 (0)89 5900 2379
Head: Paul Löhr
Series Editor: Manfred Meyer

Published by
John Libbey Media
Faculty of Humanities
University of Luton
75 Castle Street
Luton
Bedfordshire LU1 3AJ
United Kingdom
Telephone: +44 (0) 1582 743297; Fax: +44 (0) 1582 743298
e-mail: ulp@luton.ac.uk

Cover design: Derek Virtue, DataNet
Printed in Great Britain by Bookcraft Ltd, Midsomer Norton, UK

Contents

Preface

In April 1996, the *Internationales Zentralinstitut für das Jugend- und Bildungsfernsehen* (IZI) held an international conference on the premises of the Bayerischer Rundfunk, that ran under the title 'Educational Programmes on Television: What Do People Want – What Do They Get?'

The aim of the conference was to present a selection of noteworthy educational programmes produced by European television stations that had been accepted by a larger audience as being 'interesting' or 'instructive'. Furthermore, we wanted to discuss issues of the acceptance und uses of such programmes in the light of the latest results of programme and audience research. We invited research experts and asked them to focus on the following aspects:

- viewers' attitudes towards television and their expectations of it as a medium for education and learning;
- programme interests and preferences that go beyond entertainment, sports or news programmes;
- image and acceptance of educational programmes;
- types of viewers and users, differences in information processing and learning styles and their influence on television viewing behaviour.

The overall objective of the project, however, was to stimulate and expand the ongoing discussion about the future and the functions of public service broadcasting in a competitive media environment, particularly with regard to the educational remit, which is – at least according to the media legislation in many countries – still valid.

Although rich in tradition, educational broadcasting units have had to face hard times within the last few years. The basic inhouse arguments against the production or acquisition of quality educational programmes centre around the relatively low ratings for such programmes. It is the market shares that play an increasing role in the competition with commercial broadcasters. Television, it is said, is too expensive a medium to provide continuing education and specialized instruction for small segments of the population, whereas learning material for specific instructional purposes – e.g. for specialized vocational education and training – is better provided by other media such as computer teachware, CD-I or the World Wide Web.

There is, on the other hand, the educational remit for public service broadcasters. If the adherence to this principle is to make sense and be economically justified, the audience shares will have to be large enough.

Educational broadcasters have found various ways of attracting larger numbers of viewers, for example by:

- increasing their promotional and marketing activities;
- searching for popular formats to attract mass audiences for educational or educative programmes as well;
- making efforts to re-assess the educational or information needs of specific audiences; or
- going 'downmarket', i.e. trying to gain hitherto unreached audience segments, which might imply lowering the educational impact or hiding the educational intention ('education by stealth').

These and others initiatives led to quite a few success stories in educational broadcasting that we thought worth being analysed and presented as case studies, i.e. in the context of their elaboration, implementation and evaluation.

There were also indications that the reconsideration of formats and contents of the programme output – aiming at mass education rather than at small-scale or individualized instruction – went hand in hand with a new and revived concern for viewers' needs and interests, their preconceptions of the uses of television viewing in general and their different notions of learning from TV presentations.

We invited policy makers and producers in educational braodcasting, specialized journalists and researchers, liaison personnel in educational institutions and organisations that have gained experience in collaborating with educational broadcasters or have provided support for educational programmes.

The conference we considered to be only part of a documentation and publication project that was to comprise the following elements or steps:

- the documentation of pertinent literature, to be entered into our bibliographical database;
- the collation of research findings and the elaboration of state-of-the-art reviews on the aspects mentioned;
- the organisation of an expert meeting to discuss the aims and possible contents of an international workshop;
- the organisation of the international conference mentioned above;
- the publication of the conference proceedings in both English and German, perhaps in other languages as well, if competent partners could to be found.

Launched in 1994, the project had initially been publicised under the working title 'Learning from television – what do people want?'. In May 1994 we called together a meeting of experts to advise us as to whether our project would make sense and be of any use to the professional community.[1]

It was soon clear that we should not restrict ourselves to the aspect of learning. We were warned that any notion of learning – not only in connection with television viewing – would be ambiguous and hard to define. We were also told that this topic would mean warming up old soup which the practitioners would no longer be interested in. The central question was not what people learn from television or if they learn anything at all, but whether they find a programme interesting and appealing enough to stay with. It would not really matter whether there was any pedagogical intention as long as it was attractive in itself. It was made clear to us on various occasions that any attempt to patronize the audience, to make them feel that any kind of learning is expected of them, would cause rejection and 'zapping' to another channel.

This was confirmed by our preparatory reading and the consultation of various other experts – e.g. editor or producer colleagues from the Bavarian Broadcasting Corporation to which we belong.

We were requested, rather, to take practical aspects into consideration. Why, for instance, is one programme or series more successful than another, even if this cannot be explained by a favourable time-slot alone? Is success determined by presentational style or by the choice of popular subjects or trends? Does carefully conducted preparatory research or intensive programme promotion play a decisive role?

We were also frequently requested to deal with the so-called 'New Media' and their influence on the future of educational braodcasting. However, nowadays there is so much talk in all quarters of the approaching convergence of the screen media and of the blessings of two-way communication by means of digital television that we considered it superfluous to have to contribute to this debate. With the articles by Herbert Kubicek and Gerhard Eitz (Chapter 7) we have preferred to try to show where the limits are.

As is the case with most of our work, our project was to centre on publicly broadcast television, available to all or at least to the majority of TV homes without additional payment, without the need to buy expensive additional equipment. Television is still a mass medium, i.e. it is best used when messages that are important for the cohesion of a society can be

---

1 Those who took part in this meeting were: Naomi Sargant, London, Visiting Professor at the Open University; Jane Quinn, Chief Education Officer at BBC Education; Robin McGregor from the BBC Broadcasting Research Department; Dr. Barry Gunter, Head of Research, and Dr. Robin Moss, Head of the Education Department, at the Independent Television Commission; Dr. Clemens van Merwijk from the Research Department of the Teleac Foundation, the Netherlands; Philippe Mounier from the Research Department of the European Media Institute; Dr. Uwe Hasebrink from the Hans Bredow Institute, Hamburg; Armin Veihl, then Secretary of the EBU's Working Party for Educational Programmes.

potentially directed at all and not only at those who can gain access to the programmes solely by means of costly equipment.

In addition, the idea of a necessary 'universal service' is – at least in the discussion in Germany – inextricably bound up with the conception of broadcasting as a public service. This service to the public should provide programmes which try, among other things, to aim at:

- giving objective factual information and clarification as a prerequisite for an understanding of politics;
- providing new ideas for expanding knowledge and further education;
- warning against risks to health and the environment;
- encouraging intellectual activity and self-realisation;
- continuing to offer generally valid educational content;
- interpreting cultural developments as parts of a continuous process.

What we have dealt with is that part of the programmes which involves more than broadcasting up-to-date news, transmitting sporting events or – by no means unimportant – providing a pastime, diversion and entertainment.

Whether minorities or those with special interests, whether young or old, highly educated or quite simply just bright and curious – part of the audience, which is hard to describe sociologically, but quantitatively is not to be underestimated, turns to the programmes which they themselves refer to as 'instructive, interesting, worthwhile'. These are not instructional programmes in the style, for example, of the German Telekolleg or of curriculum-orientated school television. In the broadcasting stations they are registered as culture, science, factual or even counselling programmes; it is becoming far more rare for them to be run as contributions to adult education and vocational training. From France comes the scintillating term 'discovery television'. The success story of Discovery Channel comes to mind here, which proves, moreover, that imparting educational content by television can certainly be commercially profitable as well.

The contributions to our conference, and thus to this volume in our series, are intended to furnish evidence of the fact that what we subsume here for pragmatic reasons under the term of educational television is certainly not over and done with. This is shown not only by developments in France and Denmark as described by Didier Lecat and Mogens Arngot respectively. The BBC, too, whose legendary educational departments are in danger of being rationalised out of existence, has sought and successfully pursued new ways, as the contributions by Jane Quinn and Jenny King show.

Fruitful impulses for a revival of educational television might come from other production departments, for example from those responsible for science programmes, as is shown by the contributions from Hungary and Italy, from the Bavarian Broadcasting Corporation and the BBC in Chapter 5.

It was noted with special interest that some audience research departments inside the broadcasting stations are looking into the fact that many viewers apparently have very decided views on what the programmes offer in the way of education, culture and science.

The participants in the big panel discussion were prepared to reformulate their comments, fears and expectations as theses given the provocative nature of the subject, and these have been collated in Chapter 6. The contributions to this volume – taken as a whole – might offer an answer, which is: Educational broadcasting – no need to change the subject!

Acknowledgements

First of all my thanks are due to the contributors to our conference and to this book. They were all very cooperative and helpful when it came to putting the manuscripts together and converting the spoken word – often a free comment on video presentations or overhead transperancies – into a readable form. I was very glad lo learn that for quite a few of them the meeting in Munich turned out to be the beginning of fruitful cooperation afterwards.

To prepare the English version of the proceedings, we could as always rely on the efficient assistance of our experienced translators and linguistic advisers. I should like to thank Geoffrey P. Burwell for excellent translations from German into English and Norman Jones for those from French, and I wish to acknowledge the work of John Malcolm King for linguistic advice and assistance in finalising many of the English texts.

Particular thanks go to Rosemarie Hagemeister and Dieter Graßberger for their editorial assistance as well as to my other colleagues in the Institute. Without their helpful cooperation and patience neither the conference nor this book would have been possible.

This publication is the result of a first joint venture between IZI with John Libbey Media at the University of Luton. Given the fact that the relationship between editors and authors of various countries (with differing word-processing systems and ways of illustrating their ideas) on the one hand; and renowned publishers on the other are not always easy, there are many reasons to say thanks to Professor Manuel Alvarado, to Ann Simmonds and to Keith Marr in particular, who made me feel that international cooperation in publishing is the most normal thing in the world and also a pleasure.

Munich, April 1997   Manfred Meyer

1: Educational Programmes on TV – Which Audiences?

Educational programmes on television: What are the odds?

Manfred Meyer
Bayerischer Rundfunk, IZI, Munich

In 1992 our Institute, in co-operation with the Bayerische Landeszentrale für neue Medien, the Bavarian authority for private broadcasting corporations, held an international symposium on the subject 'Cultural and Educational Programmes on Television'.[1] On the last day a panel of experts were discussing – as usual – the prospects for future developments.

One of the participants in the group astonished the audience by asking: 'Whoever wants that kind of stuff any more?'. By 'stuff' was meant both cultural and educational programmes on television. The person who put this provocative question was Professor Alphons Silbermann, at that time the doyen of German sociology, living and teaching in Cologne. He no doubt wanted to recall, in a direct and forthright way, that cultural and educational programmes – at least on certain subjects and of a certain kind – are either not accepted by the majority of the audience or are not even seen by a sufficient number of the people for whom they are intended.

Educational programmes – are they really not wanted by the public? There is the other side of the coin, too: even inside the broadcasting stations themselves there are arguments against the production or the purchase of high-quality educational programmes. They mainly refer to the relatively low audience ratings. In this connection today we talk about market shares, and this indicates that we are in competition with commercial programme suppliers.

As far as the bulk of the viewers, the large sections of the general public, are concerned, it is also maintained that there is no longer any demand for general education anyway. And, what is more, television is a far too expensive medium to be used sensibly for imparting special area knowledge and continuing the education of fairly small groups in the population.

The developments in information and communication technologies have resulted in it being possible to use learning and teaching material for specific educational aims more effectively and produce it at a lower cost in the form of interactive compact discs or computer teachware.

---

1 An English version of the proceedings has been published as: Manfred Meyer (ed.): *Educational Programmes on Television: Deficiencies, Support, Chances. Contributions to an International Symposium.* Munich: Saur 1993, 284pp (available from IZI).

If the educational remit of the mass medium of television is to remain sensibly and economically defensible, the audience ratings would have to achieve a minimum level of the total proportion. We therefore have to ask whether this educational remit is still of current interest and in keeping with the times.

The educational remit

First and foremost: the educational remit – that means quite generally the requirement to offer a certain number of educational programmes – is written into the individual broadcasting laws of the German Länder, the federal states, as well as into their interstate agreements, which have actually made programmes across the borders of the Länder possible. It also applies to private companies, if they put on a full programme.

The educational remit, in some form or other, comes up in the broadcasting law of many countries in the world, from Canada to Australia, from Japan to Nigeria or South Africa. It can be found or inferred anywhere where broadcasting is understood according to the British example, as public service broadcasting, as a service for the public, as the provision of broadcasting programmes in the general public interest with an obligation to society.

It should not be forgotten that there is no educational remit in the federal broadcasting legislation of the United States or in the legislation of many Latin American countries, but that it is especially there that state, community or private initiatives have resulted in exceptionally noteworthy and successful programmes for education and the school.

Be that as it may, in Germany the educational remit is laid down in law. It cannot just be dismissed. The broadcasting stations have to live and work with terms like 'educational programme' or 'school programme'. They are apparently indispensable for planning or organisation and for reporting, for it has to be proved that the legal remit is being adequately observed and carried out. So they are also to be found in the organisational plans of most stations.

And now comes the crux of the matter: the terms 'educational remit', 'educational programme' or 'educational broadcast' are not at all defined closely by the legislator. Also, as Werner Deetz (1996) observes,[2] as far as the area of education is concerned, the broadcasting station operators have been:

> ... granted the right to define their duties themselves, ...to safeguard the institutional freedom of broadcasting ... This legal arrangement can evidently not prevent the requirements and standards for educational programmes from remaining vague,

---

2 I refer here and below to an analysis of the legal position by Dr Werner Deetz from the Legal Department of the WDR. He published it under the title 'Bildung als Element der Grundversorgung im dualen Rundfunksystem' (Education as an Element of the Basic Provision in the Dual Broadcasting System) in *Recht der Jugend und des Bildungswesens* (The Law of Young People and the Education System), vol. 44 (1996), no.1; pp 12-21.

incomplete or inconsistent. Nor can it avoid programme standards being overtly or covertly violated or not being met. As the broadcasting programmes are, however, generally accessible, they are subject to public discussion, which, in turn, can have an influence on the formation of standards and control through the socially relevant groups.[3]

Werner Deetz finally arrives at a number of noteworthy conclusions, which he entitles Basic Questions of Planning and Producing Educational Programmes. Here one reads:

> It is a good idea to define education not from the point of view of the content but of the media. Almost all subjects can be treated in educational broadcasts. The programme-makers' intention and the way in which individual broadcasts are edited and labelled for the media are in the final analysis responsible for whether a subject can be regarded as an educational programme.' And he goes on to say, with a direct relation to our subject: 'The programmes are better suited to serving educational ends as media presentations, the more they contribute to making understanding and learning possible by their position in the overall programme, their make-up and length.

Deetz concludes with a reminder to the programme and media planners: 'Educational content should and can be possible and present in all programme genres and in all forms of broadcasting and production. Global programme planning aimed at 'ghettoising', 'atomising' or 'marginalising' education do not comply with the educational remit.'

At our conference four years ago Professor Albert Scharf, the Director General of the Bayerischer Rundfunk, expressed very similar views. He, too, rejects categorisation:

> ... Education takes place not only in programmes which have up to now been referred to as educational programmes: a name which is probably now used to a lesser extent as a collective term for instructional programmes, teaching programmes, school radio, school television, Telekolleg, language courses and the like.

> ... Merely categorising into education, teaching, entertainment alone (is) not sufficient...There is an additional factor that applies to all three elements of this obligation: the democratic mentality and the cultural responsibility, and this also applies to the entertainment programmes, for example the presentation of sport or whatever it may be. Humanity and objectivity, the special features of the local region, the characteristics of one's origin, the experience of life in the surroundings – to convey all this is ... also the obligation of public service broadcasting.

---

3   Werner Deetz, ibid. p. 12.

If we accept Deetz's arguments, it also follows that all those may be come up against a rubber wall who want to derive and call for suitable broadcasts from a restricted concept of education of whatever kind.

Definitions of the educational remit fill whole library shelves. They are certainly useful, necessary and practicable for certain areas, such as school, adult eduction and vocational training. But the findings of education experts, to quote Deetz again, 'usually are no longer of any help for broadcasting, because they often deal with it [i.e. broadcasting as an organisation] only peripherally and rarely include its environment.'

Conversely, broadcasting organisations cannot wait for experts to provide them with an explanation of what education in broadcast programmes actually has to be or what its aims are.

All the same, the characteristic features of a programme, its tenor and its colour result from the manner in which the broadcasting stations – each in its own way – think about the concept of education and the educational remit and how to implement it in the programme.

The viewer: What does he want? What does he not want?

Alfred Payrleitner, Head of the Education and Current Events Department at the Austrian Broadcasting Corporation, put this – considering the media situation in Austria – in a nutshell in an interview with the journal *Univers*:

> Today all a television viewer has to do is to want, nothing else.
> And if he doesn't want, and usually he doesn't, where do I come
> into it with my educational remit?[4]

And what he usually does not want, the television viewer, is, as we know, the imparting of education – and that means in the eyes of most people 'higher education' – in short: he does not want to be taught, or to be talked down to, by television.

The attitude that television adopted towards the viewer in the 1960s and 1970s, perhaps at the beginning of the 1980s as well, was that of the Good Samaritan, who wanted to help: help the viewer to come to a better understanding of the world or of himself; help in performing the duties at home which his working life or everyday family life imposed on him as an adult.

Educational programmes on television were determined by the content and the forms used for imparting adult education. Foreign languages, bringing up children, even looking after balcony plants were included in the course programme and could hardly be taught in fewer than 10 or 13 instalments.

Almost exactly 20 years ago the EBU Working Party for Educational Programmes approved a definition of radio and television programmes for adult education:

4   cf. Univers, 1996, No. 1; p. 24.

Adult education programmes aim to give adults progressive comprehension of a body of knowledge or help them acquire skills in a defined field or equip them better for participation in community life. This should contribute to the development of the individual and increase his understanding of a changing society.[5]

The partly academic debate carried on in the 1960s and 1970s can be subsumed under the question: 'Can television teach?' But many quotations from the broadcasting practitioners as well, whose models and departmental heads came from the ranks of the 'educationists' anyway, reveal a benevolent attitude. Very frequently they were mainly concerned with the improvement of programmes for those adults who wanted to learn anyway and who turned to the medium because they needed help and guidance. If the others did not sufficiently accept this help, then they were either unwilling to be educated or incapable of being educated, or they were only interested in trivial things.

The broadcasting people, the programme companies, at any rate did their best and always endeavoured to do things better and better. One of the veterans and founding producers of the former *Studienprogramm* of the Bavarian Broadcasting Corporation is said to have expressed it in a meeting of departmental heads like this: 'Our programmes are all right, only we don't have the right audience'.

Ingo Hermann summed up what in my opinion is the decisive change in perspective at the end of the 1980s as follows:

One cannot only discuss whether television can and should educate, but one has first and foremost to ask whether people want to be educated at all, and whether they want it also in front of the screen.[6]

Education from the TV screen
What exactly is it then that the viewers should want and do not want to a sufficient extent of their own accord? Now it almost again appears that we can hardly avoid a definition of the concept of educational television or at least an approximation to it. But I shall not risk skating on thin ice and only point out that, hopefully, our panel discussion will attempt to contribute to the clarification of the concept.

At any rate there are programmes which can be marked off from the general array of news broadcasts, sports reports and light entertainment programmes such as soaps or folk-song evenings or shows. The potential audience for programmes of the other kind is the focus of attention not only from a quantitative point of view. Questions as to the possible previous knowledge of the target group, level of understanding or choice of

---

5 EBU Working Party, Communication to members, June 1976.
6 Ingo Hermann: 'Hänsel und Gretel im Märchenwald'. In: *ZDF-Jahrbuch* 1988, p.118.

format or presentation style have a different priority from that of the categories mentioned.

The common denominator for programmes of this kind, outside the category of educational television so to speak, is more likely to be found in the conditions in the run-up to the production. The programmes in question are distinguished by the fact that quite different, and in many cases even more expensive, preparations have to be made in the planning and development phase: research into current developments in science, interviews with experts, setting up special advisory bodies, consideration of viewers with special interests as target groups and, ideally, pilot tests or preliminary studies with focus groups.

Success stories
For the examples I shall be giving here we do not need the term educational television at all. They could be better subsumed under the heading which in Anglo-Saxon countries would be described as 'educative television'.

These would be television broadcasts or series in which it is often hardly recognisable that the intention is to provide in-depth information or to enlighten, that they want to implicitly stimulate the viewers to spend more time on a matter, in other words do indeed contribute indirectly to general education. Most of the better documentaries come into this category, and their acceptance by the public should give us food for thought.

Examples of successful programmes are to be found especially among magazine broadcasts, in particular health magazines and science magazines:

- The ZDF's *Knoff-hoff Show*, known not only here in Germany, in which Joachim Bublath presents science subjects and oddities from all areas of the natural sciences in a popular way, had an average audience share of 12 per cent for its six transmissions in 1995, which means each programme was seen on average by more than 5.6 million viewers.
- In Austria at the beginning of the 90s up to 2.6 million viewers were registered for the series *Universum*, or 43 per cent of the viewers. The popular series with scientific documentaries was transmitted regularly on Tuesday evenings on prime time. The grading by the viewers that is used in Austria achieved an average figure of 4.7 out of a possible 5 points – a top rating, which indicates the extraordinary satisfaction with this kind of broadcast.
- On Bavarian Television *Die Sprechstunde* (Consultation Hour), a health magazine, was for years the most successful programme and achieved ratings of 20 per cent and more.

In the following, I shall give some unusual examples from Britain treating topics that one would not usually think of as subjects for light evening entertainment:

7

- *A Small Dance* was a one-part educational drama produced by Thames TV in 1992 that told the story of a teenage girl that got pregnant and abandoned her baby. Broadcast on 8 p.m. primetime, it captured an unexpected audience share of 49 per cent, i.e. 11.1 million viewers. It was accompanied by supporting publications and a telephone helpline (300 immediate calls) advising on teenage pregnancy, contraception and family violence.
- Also in 1992, Yorkshire TV transmitted *The Last Cigarette*, a 90-minute light entertainment special, on a Sunday in March at 10:40 p.m. on the occasion of the National No Smoking Day and repeated it even later in August. Immediate response to a telephone helpline to the repeat broadcast was over 60,000 attempts; 25,000 information packs were distributed on request and to self-help groups.

So it is obviously the great problems and vices which affect many people and thus rouse the viewers and attract their attention; but not only that:

- *Play it Safe*, a BBC Education series of a documentary followed by eight 10-minute programmes on child accident prevention counted 9 million viewers when it was shown in 1989. It was supported by a range of back-up material and linked with a national campaign. Here, too, the demand for support material and more detailed information showed that the BBC had, so to speak, hit the mark with its choice of subject and format.

Programme support
That a fairly large number of viewers are reached by broadcasts of this kind is certainly not only connected with the degree of concern resulting from the choice of themes, but to a great extent also with professionally conceived programme support measures, which is another key concept in connection with educational programmes and their acceptance. This area was the internal subject of the 1992 MediaNet Conference.[7]

How much is it worth to the viewers?
Sceptics would now say that concern or activation end when the people are challenged, especially if they are called upon to open their purses. Some examples on this, too, which do not support this view:

- A course on Chinese language and culture (*Hi Non*) was offered by the Dutch educational channel Teleac in 1988; 14,000 packages of support material, including 2 books with 800 pages, 17 audiotapes with listening exercises, were sold at 275 Dutch Guilders each.
- *Legacy* was a six-part series of one-hour programmes produced by the British independent company Central TV in 1991. It explored the origins

---

7   cf. note no.1; programme support in connection with school television broadcasts is dealt with in various contributions to Manfred Meyer (Ed.): *Aspects of School Television in Europe. A Documentation.* Munich: Saur 1992; 596 pp (available from IZI).

of civilisation in the West, Central America, China, Egypt, India and Iraq. Although it was shown on Tuesday nights at 10:45 after the late news, the series attracted audiences from 2.1 to 2.9 million viewers, achieved an appreciation index higher than the average for this category and stimulated – provable – further activities such as discussing the issue, visiting a museum or reading a book; over 20,000 asked for the support pack with information sheets and paid £1.90 for it.[8]

More fees for educational programmes?

People seem to be willing to pay in order to be served with educational programmes on mainstream TV – at least in the UK. In a study carried out in 1989, the BBC Research Department had the audience attitudes tested on a hypothetical system in which certain individual programme categories would have to be paid for. The research question was:

There would be a basic licence fee which … would allow you to see:

ITV – Channel 4 – Most of BBC1 – Most of BBC2.

For certain programmes on BBC-TV there would be an extra charge. You would choose:

– either to pay extra to see them;

– or not to pay extra and not be able to see them.[9]

The genres with the highest proportions saying they would be at least 'quite likely' to pay under such a system were Films (68 per cent), National News (66 per cent), Nature Programmes (61 per cent), Documentaries (53 per cent), before Serials/Series (55 per cent), Situation Commedies (51 per cent), and Sports Programmes (49 per cent).

After all, roughly one third (35 per cent) would pay for Educational Programmes, which is slightly more than for Children's Programmes (32 per cent) or Science Programmes (31 per cent).

Discovery television

The true success story of the late 80s took place in the USA. It is the story of The Discovery Channel, which was set up in 1985 with the aim to offer the best in documentaries produced for television.

The concept of its founder, John Hendricks, is based on a succinct statement: 'Man's thirst for information – man's curiosity about himself and the world around him – is universal.' And for him there is apparently no doubt about the best way of quenching this thirst: 'People are curious about the world around them and television is a great medium to satisfy that curiosity…'[10]

8   cf. Robin Moss: 'Hunting the Snark: the Search for the Q'. In: *Journal of Educational Television*, 18/1992/2-3, pp. 107–116.

9   John Samuels: 'Public Attitudes to the BBC and its Funding'. In: *BBC Broadcasting Research Annual Review*, Number 15, 1989. London: Libbey 1989; pp. 73–84.

10 Quoted from *The Daily News*. MIFED 1995, No. 6, p.133.

After only five years Discovery Channel could be received in more than 50 million cabled homes. Today it is over 63 million in the USA and several millions in Britain and Ireland, Belgium and some Scandinavian countries. Discovery Channel has also gained a foothold on other continents. One looks in vain for the classical course programmes on Discovery. They can be found on the Learning Channel, which was set up in 1990 and can now be seen in Europe as well.[11]

What interests here is the obviously skilfully chosen, because attention-grabbing, title: Discovery. The French counterpart *Découverte* is part of the logo of the French educational channel *La Cinquième*, which started up in 1994 and which occasionally refers to itself as 'la chaine du savoir, de la connaissance et des découvertes', a channel therefore for imparting and expanding knowledge and for discoveries.

In 1995, the president of *La Cinquième* Jean Marie Cavada founded an international association entitled International Association of Educational and Discovery Television Companies (original title: *Association internationale des télévisions d'éducation et de découverte*). On 20th April 1996 it held its first general meeting in Cannes.

[NB: The French publishing house Gallimard puts out one of the most successful series of paperbacks entitled *Découverte*s with the highest standards of artwork. The German partner edition is entitled *Adventure Story* and is published by the Ravensburger Verlag. The publisher promotes it with the slogan: 'The story of the world, as exciting as a reportage, historically documented in words and pictures', a marketing slogan that could just as well be used for a television series like *Terra X*.]

The ZDF series *Sphinx* is subtitled 'The secrets of history'. Television titles like *The Research Adventure* (ZDF) and *The Science Adventure* (SDR) also hold out prospects of being gripping and exciting programmes. The Bavarian Broadcasting Corporation is working on a new series titled *Scientific Mysteries of the Universe*.[12]

These titles are not chosen haphazardly; those who choose them know why. We are moving in a semantic field that has nothing to do with a curriculum for formal or non-formal education: adventures, discoveries, mysteries, interesting and sensational subjects from the worlds of history and science. It is a way back to the origins of journalism. There experiences are offered and accepted which tend to touch on the affective domain. Programmes of that kind are accepted not because they are 'instructional', but because they are interesting, they arouse curiosity, they 'turn you on', to adopt a word from the jargon of young people.

The interest
In his novel *Doktor Faustus* Thomas Mann has his hero, Adrian Leverkühn, ask: 'Do you believe that love is the strongest emotion?' – 'Do you know a

---

11 See the article by Joyce Taylor in this volume, p.55 et seq.
12 See contribution of Ulrike Emrich and Rainhold Gruber in this volume, pp 156.

stronger one?' asks his friend and chronicler. 'Yes,' is the answer, 'interest.'[13]

The viewers apparently react positively to your wanting to arouse their interest. They want to be taken along on a journey to the unknown, the undiscovered. They seek experiences, educational experiences, if you like, and the closer they are placed to the prime time, the easier it is to get on board and go on the trip. Here it is no longer a matter of instructional material, of systematic knowledge, of a coherent and sound explanation of the world. Nor is it a matter of coping with one's daily stint of learning, of acquiring knowledge that can be examined.

Adults learning

In studies into the use approach, 'learning' was often specified as one of the gratifications that was given to select from in the case of television use. In a study that was carried out by the Independent Television Commission in 1991, one of the answers to choose from among the reasons for watching television was: 'I think I can learn something'; 66 per cent (on rank five) said this was why they watched television 'often' or 'occasionally'.[14]

In our context we have to ask what people mean when they speak about 'learning' in connection with the TV screen. If a conclusive answer could be found to this question there would be a fresh chance, perhaps the crucial one, to narrow the gulf between a programme offered and its acceptance. I only want to outline one of the possible paths to follow.

In 1971 the Canadian Allen Tough published the results of a study under the title *The Adult's Learning Projects* in which he provides evidence that every adult carries out at least one or two and on average about eight learning projects a year that he has organised himself.[15] He defines learning project as a series of episodes which are related to one another and are consciously directed towards acquiring and retaining knowledge or skills. Only what lasts at least seven hours is considered to be an episode within the framework of a learning project. On average the test subjects spent about 700 hours a year on learning projects.

As far as the content is concerned a learning project can relate to very different areas of life, to interest in one's work or one's hobby, family life, home and sport, nature or culture and historical epochs. Only about 5 per cent of all learning projects are directed towards obtaining certificates or similar formal recognition. The motives are in the main curiosity, interest or fun. Tough's empirically obtained findings, supported by replicate studies, are not the only ones that have changed our knowledge about adults' learning. In our context here it is significant that self-controlled learning in the life of adults is a widespread, natural and everyday strategy.

---

13 Thomas Mann: *Doktor Faustus*. Frankfurt/Main: S. Fischer 1963; p. 76.

14 Barrie Gunter; Carmel McLaughlin: *Television: The public's view* London: Libbey, 1992; see pp. 26-27.

15 Allen Tough: *The Adult's Learning Projects. A Fresh Approach to Theory and Practice in Adult Education* Toronto: 1979 (2nd edition)

There are quite a few indications that an enormous scattering range of different ideas of learning are hidden behind the statement that you can learn something from television.

Possibly the lack of understanding in this area is proving to be one of the decisive desiderata, as far as our knowledge of the interaction between viewer and television programme is concerned. Maybe it is here that television research's mystery of the universe lies, waiting to be solved. It is sufficient for the time being to give more thought to the change in perspectives that Hans Paukens recommended to us here four years ago:

> Up to now education on television has been based on the premise that imparting knowledge, providing instruction, presenting and structuring are all important. A pedagogical teaching/learning situation or communication situation is taken for granted.

> We have known for some time from communication research ... that reception is determined by a large number of factors, whereas acquiring knowledge, i.e. learning from the material presented, is dependent least of all on the intention and structuring of the individual communication content....

> It therefore appears important ... to concentrate for a change on the acquisition process of the audience. It would mean starting with the viewers and thinking about when, where and also how educational processes occur in the case of television, how the viewer acquires knowledge (from TV) and with which learning strategies this takes place; how, for example, he or she establishes a link between the subjects and contents presented, on the one hand, and his or her life-world and life-plans, on the other.[16]

Perhaps some things have become clearer to us after four days. Perhaps we shall go away from here with a fruitful feeling of uncertainty as far as our ideas about the viewer are concerned.

Manfred Meyer *is information specialist and deputy head of the Internationales Zentralinstitut fuer das Jugend- und Bildungsfernsehen (IZI), a documentation and information centre at the Bayerischer Rundfunk (Bavarian Broadcasting Corporation), founded in 1965. His main interests are: forms and functions of educational television and radio programmes, educational broadcasting research, television for children and young people, research into the effects of broadcast media. He has published various reports and books on aspects of educational broadcasting.*

16 Hans Paukens: 'Cooperation with German broadcasting organisations: The experience of the Adolf-Grimme-Institute'. In M. Meyer (Ed.) *Educational Programmes on Television*. Munich: Saur 1993; p. 139.

Getting closer to the audiences:
The BBC experience

Jane Quinn
BBC Education, London

Let me open with a provocative statement: We are moving into an audience-led future, one which is based on a detailed understanding of the interests of a general audience, and then of the interests of particular target audiences within that main set of viewers. The audience is king or queen. We build our programmes around our knowledge of how they talk about different subjects, what they would like to see more of, and – with regard to educational radio and television – what they are most likely to learn from.

This vision of a future which is principally audience-orientated is being widely talked about. Michael Jackson, controller of BBC2, said in his speech to the Royal Television Society a few weeks ago:

> The greatest danger in broadcasting is to be out of touch with reality. Reality – this means in our context 'the audience'. Television is not about addressing people from on high; it is about connecting the intelligence of the viewers with the intelligence of the programme makers. Public service television is more relevant today, not because of the brilliance of today's generation of programme-makers, but because society has forced us to think in more complex ways.
>
> Society is more diverse, and the BBC can no longer be a drill-sergeant of taste. But precisely because of the new complexity of the world, the BBC is more and more vital as a 'meeting place' – a democratic forum – 'a confirmer of citizenship'. In other words, a place where viewers can have a shared experience of learning which connects with their experience of life and reality.

But what exactly are the debates around broadcasting in an audience-led future? There are arguments in favour of producing educational programmes led by researched audience preference, and there are arguments against it. One might hear something like this:

For: 'For years we've had TV and radio producers making
        programmes *they* want to make but *the audience* doesn't want
        to view or listen to. In a media environment dominated by
        ratings we can't afford this luxury any more.'

Against: 'Yes, but that's part of the producers' art; they can spot trends and needs before anyone else and can let an audience know about new things. They're creative people.'

For: 'Yes, but to reach an audience you have to understand their starting point and build from there.'

Against: 'But often audiences don't know what they want. Successful programmes have the shock of the new. You won't get that from audience research.'

That should serve as an introduction to the debate, and it is up to the reader to take his or her side. I shall delve a little deeper and look at how a range of educational audiences are identified, and how they are reached within BBC Education.

During the last few years, many developments have taken place in BBC Education. In research terms, I can categorise the results of these changes in four stages:

Stage 1: *A changing awareness of the educational audience*
This is best illustrated through the triangle below:

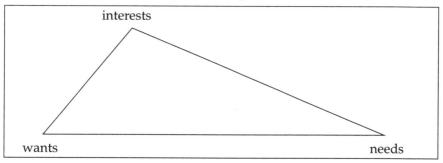

Before the development of this triangular model, the determining of the type of educational broadcasts we transmitted was almost exclusively *needs*-based. It was founded on our understanding of what educational professionals felt were the key areas of educational and social needs in the audience. It was undeniably a view from the top.

The triangle, therefore, represents a development in our thinking towards understanding the audience. An audience may have *wants* which might not correspond with a needs-based hierarchy: to learn French, for instance, to learn cooking, to understand information technology, or to gain knowledge of child development.

And, of course, they also have *interests* – in everything from bird-watching to wine-tasting to looking after their pets. And interests are often the greatest motivation to learn of all. If, as broadcasters, we are trying to reach an audience and move them along a learning spectrum, we need to consider each of these – needs, wants, and interests – in deciding the content, format and scheduling of the programmes.

Stage 2: *Can we prioritise?*
The next stage took a slightly different approach. It was an intensive period in which we experimented with ways of prioritising the most important subjects. This took into consideration comparative degrees of educational need in an audience-defined list of areas such as relationships, business and languages; it looked at social trends as an indication of audience interest, and it looked at current supply across all the channels to see if the audience was getting sufficient programming to meet the interest/need level identified. This led to a list of priority subjects within which commissioning decisions could be made.

Stage 3: *Moving viewers along*
At the same time, we were working out a continuum of educational effectiveness. This looked something like this:

Passive					Active
viewing programme	making decision to view another programme in the same area	talking to friends/ colleagues about the programme	sending off for a booklet or ringing a helpline or information line	taking an open learning course	joining a college course

It was dependent on the previous experience of the viewers at the time of viewing and how the programme resonated with this, and the opportunity provided by the broadcaster to access follow-on information, whether through leaflets, booklets or helplines. This represents an educational developmental movement from passive to active.

Stage 4: *Detailed audience understanding*
This is the current stage. It is based on a belief that a linear list of priorities does not give the commissioning team which wants to make informed commissioning decisions sufficient understanding of audience interests. We are on the brink of a more complex research exercise, which will look something like the following diagram.

This diagram brings us right up-to-date and provides us with the direct context of the conference address. It is worth emphasising, however, that research within the BBC is a dynamic process that will undergo more changes as it evolves.

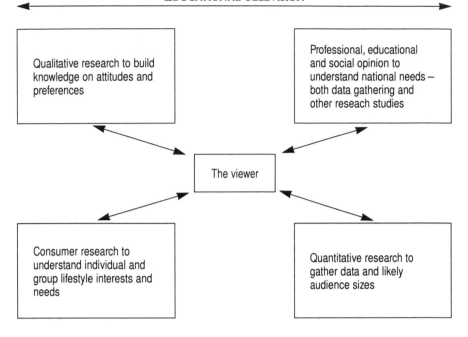

To sum up: research carried out by our research department before pro-grammes are commissioned is, no longer, exclusively about educational needs and trends as defined by professionals and experts.

Professional educational opinion through permanent committees and occasional focus groups is still an important factor in the research mix, but so is qualitative research both pre- and post-programme, market research and consumer research, to give us background information and data around particular programmes. All this provides a rich and complex back-ground of information, preferences and ideas.

Out of this process comes a framework against which commissioning decisions take place. But that is the easy part. Delivering programmes which use peak viewing time slots to reach a target audience to inform, entertain and achieve their educational objectives – all this takes a magic mix of knowledge and creativity, against a background of profound audi-ence understanding.

I am going to comment on a few examples from our recent output to show how this has taken place.

Read And Write Together

Read And Write Together was a week of programming broadcast in February 1995. The central programming focus of this season was three 60-second shorts on BBC1, scattered through the schedule at peak viewing time. The aim was to use BBC1, the popular BBC channel with viewers drawn from across the socio-economic range, to reach parents who might be having dif-ficulties reading with their children because of their own literacy problems.

Research had shown that a great deal of reading problems started in families where reading interaction did not take place in the early years, and the original impetus for family literacy work came from *Tom Strick*, an American academic. It was taken up by the Basic Skills Agency (ALBSU) who, with government funding, set up a national network of family literacy centres throughout England and Wales, in primary schools, where parents and children could come, outside school hours, for reading tuition. So by the time the BBC put the programmes on the air, there was a national infrastructure of centres in place.

The aim of the programmes presented us with the problem, however, of how to reach those people, of the 6 to 8 million people who watch BBC1 each evening, who found reading difficult without being patronising, building up feelings of guilt and failure, or indeed alienating the rest of the audience.

The executive editor contacted Bartle, Bogle, Hegarty, one of the leading advertising agencies in the UK, to design and produce the shorts with both a general audience and the target audience in mind.

They came up with three separate 60-second promotional shorts. The response from the audience was staggering. Over 5 million people, i.e. 70 per cent of the target audience, saw at least one of the shorts, and over 300,000 people rang the information line for a pack to read with their children. The Basic Skills Agency were overwhelmed by the response, and the Controller of BBC1 was delighted at having the programmes on his channel. This was a highly motivational literacy campaign, directing people off-screen to more specific learning while using the BBC's mass audience channel.

The Trouble With Men

A slightly different example on BBC2 was *The Trouble With Men* – a season of television and radio programming stretching across a week on men's health, broadcast in March 1996. Here, the research we carried out showed over and over again the need to encourage men to understand their own, most common health problems and to seek help if necessary. Part of the challenge in broadcasting a successful season would be to find a format which would reach, and appeal to, men between 25 and 55.

BBC Bristol and BBC Education came up with a range of different programmes which were transmitted on BBC2 and Radio 5 live in a week during March 1996. They covered health problems such as impotence, infertility, depression, sexually transmitted diseases, Hormone Replacement Therapy for men, or testicular cancer, the latter being of particular importance since about 50 per cent of all patients do not go to their doctor until the cancer has spread.

Sixty helplines at three centres were open each evening during the week for calls, and an e-mail counselling system via Internet was set up by our partner agency Broadcasting Support Services for the first time alongside a broadcast of this nature. This was because the target audience for these programmes so closely matched the profile of Internet users.

The *Male Survival Guide* was a series of six ten-minute programmes which formed the backbone of the season, adopting a style which resoundedly and directly reached the target group. The programmes showed a combination of 'in-yer-face'-programming, deliberately macho in tone, with clear, unambiguous statistics and individual men speaking about their problems.

BBC2 is the BBC's less populist channel. It reaches viewers from upper social strata (professional, managerial and white-collar occupations; ABC1) with a male bias through a rich mix of cultural programmes – science, documentaries, arts programmes, politics, drama and comedy. It experiments with new formats to reach new audiences. *The Trouble With Men* drew audiences of around 2.5 million on average for the slots in which the programmes were placed. But of the 5,300 callers to the helpline, 85 per cent were male (in the area of health programming where callers after TV programmes are predominantly female), of which 88 per cent were calling about themselves and their own health problems, not on behalf of 'a friend'.

Doctors have been phoning relentlessly since the season, with news that the number of men in their surgeries has increased. (We had sent out a leaflet to doctors before the season was put on, warning them that this might happen.) Over 7,000 copies of an accompanying book have been ordered. So *The Trouble With Men* presents a model of a targeted season, on BBC2, reaching a predominantly male audience with direct health education messages.

The research groups we ran after the season showed that the particular format of 'real' men talking about their health, combined with bald statistics and medical explanation, appealed directly to the male audience, including the 16- to 24-year-olds – a group which is often so difficult to appeal to.

The Learning Zone

My third example of a smaller, more traditional education audience is drawn from *The Learning Zone*, the new educational service transmitted during night-time between 12.30 and 5.30 a.m. on BBC2. It aims at providing programmes intended for recording and then later usage in colleges and schools, and it is a rich new educational resource, combining education for schools, programmes for further education colleges, study seasons for committed learners, a strand of programmes for business and work, and Open University courses.

Within our service for further education colleges (FETV), there are currently no originations, but there is a strand called *Short Cuts*. Each Short Cut is built up around a particular curriculum need – it may be customer care, information technology skills or race portrayals – and the BBC's rich archive of programmes is then, quite crudely, mined, to put together short sequences for use by lecturers. One may therefore get combinations of comedy, drama and documentary juxtaposed with education to give flexible, customised resources for teaching.

The idea for *Short Cuts* grew out of research showing that lecturers needed short, 5- or 10-minute pieces of programming, which they could use flexibly to fit in with different qualifications and different kinds of courses. Longer programmes where they had to spool through, select and edit before usage were actually presenting a barrier. It was also clear that lecturers preferred to record at set times rather than catching part of the often changeable general schedule. So a predictable night-time service was created in response.

The Learning Zone has only been going for six months but early research results attest to a high recording ratio in colleges.[1] The target audience is the 650 further education colleges in the UK, with carefully tailored programming drawn from our archives to reach a clearly defined and researched formal educational need, and that initially targeted group has now spawned others. Through focus groups and by visiting colleges, we are working closely with the educational world in order to refine these Short Cuts to make them more immediately usable. From this year, *The Learning Zone* is reaching into Europe on BBC Prime. We will wait to see how it is received.

Running in parallel to the development of tailored zones for small, identified educational audiences is a determination to increase interaction with our audience. Interactive media have a special role in learning, and we have increasingly been producing CD-ROMs alongside our programmes where research indicates that there is a market for them. This is most clearly developed in schools with titles like *Romeo and Juliet*, the French programme *Clementine*, *A Midsummer Night's Dream*, *Geodome* and *Japan 2000*.

1   Cf. the paper by Jenny King in this volume, pp. 79.

Similarly, pages on the World Wide Web that extend interaction with the audience around our programmes are now the norm rather than the exception. A new multi-media centre at our head quarter White City is poised to lead developments in the new media within the BBC.

So, to conclude, if there are two qualities which characterise the move towards greater audience responsiveness, they are a commitment to research and to innovation. As broad-band technologies offer the opportunity for greater sophistication in programme quality besides greater variety and choice to the audience, the chance to get closer to our viewers increases – with appropriate, planned and clever programming and support activities. But we *do* need to be ready to accept the challenge, and we *do* need to listen to the audience.

Jane Quinn *is Chief Education Officer, BBC Continuing Education for Adults. Since joining the BBC, Jane has initiated many research projects into educational broadcasting. These include how people learn from TV, the use of helplines, the portrayal of older people on TV, and a wide range of post-transmission research into audience response to particular programmes. She heads a team of Education Advisers who work closely with programme makers to identify key areas for broadcast, understand the needs and interest of audiences, liaise with the educational world, and initiate a diverse range of support materials.*

Knowledge and discovery:
The conception of *La Cinquième*

Didier Lecat
La Cinquième, *Paris*

Introduction

The economic crisis experienced during the current decade has placed France in a state of weakness which has hardly been known since the beginning of the 1950s. At the end of 1994, the gulf became visible separating those who have frequent access to the delights of France's wide-ranging cultural scene and those who have to be satisfied with what the television channels supply them more or less free of charge. France is witnessing a resurgence of illiteracy, poor scholastic performance, the negation of certain cultures and the emergence of ideologies.

For many French people, television is the only window on the world. Television, like the language of Aesop, can offer the best and the worst of things. Following years of discussion, a new television channel, *La Cinquième* was established as the 'channel of learning and knowledge' in December 1994. The channel's aim is to make available very high quality programmes to everyone, both those who have multiple access to knowledge and those who do not have the same chance. *La Cinquième* is committed to being a 'popular' channel (in the sense of: channel 'for the people') promoting hope, social cohesion and cultural dignity.

Presentation of *La Cinquième*

The birth of an educational and popular TV channel

Before the arrival of *La Cinquième*, it was difficult to find any pronounced attitude towards educational matters in French television programmes. In fact, there is no quota for programmes of this kind in the charters of the television channels.

As the channel for 'learning, training and employment', *La Cinquième* has an original place in the French audiovisual landscape. Compared with the other non-specialist terrestrial channels which provide entertainment and information, it is emphasising its television identity as an educational and, in the real sense of the word, 'popular' television channel. Its daily aim is to make knowledge and culture accessible to all and, in particular, to those who, for economic, social or geographic reasons, are the furthest away from such access. In this sense it is an authentic public service station.

The educational dream

La Cinquième's aim is not to become a substitute for the school or university, but to provide a quality educational programme that is complementary in nature. Its role is not to award diplomas but to prepare the ground for the stimulation of intellectual curiosity.

La Cinquième's educational aims constitute a response to a deep need experienced by the general public. In France, as elsewhere, the desire to learn and to have access to knowledge is immense. The success of foreign educational television has been confirming this for years. When received by the maximum number, television is a formidable tool in the transmission of knowledge – and is therefore of public benefit.

La Cinquième is thus invested with extremely useful mission aims. But while it wishes to be seen as stimulating the educational process, what this 'popular' channel desires above all is to give everyone an appetite for and an enjoyment of learning.

Definition of La Cinquième

Let me first of all point out what La Cinquieme is not:

- La Cinquième *is not a cultural channel for the elite.*

  It is the opposite. Its aim is to give to the maximum number an appetite for knowledge and a stimulation of their curiosity, as well as that openness to the world which gives meaning to freedom. Its objective is to make a contribution to defending and developing employment by providing better information concerning the working world, businesses, and job training procedures.

  In this way La Cinquième is putting itself at the service of the general public and is endeavouring to respond to their needs.

- La Cinquième *is not a school television channel, and it is not a substitute for teaching at school or university level.*

  The programmes of La Cinquième are rather to be seen as complementing the work of the schools. It works hand in hand with those playing an active part in the educational community and wishes to be seen as providing an accompanying service for teachers in their daily practical work. Moreover, it has already met with a vigorous response in the educational world. La Cellule pédagogique (educational cell), a body composed of educational experts, and its Observatoires académiques (academic observatories), which provide access to academic institutions, form a unique structure in French television – bringing together teachers, educational experts and the parents of pupils, who make an effective contribution towards developing our programmes. By stimulating enthusiasm for knowledge, it is making education one of the most important values of our society.

- La Cinquième *is not an elitist channel.*
  La Cinquième is a terrestrial service which can be accessed by everyone in France. It is directing its efforts towards providing everyone with educational programmes which are rich, substantial, and varied in content, and at grips with real conditions in an increasingly complex world.

What, then, is *La Cinquième*?

- La Cinquième *is a channel for the general public.*
  The language it uses does not create barriers between it and the general public. Its tone is not stilted, and its style is that of modern television for young people. *La Cinquième*, a channel devoted to education and the provision of knowledge, is meeting a demand felt by its audience, by all audiences. For all those who were not able to attend a course of study, for all those who are looking for a different kind of television and for all those who have the wish to learn, it is providing televisual sustenance which brings both enjoyment and knowledge.
- La Cinquième *is a lively, dynamic channel.*
  Our programmes are consistently modern, lively and dynamic. Its short and simple transmissions arouse curiosity and a desire to learn without ever becoming boring. It has rejected 52- or 90-minute programme modules and adopted the rhythm of life at the beginning of the 21st century: an active, lively, greedy rhythm that passes from one subject to another at a demanding and rapid pace.
- La Cinquième *is a channel that is capable of development.*
  It allows the maximum number of people to be in touch once again with the meaning of things and events. It makes possible the advent of a society that is more adult and more balanced. *La Cinquième* aims to bring about a deep modification in attitudes towards television by encouraging viewers to adopt an active and participatory attitude. It applies the most modern technologies and thus seeks to play a pioneering role.

Realisations

The programme schedule: a complementary service

La Cinquième, as an educational channel, was entrusted by law with specific aims concerning education, learning, young people, services and employment. While competition in the French audiovisual scene often encourages television channels to schedule the same style of programmes, *La Cinquième* sees itself as proceeding very definitely in the opposite direction.

Providing the French public with an extremely well-filled and diversified schedule, comprising around 40 programmes a day, *La Cinquième* is and will remain a 'complementary' channel, in accordance with the aims of its charter. In the months to come its aims will be to emphasise its different nature while improving its programmes even further. Programmes will continue to develop smoothly, its scheduling endeavouring to establish regular viewing habits among its audiences and to gain their loyalty by providing maximum satisfaction. The educational programmes and those aimed at educators are already one of the channel's successes with the range of programmes transmitted as part of the *Ecrans du savoir* (knowledge on screen) programme slot.

Les Ecrans du savoir covers all fundamental branches of knowledge (mathematics and history, economics and geography, literature, philosophy and science). But their constant guiding principle is to combine enjoyment with the provision of knowledge.

La Cinquième also deals with preventive health care, the environment, the fight against social exclusion, knowledge of institutions and civic education. All these topics, approached without heavy-handedness by means of reports, descriptions of personal experience and discussions, can provide televiewers with concrete help in finding their bearings in the complexity of the surrounding world.

A major effort has been made to emphasise questions relevant to the world of work and job training, with a daily programme being scheduled at midday. With regard to the documentaries and magazine programmes on travel and adventure, art, culture, geography and history, they have since the very beginning gained the approval of an audience who are becoming increasingly loyal and increasingly numerous.

With regard to the future, *La Cinquième* is affirming its desire to highlight current events through special scheduling which will devote a whole afternoon, a whole day or a whole weekend to dealing with all the aspects of a current issue and in this way to breathe new life into the channel. New life will also be produced by a more frequent use of live transmissions to make the schedule more attractive and varied.

Finally, a very important effort will be made to interest children, especially those between 3 and 7, who from now on will have a programme produced for them every morning.

Promoting discovery and the desire to learn

La Cinquième regards its cinema policy as being different and innovative. Thus short films now have a place on the channel in a weekly 26-minute magazine programme allowing young directors, tomorrow's film-makers, to present their productions. In this way *La Cinquième* is remaining faithful to one of its aims, which is to support and discover new talents of the cinematic art.

Affaires publiques (of public concern), a programme devoted to instruction in civics, which is screened in the educational slot known as *Ecrans du savoir* (see above), has been widely welcomed by the teaching body. *MAG 5*, a magazine programme devoted to travel, adventure and information for young people aged between 15 and 30, deals with topics connected with trends, fashion phenomena, new sports and jobs in innovative areas. It is also experiencing real success.

Developing live transmissions

Also worthy of mention is the growing success of documentary programmes dealing with travel and adventure. They allow televiewers to escape from the daily routine, giving them points of reference or landmarks relating to events taking place elsewhere in the world, and bringing within their reach exhilarating human adventures. *A tous vents* (under full sail) presented by the sailor and navigator Titouan Lamazou deals with maritime routes. This group of programmes has been rounded off by the arrival of *TEVA*, presented by the son of Paul-Emile Victor, who retraces the journeys of the great explorers filmed all over the world.

One of *La Cinquième*'s successes is to have found an original note in its approach to subjects with a range of programmes different to those of the other terrestrial channels.

For this reason, respected figures in their own fields – scientists, sportsmen, adventure-seekers – have made available their skills and their knowledge to help to fulfil the channel's mission aims (education, job training, the joy of discovery).

Audience Results

After an existence of 16 months, *La Cinquième*'s success is continuing to grow regularly. From 3 per cent in March, its market share – one of the indicators of its success – went on to move from 4.6 per cent in August to exceed the 6 per cent level on certain days in July. It has thus done better than even the most optimistic scenarios had forecast. A survey carried out in May 1995 by SOFRES for the Ministry of National Education reveals that a quarter of teachers have already used *La Cinquième*'s programmes as part of their lessons, that 10 per cent have recourse to its programmes once a week and that 93 per cent now rate it as tending to be 'interesting'.

Taking all audiences together, IPSOS Média measures an average of ratings attributed to programmes as being 8/10, explaining that the approval index is considered to be good from a level of 7/10. As far as the interest rating given to programmes by audiences was concerned, it is estimated by the same institute to be 47 per cent (a rating above 40 per cent is regarded as excellent).

La Cinquième's task now is to consolidate these encouraging results and to provide itself, as rapidly as possible, with the dimensions it is now justified in claiming for itself, to get the country, which places so much hope on education and job training, out of its crisis.

Consolidation and development of *La Cinquième*

Following the period of its establishment beginning in 1995, *La Cinquième* has now entered the phase of development and consolidation.

La Cinquième will have to make it easier for our country to become more open to the outside world and, at the same time, to help to make France better known outside its own borders. For this purpose discussions are under way with cable operators in several foreign countries (both francophone and non-francophone) interested in taking our programmes.

Simultaneously, contacts concerning exchanges, coproductions and other forms of cooperation are being established with different educational channels in the world. In fact, *La Cinquième* took the initiative in creating AITED (International Association of Educational and Discovery Television Companies). This association groups together about 50 television channels with the final aim of creating a separate market specifically for educational programmes.

La Cinquième must use all possible means to increase access to knowledge:

- The first 'window' in its strategy to achieve this are information spots giving details of *La Cinquième*'s programmes that are transmitted by the other French television channels.
- The second window is *La Cinquième*'s range of educational programmes on its different networks.
- The third is the transmission on *La Cinquième* of programmes of educational value which will attract the interest of other networks (cable and satellite channels, job training organisations, telecommunications networks etc.), networks that would constitute the means of access to knowledge.

Thus, for example, a company wishing to promote an interactive compact disc dealing with a visit to the Louvre Museum could show on *La Cinquième* an extract of the type of visit to gallery X or Y , and then refer to the product that it has conceived.

This final component in *La Cinquième*'s programming is decisive, as it allows access between the system and the other networks, thus giving it multiple effectiveness and a greater ability to react to future developments.

Conclusion

One year after its launch, it is possible to make an initial interim assessment of this new public television channel. *La Cinquième*, like the most recent stations in this sector, had counted on a much more modest level of viewers than that which has actually been achieved for the daytime programmes screened by this channel. In fact, the number of viewers is impressive for programmes as demanding as those concerned with modern languages, philosophy, preventive health care, sciences, human or animal biology, and history.

The creation of *La Cinquième*, a channel for popular education, culture, travel and adventure, makes up for the substantial amount of time lost by our country in this field in comparison with the USA, Canada, Japan, and

– initially – Israel, where the first of these channels was established.

It addresses itself to the general public, the most important concentration of those who, for various reasons, did not receive further education, who have no access to modern job-training facilities, who have a poor knowledge of life in the countries surrounding France and of the solutions they provide to their own problems.

It is evident that *La Cinquième* shows respect above all for the least elitist social groups in our country by promoting the development of each person's intelligence, and not by flattering the most commonplace element in our make-up. It is because of this attitude of respect that this channel has found its right place. Its programmes must retain an approach that is modest but the very opposite of long-winded, realising the wishes of our audiences by taking a chance on the idea that everyone is intelligent, whatever his social position, but that few have the means of improving this position.

Didier Lecat, *a television and radio journalist by profession, is Director of Partnerships and Cultural Projects at* La Cinquième *and Director General of* La Cinquième Développement. *He is also co-founder and at present Secretary General of the International Association of Educational and Discovery Television Companies (AITED). Before joining* La Cinquième *he held appointments, among others, as Director of Communications at FNAC, as Director of Communications and Development of the Cité des Sciences et de l'Industrie de la Villette, Paris, and Director of Road Accident Prevention.*

Restarting educational broadcasting in Denmark to meet the challenges of the new technological environment

Mogens Arngot
Danmarks Radio, Copenhagen

Modern life has at breakneck speed become far more complex, demanding a comprehensive view. Our consciousness (or rational self) – worshipped in most cultures during the past couple of thousands of years – is no longer sufficiently well-equipped. Its capacity is too low and slow for modern life. We must increasingly relate to immense complex problems and situations to keep abreast of events.

This is of little regard, as we have the potential within ourselves. Our sub-consciousness has enormous power. We are able to pick up and handle many hundred thousand times more information in our sub-consciousness than in our conscious lives. Consequently we must begin to step up the cultivation of the sub-consciousness or intuitive way of thinking. We must trust it to a much higher degree, learning how to use it. In other words we must learn intuitive and complicated patterns of reaction towards complex problems. Moreover, we must learn that there are not necessarily rational and controllable answers to all problems. This will be a major task for education in the next few years.

Why am I telling this to you TV people? What does it have to do with my own new educational television department at the Danish Broadcasting Corporation?

The above applies in several ways. One connection is that images – particularly the living images of television – represent an eminent tool for intuitive learning. Second, the educational department 'TV ÅBEN' (TV-Open) has been set up during the past few years under the strong influence of the enormous re-adjustment offered to education by new technology.

The revival of educational broadcasting

Allow me to return to images and intuitive learning later, but first I would like to tell you something about TV-Open. TV-Open is a new programme department at the Danish Broadcasting Corporation: its main task is to broadcast educational programmes besides offering individual citizens and institutions access to DR's television channel if they wish to inform, take part in a discussion or just regard the world in a way diverging from the normal perspective of ourselves, the public broadcasters.

The Danish Broadcasting Corporation previously had an educational department producing and broadcasting both radio and television programmes for schools and adult education. The department was originally a part of the normal activities of DR and as such financed by the license fee, but then the Ministry of Education undertook to finance the entire department in the middle of the seventies. In the late eighties the Ministry of Education initiated a process of cost-cutting, when it was decided to remove the finance intended for educational broadcasts. As DR did not wish to assume the financial burden, the department was closed down in 1989. Since then the question has frequently been raised of re-instituting educational broadcasting in the financial network of DR. Many felt that educational broadcasting was a clear-cut obligation for any public service broadcaster.

The direct stimulus for the revival of educational broadcasting in Denmark was the decision by the Ministry of Education to begin exploring opportunities for providing 60,000 adults with new training facilities by the year 2000. The result was that the politicians decided to step up adult and further education in Denmark by establishing 10,000 new training opportunities per year – in both vocational training and general adult education, as the result of which the Government had to work out how this could be achieved. The ensuing report demonstrated that the only economical, feasible way was to include the electronic media used for distance and mass education, suggesting that the educational institutions should have access to DR's transmitting facilities at their own risk and responsibility.

It was this suggestion that caused DR to take action. Naturally, we did not want to relinquish broadcasting time without having any influence on the programmes and any way of preserving our control over broadcasting time. Hence it was decided two years ago to resume educational broadcasting on DR Television for a temporary trial period of 4 years.

Since there were not many funds available for such activities, the proposal of co-operation with interested parties outside DR was submitted, with regard to both programming and financing. Such parties might be educational institutions, various ministries or government departments, on the one hand, or major companies and institutions with a vested interest in having their educational video programmes broadcast, on the other – irrespective of whether they were produced by the institutions themselves or purchased from an independent producer. The aim was of course that these programmes could be used as a part of the education facilities, thus reducing the need for teachers.

Co-operation with educational publishers or video producers was also envisaged, who would have a commercial interest in selling back-up material, books and/or videos, for the television programmes broadcast by TV-Open.

Working Principles of *TV-Open*

The principle of TV-Open is that the department makes itself available and helps to acquire, produce and broadcast television programmes on DR's television channel.

- TV-Open has a minor budget of its own for purchasing and developing educational programmes, but it is not intended that the department should normally produce programmes itself.
- TV-Open offers broadcasting time, help from media experts in the development of ideas and programmes, advance publicity and launching of programmes and assistance in the co-operation between producers, publishers and others involved in a project.
- TV-Open will first and foremost contribute to the development and acquisition of educational programmes, while the development of ideas, the financing and the production is mainly assigned to institutions, organisations and others offering education in our society.
- TV-Open willingly assumes control of production, adopting a consultant role in the production process, should authorities, organisations, publishers or educational institutions lack experience and require our help.

As mentioned above, we have also applied the idea of the open principle in two other areas offered by TV-Open:

- The first area is open access to the television channel for institutions, associations and organisations having information they would like to distribute to the entire Danish population; for health campaigns (on alcohol or AIDS, child-care etc.), information on conditions and relations within the EC, social problems in third world countries and new documentary films available free of charge in public libraries.
- The other area is open access for ordinary people who have produced a small video dealing with a topic they are really interested in or expressing their opinions or feelings.

The only requirement in these two areas is that on no account must any kind of advertising be shown and that nothing must be said or shown contravening DR's rules on proper broadcasting or the Danish penal code. Apart from that there is complete freedom of expression in the time-slot allotted to these kinds of programmes, amounting to four hours of first-time broadcasts and four hours of repeats per week.

In the area of general adult education TV-Open is first and foremost an opportunity to make broadcasting-time available to independent producers and others offering television programmes in the field of general adult education. Naturally, users can also approach us to make their needs known, suggesting the purchase and broadcast of programmes catering for their specific interests, as can individual people wanting to use the programmes in the privacy in their homes as well as groups of users from adult education centres and education associations or participants in vocational training.

Courses for adult education

The contents of the programmes in this kind of adult education will normally concern people's leisure-time activities or family life, the citizens' aim to gain proficiency in foreign languages, cultural and economic affairs, 'Do-It-Yourself' courses and knowledge about new technology. The programmes may either be targeted at teacher-guided education, for example in evening classes, or they may be intended for private study in the home.

Our programme *Piano School* is a typical example. It addresses 'false beginners'. The series comprises ten 15-minute programmes, produced on a lean budget by ourselves. The total cost amounted to only 200,000 Danish kroner (£20,000 approx) for all 10 programmes.

We embarked on a joint-venture with a publisher who took care of the accompanying booklet, and we also co-operated with a video production company that published the 10 programmes on video. In both cases we received royalties. So far 10,000 booklets and 5,000 videos have been sold; our production costs have been more than covered.

Another typical example is a series of 'Do-It-Yourself' programmes we are broadcasting just now. An independent production company inquired whether we would be interested in purchasing 12 'Do-It-Yourself' programmes very cheaply. With the letter of intent we had written to express

our interest it then approached a chain of shops selling all kinds of construction material as well as material and tools for DIY people, asking whether they would be willing to participate in the financing of the programmes. The only benefit for the chain would be an acknowledgement in the credit-list after the programmes. The chain agreed, so the programmes were produced and brought to us. We viewed the programmes and having found the quality satisfactory, we bought them at a very reasonable price. Let us look at an example.

Although we are not allowed to show commercials on DR TV by law, we may purchase programmes from anybody. This applies even if commercial contributors to the financing are mentioned in the credit list, provided the programmes are judged to be satisfactory by an independent editorial body.

Further education and in-service training

Concerning further education and in-service training, TV-Open is available to the entire system of further education and in-service training in Denmark. The educational programmes from TV-Open are not meant to be a substitute for teacher-guided education. The tradition of educational theory for adult education in Denmark is basically founded upon the idea that professional learning takes place in a social environment and that a positive social experience is an essential condition for good learning results. Teacher-student interaction constitutes the foundation of the learning process.

It is therefore imperative that the television programmes should be a tool in the learning process, rationalising and supporting the teachers efforts, partly by saving confrontation time in the more trivial parts of the teaching process, partly by reinforcing the teaching process in the cases when audio-visual communication can improve the result.

For major groups of people with a short formal education the visual substructure of the teaching will contribute towards breaking down barriers created by reading and writing difficulties, for example.

It is an enormous task to persuade the Danish educational system to take advantage of the very great opportunities offered by new technology, including television. New technical equipment must be purchased, software and educational programmes must be developed to substitute, sustain or supplement pure teacher-guided learning. Last but not least, trainee teachers must be taught how to use the new technology, and – an even greater challenge – the entire teaching profession must be re-educated.

But after a couple of years of constant work TV-Open is now well underway. We have already broadcast a number of smaller programme series intended for in-service training; now we are working on a number of major series. We spare no effort to find projects in which different media can work together.

A current example is a series produced in co-operation with the (Danish) Foundation for a Better Working Environment. The series of four live programmes was a part of the training for safety stewards. All major Danish workplaces are obliged to have safety stewards, who have to attend a course in safety-requirements every year. By producing this education as a television course and thus keeping the safety stewards in their normal working environment where they view the television programmes, it is possible to produce the course for only a third of the cost of a normal course, when participants have to travel to a training establishment.

The safety stewards were brought together on the shop floor for two hours on four Wednesdays. First, they watch the live programme which they can then phone in to with their questions and comments. The written material is distributed to them in advance, teletext being used for supplying additional information. It is possible immediately after the broadcast to contact a number of teachers via phone, fax or on-line. There are also plans to broadcast live radio programmes with questions phoned in to a panel of experts on the evening of the same day when the programmes are transmitted.

New digital technology will shortly present undreamt-of possibilities for television to produce different kinds of interactive education, both via cable and satellite, at the outset mainly by the use of the telephone or CD-ROM. TV-Open is well underway, having initiated a few projects of this kind, but I am not yet able to give more details.

Success in development
When TV-Open started just under two years ago our output was one hour every afternoon from Wednesday to Thursday. With a staff of eight and a

budget of approx. 4 million Danish kroner (£400,000 approx) for the first half a year we managed to broadcast 50 hours of programmes. Since then we have moved very fast. Our current output is 20 hours per week, including 10 hours of repeats. According to our estimates, we will broadcast all in all about 650 hours this year with a staff that has been increased to 25. Our total budget amounts to 12.5 million Danish kroner (£1.8 million approx).

TV-Open was intended as an experiment that should run for four years, after which time it was to be evaluated. But we have been moving so fast (and in all modesty we have been so successful) that the evaluation took place late last year. The result was that TV-Open was established as a regular television department on January I this year.

TV-Open broadcasts to narrow target groups, which explains why we occupy marginal parts of the programme schedule, namely late in the evening, Sunday mornings, and weekday mornings and afternoons. Of course, we cannot attract a large number of viewers to our programmes. Our share is on average between 0.5 and 3 per cent. Beginning this autumn, DR will open a new channel during prime time (from 8 p.m. to 11.30 p.m.) and TV-Open will appear on this channel at least twice for half hour each week.

Images and intuitive thinking

Now I would like to return to the subject of images and intuitive thinking including my ideas of what will be incredibly important for us as technological mediators of education. Allow me in the next part of my presentation to rise a little above the plane of logic and strict rationality. I will begin by drawing a couple of small period pictures.

1. The first picture deals with language.

Communication is a resource. The one who possesses communication possesses power. The word, written or spoken, is a tool for communication and thus for power. The elite has therefore always tried to take possession of the word and outlined exclusive rules for its use. Every time the language moves in a undesired, undisciplined direction the reins are tightened. Most of us experience language as a mechanism of oppression, imposing restrictions on what we think or feel: a mechanism we are incessantly forced to struggle against.

It is said that the language is kept in a tight and regular rein because it can then be used for the clear and pure intellectual communication of ideas, passing from one bright mind to another. Precise and regular language results in a precise transmission of information.

But language is not reality. As a matter of fact it is completely detached from reality and the abstract. The written word is worse than the spoken, but both are incredibly far removed from what things look, feel, smell and sound like. Pictures, on the other hand, are very concrete. I will return to that later.

2. The second representation of real life is also based upon the Danish school.

We are all living in a 'you-shall-not-implement-anything-unless-you-are-able-to-control-it' society. At school this is reflected in the fixation upon the curriculum and degrees. For many years there has been a wish to do something else. Experiments with statements instead of marks have been tried, the problem-solving ability has been trained in replacement of fingertip knowledge. Emphasis has been placed on the process and collective action instead of the product and the individual.

The Danish school is still ruled by the curriculum, however, by the same abstract linguistic learning/control method without any contact with reality. The tools have not changed.

It has not been possible to go any further than checking whether pupils acquired some abstract knowledge temporarily. Whether the learning will leave any trace of suitable behaviour has been impossible to ascertain.

Here I have referred to the primary and lower secondary school, but what I have said applies by and large to all Danish educational institutions. The wish to control the pupils' acquisition of knowledge compels all learning to pass through the narrow funnel of consciousness and linguistic abstraction.

3. The third picture deals with our private lives in which we will simplify our way of making decisions.

Human beings will witness the problems and problem-solving in their private lives computerised to an increasing extent. Once their personal profile, social and economic situation have been coded and fed into the computer, decisions concerning purchase needs, diet, contact with authorities, vacation, heating, relations with society, the programme to see on the telly and many others will be removed. It will all be handled by the computer.

But by computerising the way of presenting problems, the problems will however be individualised and removed from their social connection – and the training in dealing with various life situations will be lost.

At the same time the reality of today's society becomes more and more complicated, demanding special knowledge in an endless number of areas. The ways of presenting different problems will tend to become isolated from each other in the computerisation process, causing mankind to lose a global view of matters.

Society's *demand* for the ability to re-adjust and for flexibility will then reflected in the ability to move from one little box to the other, not in the ability to realise, analyse and react appropriately.

We will, however, continue to be human beings with a need for social identity; our need for being together socially and having a reference to a certain group of people that can offer a feeling of belonging and identity will still be there – even outside the close family-circle.

This could give rise to the apprehension that we will then require social training and training to identify problems for the purpose of living both a private and social life in the community.

And now we have arrived back at the point I started on in my introduction: *intuitive intelligence* – or the intelligence of the sub-consciousness. I believe that in the years to come we will experience a growing alertness towards, and an upgrading of, intuitive capacities.

Our consciousness – our logical self – cultivated during the past couple of thousands of years is no longer adequate. Its capacity is too low, too slow for modern life. We must increasingly relate to major complex problems and situations to keep abreast of events. The word, both spoken and written, is too sluggish to be of use.

But that does not really matter because we have the potential within ourselves. The sub-consciousness has a tremendous power. We are able to absorb many hundred times more information directly into our sub-consciousness than if it passes through our consciousness.

Images and the communication of images – our world as television people – are so loaded with information that by and large they cannot be used in the consciousness. But they certainly can be used by the sub-consciousness.

We must therefore now begin to cultivate the sub-consciousness – the intuitive – much more. We must trust it to higher degree. We must learn complicated patterns of response to complicated problems, where the capacity of the consciousness is too low. We will increasingly learn by experience than by means of the rational and conscious work of the mind.

Of course, this is not at all new information. We have come by most of what we have learned and what we are able to do by experience, virtually without using our consciousness. But that has not yet been recognised. For thousands of years man has cultivated the intellectual and rational mind in the belief that consciousness was in command.

But we are still – to a very high degree – directed by the intuitive mind. So far the intuitive mind has not been sufficiently utilised. The problem for both religious and political societies has of course been that the intuitive mind is difficult to control and in particular it is not as dirigible as the consciousness of the people.

What does this intuitive focusing mean to us as producers of software for the information society?

1. Very rationally, logically and consciously controlled information and technology will be downgraded. Images and visually endowed information will be given a higher priority.
2. Two-way communication will gain higher priority; interactive facilities in the communication of information will play a key role, i.e. the receiver of the message must have opportunities to influence both the course of the information and the format of the information itself.
3. The operation of the receiving equipment must be concrete, in touch with reality, which implies that it must be voice- or motion-controlled, not intellectually controlled.

To be more specific let me return finally to my former three small pictures of real life. If we begin with the thesis on language and consciousness, the development will lead us away from the clear, distinct and factual transmission of information between human beings. This does not mean that we will not need this kind of interaction – at least not temporarily, but it will lose its importance.

The receiving equipment, the built-in computer and TV receiver, must be able to perform on both the micro-level and the macro-level. It must be able to jump fast from the concrete, isolated and precise linguistic level to a visual level describing totalities and coherence.

Concerning the thesis about our culture of control, tendencies towards an easing-up of the process can already be seen. The exact sciences are for example currently opening up towards the non-exact humanistic sciences: it is accepted that there are things that cannot be explained logically and finally – but only can be experienced and used intuitively. This will mean for us in our capacity as information-workers that the users will need or demand a contributory influence on *which* information they want and *when* they want it – and, last but not least, *how* they want it.

It sounds like a paradox – but the unconscious user makes demands. The most important demand will probably be that the user will have a contributory influence while the transmission of information is taking place. And as a result of this, people will share the responsibility for what they receive and where they are going. And in the process, the aim that is fixed in advance and controllable and consequently the present culture of control will gradually be relinquished.

Finally the thesis about private lives. The information instrument (the convergence of the computer with the TV receiver) will in future be able to accomplish increasingly concrete tasks, thus loosening the accomplishment of the tasks from a social context. But our social lives still require our ability to perform social tasks aptly, and in our economic lives and lives in the community there is a downright need for these abilities.

So, in my opinion, there will be a need for training comprehensive thinking and comprehensive behaviour via the computer-cum-TV receiver as a counter-measure to prevent the mechanisation of problem-solving.

There will quite simply be a need for training the ability to react appropriately in complex social situations outside the sphere of the amputated conscious mind, which means nourishing and stimulating intuitive ability.

We have been bound by the much overrated consciousness for many hundreds of years, but I believe that in the years to come we can begin to liberate ourselves again from its constraints – paradoxically, compelled by the development of information technology. I, for my part, look forward to taking part.

Mogens Arngot *is Head of the Department of Education and Public Access, a division of the Danish Broadcasting Corporation (DR). He obtained a Master of Communication degree in 1982; subsequent studies and research work culminated in a thesis on 'The influence of television on the viewer, especially in the area of education'. Since 1984 he worked as a television producer for the department of education, later for the department of documentary of DR. In 1994 he was appointed Head of TV-Åben (TV Open).*

2: Success Stories of Educational Programming

Riddles of the world – explained and understood?

Wolfgang Homering
Department Culture and Society, ZDF, Mainz

Once the well-known literary critic Marcel Reich-Ranicki expressed himself on his various roles in a talk show as follows, 'Years ago I was made fun of as a pedant, today I am called an entertainer: I would like to be both and I enjoy being both.' A public service television corporation is in much the same situation. There is an information and educational remit which the public service systems in Germany have devoted themselves to with energy and commitment since their foundation. In times of competition with the commercial companies, however, the viewers are turning their backs on these educational programmes.

We at the ZDF can tell you a thing or two about that. Our special situation of possessing only one channel on which we have to broadcast a complete programme has made it difficult in recent years to find a suitable place for this category of programmes. We have never been able to fall back on a second channel and set up a niche for a target audience which, although only small, regularly and with commitment makes use of this programme genre and, I hope, profits from it.

This landscape has been dried up by raw winds. The viewers stayed away, no doubt because it is more refreshing to listen in to a seemingly true-to-life talk show in the afternoon or early evening than to deal with didactically edited analyses and processes. We at the ZDF have been forced to experience this in a very drastic way. So something completely new had to be thought up and radically implemented. If we wanted to impart important themes, so-called 'educational content', in an objectively precise and intelligible way, we had to proceed differently. So we decided, after carrying out thorough research into the viewers, to try and produce programmes with the following features:

- transmission times that are easy to remember and remain unchanged;
- the best transmission time available;
- clear content which is easy to grasp and suitable for gaining the viewers' interest in definite areas of life, which, if you like, could be termed classical educational content.

These areas are, to mention only a few: historical subjects, areas of natural science, the history of art and culture, the myths and legends of mankind and the threats to and beauties of earth's nature.

Fixing the transmission time to Sundays from 7:30 to 8:15 p.m. has given this evening time a clear image. We do not describe these broadcasts as educational programmes. We offer the public subjects which are worth watching and thinking about. What the viewers make of them is something we leave open.

Allow me to quote the Head of the Culture Department, Dr Hans Helmut Hillrichs, to elucidate these programme planning decisions:

Since the end of the 80s the following development has been emerging in the *documentary* area of the Culture Department:

1. Giving up an *educational programme* anchored in the programme with a weekly documentary, but which remained ineffectual and whose audience dwindled on account of its rigid, often academic conception.

2. The gradual revision of the documentary programmes, the aim being not to appeal exclusively or chiefly to a specialised audience that was interested in literature, art or culture, but to choose and develop the subjects so that they reached not just the small group of those with previous knowledge, but also viewers whose interest could *potentially be aroused*.

3. The findings [of the ARD/ZDF study 'Culture and Media'[1]] … have contributed towards getting away from certain editorial truisms which say that one has to enlighten the viewer as fast as possible and condescendingly instruct him on what one already knows oneself. Instead, a different attitude also became possible: no longer to regard the viewer as a recipient of certain lessons, but to go on a journey of discovery with him almost as if he were an equal partner.

   There was only a single programme form that had successfully demonstrated that: namely, the series *Terra-X*. Attempts to achieve a development here were now made in various departments, especially in the department Culture and Society, but also in the Literature and Art department and finally in the area of science and technology, where in the *Knoff-hoff-Show* a model was developed, which, although completely different, was quite comparable to the successes of *Terra-X*. These attempts can be brought together under the motto: Making it possible to experience science, history and culture.

4. In addition to the three above-mentioned development trends there is a fourth very important current, viz. a rising demand and a noticeable increase in competence in the area of counselling broadcasts. The health magazine *Practice* should be mentioned here as should the *Contact* broadcasts from the department Church and Life, which produced a considerable response from the viewers.

---

1   Frank, Bernward; Maletzke, Gerhard; Müller-Sachse, Karl H.: *Kultur und Medien. Angebote – Interessen – Verhalten.* Eine Studie der ARD/ZDF-Medienkommission. Baden-Baden: Nomos 1991 (Schriftenreihe Media-Perspektiven Nr. 11)

The impact of these four lines of development can be summed up as follows:

- They have led to the fact that the Main Department Culture has found its skills and qualities to a greater extent in the area of what is *popular* and less in serving a limited specialised audience that already has some knowledge of the subject.
- They have moved culture closer to issues of *life and survival.*
- They have resulted in vitalising and up-dating *the concept of culture which is understood in a broader sense* and which is based on the generous subject canon of the Main Department.
- By creatively crossing the borders between the individual subjects and areas they have led to an increase in new themes, but also new narrative styles and presentation forms.

With the potential viewer for our new series in mind, Dr Hillrich referred to another finding of the ARD/ZDF study 'Culture and Media', which he summarised as follows:

> The 'culture specialist', who is only interested in a narrow cultural segment, is the exception, while the 'culture generalist', who is interested in areas bordering on his main interests, is the rule. In addition, this study indicated a potential target audience in the order of 12 per cent whose interest in culture in the broader sense could be aroused, and gave television at least limited chances of overcoming traditional access barriers to cultural programmes and of also bringing those closer to culture whose socialisation and way of life had up to then kept them away from it.

The programmes that we have conceived on these lines succeeded in meeting, to a greater extent than we expected, the wish of people to be both informed and 'educated'. The response to this series was and is still astonishing. More on that later.

The form of the documentary plays a decisive part. The willingness of viewers to allow stories to be told to them, to accept a narrative style that is easy to grasp and follow, was not surprising. The intellect and the heart are addressed, and only in this combination can attention be captured in the torrent of programmes that overwhelms the viewers.

I should like to give three examples. Let me begin with a newly conceived series which we have named *SPHINX – The secrets of history*. In the history of the world there have been spectacular events and historic personalities who still stimulate people's imagination even today. The reasons for this fascination remain largely obscure. This fact is the peg on which we have hung the documentaries planned for this series, which ran with great success and a lot of extra work. The need to interpret the secrets of the world is very pronounced, even in people without any awareness of history. So in the first series we focused on figures, on personalities, with whom a broad audience is familiar on account of their being especially well known. We serve up a stereotype and destroy it at the same time. It is from this suspense that stories live. Some of the subjects of this series were *Cleopatra, Hannibal* and *The Huns*.

The series which ran the longest on the ZDF under the assumptions just described is at the same time the best-known: *TERRA-X – Vorstoß ins Unbekannte* (TERRA-X – Venturing into the unknown). This series has

become an integral part of Sunday evenings, and the themes it deals with have been very well received. The stimulus to mental speculation rates highly, not for the sake of sensationalism, but in order to pursue further the serious approaches to the subjects with the help of science.

One broadcast had as its subject *Death in the Bulrushes. Moses and the miracle of the desert.* Theologians, archaeologists, geologists and oceanographers have in recent times again been intensively investigating spectacular miracles in the Old Testament. Are they fantastic exaggerations or an impressive propaganda for an important new religion? Whether it is actually legitimate to back up the reports of miracles using the yardstick of science is another question. In this series we attempted to do so; God's greatness and his miracles are not diminished when we humans recognise that the force of nature's laws assumes dimensions which border on a miracle.

Scientific connections are frequently presented in our television studios. Imposing experiments are performed which are also quite impressive in pictures. This usually happens in a very entertaining way and to the amusement of the viewers; the 'aha' effect is similar to that achieved by a conjuring trick. Our science series *Knoff-Hoff Show* is evidence of this.

Another form was tried out with the three-part series *Sun, Moon and Stars.* Research into the sun, moon and stars and its findings have been presented to the public again and again, rarely, however, from the point of view that the sky came down to earth and mixed with the humans, shaped their thought, their actions and above all their language, their religions and their everyday life. Sun, moon and stars have entered myths and fairy-

tales, churches and nurseries, inspired poets, thinkers and designers. In our country the story of our relationship with the cosmos has always played a role. That is what is to be presented in these three documentaries.

Who are the viewers of these broadcasts? In the meantime we have accurate information. I should like to give you some important data on this which were obtained for the *SPHINX* series in 1995. These data also apply, with slight variations, to the other series transmitted in this strand on Sundays at 7:30 p.m.

On average each broadcast was seen by 5.48 million viewers, 2.98 million women and 2.5 million men. The market share was 17.7 per cent. In view of the strong competitive programmes this is a very good position. Of these viewers 12 per cent have 'Abitur' (school leaving certificate for university admission), 4 per cent are simple workers, 5 per cent skilled workers, 9 per cent have an elementary school education with vocational training and 14 per cent live in a household on their own. These are some of the viewer categories out of a list of 30 that were examined.

These also included the age structures of the viewers: 160,000 of the 6- to 13-year-olds watched, 90,000 14- to 19-year-olds, 430,000 20- to 29-year-olds, 730,000 30- to 39-year-olds and 550,000 40- to 49-year-olds. The 50- to 64-year-olds with 1.57 million and those over 65 with 1.92 million viewers make up the largest groups. Now it is an important task for us to win over the support of more younger viewers.

One or two things have got going for the broadcasts considered here. Specialised support material is on offer for almost all the programmes; back-up books, CD-ROMs, reading lists from the foundation *Stiftung Lesen*, video cassettes and manuscripts.

Productions cost money. To secure the financing, we made agreements with partners, who do not fail to join in the discussions on the content, e.g. with ORF, Canal+, The Discovery Channel, The Learning Channel, TV Ashai Japan, Australian Broadcasting Company, the National Geographic Society, to mention only the most important.

In conclusion I should like to note that responsibility for all the broadcasts in this series rests with one department, the Culture and Society department, which continues the tradition of its predecessors, the Education department and the Culture, Education and Society department.

Wolfgang Homering *studied for his diploma Philosophy and Theology at Salzburg University. From 1973 to 1977 he worked in the area of out-of-school education for young people at various institutions; from 1977 to 1980 he studied Media Didactics at the Fachhochschule in Cologne (diploma). Since 1985 he has been an editor in the Culture and Society Department where documentation series like* TERRA-X *and* SPHINX – Secrets of History *are produced. Before this, he worked as an editor at the ZDF Education Department, producing children's programmes like* Rappelkiste, Neues aus Uhlenbusch, *and* Löwenzahn.

Baby It's You

or: How the 'wild animal' in your living room becomes a human being

Karen Brown
Channel Four Television, London

This 6-part educational series is a good example of the kind of programmes which Channel 4's education department commissions. Popular and accessible, it aims to beguile viewers first, and then to educate. The fact that its first aim is to please does not mean that the educational aspirations are any less clear.

This series tried to show the development – physical, mental and social – of the young human, starting at birth and working carefully through the first three years of life. The subject was examined from the baby's perspective. What emerged was not a 'How to Bring Up Your Baby' series but rather a series which, although equally helpful to parents, would build an understanding of the nature of the human species and why babies and young children behave in the way that they do.

As the programme makers wrote: 'A baby achieves more in the first two years than the rest of its life, … in 15 short months, a baby achieves in miniature what it has taken the human race thousands of years of evolution to perfect – turning the skeletal structure upright and moving about on two legs.'

The series was made by the independent production company Wall to Wall, and it had high production values and a generous budget of about one hundred and twenty thousand pounds sterling per half hour. This was only possible because of a co-production deal, a three-way partnership between The Learning Channel, the distributors ITEL and Channel 4.

I was the Commissioning Editor responsible for the series as well as for other adult education programmes on Channel 4. It may be of interest that The Learning Channel and Discovery are my closest co-production partners and the relationship allows us to achieve more than we could otherwise hope to.

The series was scheduled during peak transmission at 8.30 p.m., midweek just when people come home and expect to be diverted after a hard day and just when the other channels provide the strongest competition. Its average audience was just under 3 million viewers and it made it into Channel 4's list of top 20 programmes several times. It achieved a high audience appreciation index, and in particular it was appreciated by young people and by women.

As the baby starts to refine her speech, she has to learn the correct mouth shapes to produce the sounds she wants.

There is an old British proverb which says: never work with children or animals. But the producers wanted to adopt the approach of a wildlife film and to observe the babies in the same way as animals and to try to capture each phase in their development. After some experimentation, it quickly became clear that the filming process would need to draw more from the techniques of drama than from those of wildlife films.

They had to find a method of working which would enable them to match the academic knowledge of child development with the naturalistic behaviour of young humans. They had an extended period of pre-production when they worked out the key moments of development. Then the production team advertised for a cast of some 25 babies. There was no shortage of volunteers! Babies of different ages and different stages of development were cast.

In their desire to be authoritative and informed by the latest scientific research, the production team had won the support of Annette Karmiloff-Smith, a Professor of Psychology,[1] who became series consultant. She understood the challenge of helping to turn the academic work into clear, simple visual information. She also wrote the book which accompanied the series.

The themes were pursued chronologically in each programme from birth and early life up until three years old. Then the directors set about working out how they could illustrate the various facts which they wished to convey in each programme unit. In some cases this was not an easy task; for instance, when it came to illustrating how we learn to reason, plan, and solve problems.

And it is even harder to describe in words the kind of imaginative solutions they came to. To display different crawling techniques they used specialist camera equipment and glass to observe the babies' crawling action from underneath. The most unusual of our performers was undoubtedly the 'bottom shuffler'.

---

1 Professor Annette Karmiloff-Smith, Professor of Psychology at University College, London. She is also a Fellow of the British Academy. Formerly a research collaborator of Jean Piaget and Bärbel Inhelder, she is a Senior Scientist with a Special Appointment at the Medical Research Council's Cognitive Development Unit in London.

BABY IT'S YOU

How the 'wild animal' in your living room becomes a human being

Baby It's You, a major new six-part series, will change your mind about babies forever ...

Baby It's You takes the viewer inside the baby's world, using natural filming techniques usually reserved for polar bears and elephants, to reveal the processes behind the miraculous transformation from a helpless organism to a walking, talking, thinking human being – revealing an arduous, frustrating and often terrifying journey.

THE PROGRAMMES: walking upright, using tools, talking. thinking and making friends – characteristics that define us as human beings and seperate us from the rest of the animal world. Each of the six episodes of *Baby It's You* look at one of these 'human' aspects and traces its development over the first years of life.

Programme 1: IN THE BEGINNING

From the very first moment after birth: how babies see, hear, smell and taste. How the newborn prefers to look at and listen to people more than anything else, how he motivates other people to care for him ... and how, through them, he starts to make sense of the world around him.

Programme 2: FIRST STEPS

Observes the long, sometimes painful, often gleeful struggle to sit up, crawl, struggle around aided by furniture and finally to make that one small step for man.

Programme 3: TAKING HOLD

From the primitve grasp of the newborn to the creativity and dexterity of a two-year-old. We reveal how the baby learns to co-ordinate hand and eye, pick up objects and drop them and how these skills are put together with the tools of everyday life: spoons, toothbrushes and pencils.

Programme 4: WORD OF MOUTH

From the first gurgles to the ingenious story-telling of a three-year-old. How a child learns first to communicate and then to talk – at first to herself and then to everyone else.

Programme 5: THE THINKER

What exactly does a baby learn when he empties the contents of a cupboard onto the floor? What happens in a baby's mind when she 'feeds' her dolly? How do children learn to reason, plan and begin to solve problems?

Programme 6: YOU AND ME

The final programme looks at how babies develop one of the most tricky human skills of all: getting on with other people. When do children develop a sense of self? How do they understand the feeling of others? When do they start to make real friends?

First broadcast:	4th April 1996; 8:30 – 9:00 p.m.
Series Producer:	David Hickman
Executice Producer:	Alex Graham
Directors:	Leanne Klein, David Hickman
Production Company:	A Wall to Wall television production for Channel 4, Discovery Networks & ITEL
C4 Commissioning Ed.:	Karen Brown

Excerpt from a Press Release

48

More difficult than these general informational scenes was capturing the crucial moment of development in the first tentative moment that the child achieved it. However, the parents attended a briefing seminar where the behavioural stages were explained to them and they were told when they might expect them to take place.

Back at home they were asked to phone in whenever one of these developments looked as if it was about to happen. The parents also kept a record in their child's personal development diary which was used to inform both the series and the book.

It was a telephone call which enabled the cameraman to capture the moment when one of the babies first learned to use a pincer movement with its thumb and index finger. No other animal has this ability and it develops into the skill of fastening buttons and bottle tops, using pens and paintbrushes. In the film you see a child carefully trying to pick up sultanas between finger and thumb, gradually perfecting her control until she is able to feed them one by one into her mouth.

This kind of determination on the part of the programme makers and their subjects is, of course, not unique in the history film-making. There is a story which I believe to be true of a wildlife cameraman who waited twelve months to capture a female orang-utan at the moment that she came free from caring for her young. He wanted to capture on film her action of picking up a stone and using it as a tool to crack a nut. On this day, finally, after a year of waiting and observing, she did indeed pick up a stone and use it to crack a nut. But at the crucial moment his film ran out and he had to re-load the camera.

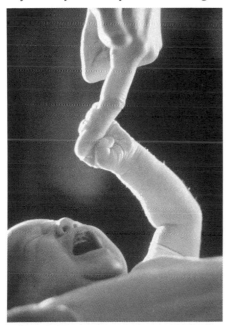

The frustrations of working with children do offer some remedies which may not be available to wildlife cameramen. In the programme on reasoning, Polly's ability to put thoughts together to achieve her aims was illustrated by a sequence where she gazed up at a biscuit tin out of her reach. Then a thought struck her and she pulled up a stool, stood on it and climbed onto the kitchen counter and up to the tin. Moments later she was rewarded with the fruits of her newly acquired reasoning power and we saw her happily munching her biscuit. In fact, this took many takes to achieve, but

The newborn baby demonstrates the grasping reflex.

49

the production team were ably supported by Polly's ability to act naturally in front of the camera and her appetite for an unlimited supply of biscuits.

The achievement of *Baby It's You* was that it found a way of presenting information about child development in a non-didactic fashion by inventing a grammar which allowed the audience to see it all for themselves. At the same time it succeeded in charming and entertaining the audience.

Nearly all Channel 4's adult education programmes are transmitted in peak time. History, health, social issues, campaigns, special interests and educational features like *Baby It's You* all form part of the brief. The aim is to reach out to the audience and win them over to watch programmes about subjects which they might not have considered interesting or important. These and other Channel 4 programmes are supported with booklets, telephone information lines, discussions on the Internet and various other schemes, all under the editorship of Paula Snyder.

Karen Brown *joined Channel 4 in 1987 to work in the News and Current Affairs Department. In 1992 she became Commissioning Editor for Education, responsible for developing Channel 4's educational strategy including its programme support, and for commissioning campaigns. The output ranged from philosophy to health, and from food to archaeology, including the Basel Prize winning* Time Team. *She recently became Controller of Factual Programmes with overall responsibility for approximately 35 per cent of Channel 4's output.*

Kapusta –
A first-aid course in Russian

Roman Schatz
Finnish Broadcasting Corporation (YLE), Helsinki

The Foreign Language Department of the Finnish Broadcasting Corporation (YLE) produces mainly instructive educational television programmes. The acceptance for language tuition is very great in Finland – it is not difficult to imagine: with a mother tongue like Finnish it is absolutely essential to learn foreign languages, and so since 1963 there has been a department which has specialised in the production and adaptation of language teaching programmes. Roughly 20 per cent of the Finnish population attend an adult education centre every six months, and over half of them enrol in language courses. At 80 per cent of the adult education centres programmes are used which we have produced or co-produced.

In the following, I shall describe a Russian course called *Kapusta*, a 'first-aid course for Russian ', as we call it. But first I should like to briefly outline the present status of Russian as a foreign language in Finland and the relevant historical background.

For some years Finland's neighbour has no longer been the relatively predictable, centrally controlled Soviet Union. Instead, there is now a rapidly changing structure, which has a border with Finland about 1,500 km in length. A quick look at the map should therefore suffice to make it clear that Russian is an important foreign language in Finland. Nevertheless only around 1 per cent of Finnish schoolchildren choose Russian as a foreign language. The barter system that existed with the Soviet Union has broken down, so it is no longer possible, as it once was, to find a partner in the Soviet Union simply through a central institution. Now every company has to make and maintain its own contacts without the benefit of a central structure, and to do this proficiency in foreign languages is necessary.

From 1806–1917 Finland was part of the Russian empire under the Czars, an autonomous grand duchy, and it is not surprising that there is still some prejudice against the Russian language. In the Second World War Finns and Russians fought against each other, and the old teaching material from the communist times is full of unintentional humour.

In 1995 there was a relatively large-scale campaign to revive interest in Russian. President Martti Ahtisaari acted as patron. On joining the EU

Finland had recommended itself as a country with an extensive knowledge of Eastern Europe, and Finland's eastern border is the only common border between the EU and Russia. So that the promise 'We know what's going on in Russia' does not turn out to be an empty shell, it must now be ensured that Russian is learnt voluntarily and with motivation in Finland. It was against this background that we therefore began to produce *Kapusta*, a television series of eight 20-minute programmes, in order to break down prejudices, to motivate the public and to enhance the negative image of everything that has anything to do with Russia and Russian. Our message is: Russian is modern, Russian is pop, Russian is sexy.

We have consciously tried to do something different with the Russian language this time. The course package, the back-up material that is part of *Kapusta*, comprises an audio cassette, a disc with several games, a CD-ROM with an animated adventure game in which you are abandoned in a Russian city and then have to cope with the situation, and two books. Arto Mustajoki, vice-chancellor and professor for Russian at the University of Helsinki, was responsible for the didactic concept, and in the course of the production he turned out to be a surprisingly humorous person.

In these eight parts it is a matter of decoding the Cyrillic alphabet, or making it digestible, and of operating with a vocabulary of two to three thousand words that is recognisable, immediately and without any previous knowledge. In addition, simple everyday Russian phrases are taught: greetings, thanks, apologies, asking oneself simple questions.

We have tackled the matter with a lot of self-irony and have tried to bring

52

important Finnish people into the programme, to satisfy the play instinct and to make the whole thing as easy-going as possible – bread and games.

'Kapusta' means in Russian 'head of cabbage', and that is the logo of the whole series, but it has nothing to do with the eating habits in Russia. *'Kapusta'* also means in Finnish slang 'head', 'bean', 'dome', and in some east Finnish dialects *'Kapusta'* is a wooden ladle as well. And in Russian slang it also means 'cash', 'lolly', 'dough'. So the motto of the whole media package is: Get Russian into your bean – and if need be, with a ladle. And a cabbage serves as the logo.

The eight parts are magazine broadcasts with different elements. There is a magician who effectively conjures up the Cyrillic letters; there are play-ful and amusing phraseology sequences; there is a plot, in which Mato Valtonen (a musician from the well-known 'Leningrad Cowboys') is forced to learn Russian by his mother. At the end of each programme prominent studio guests play a computer game in which they can win a million rou-bles as the main prize, that is about US$ 200.

Other prominent Finnish figures are Nina Björkfeldt, a specialist in Russian and a former Miss Scandinavia, Pilvi Hanhikorpi, the Finnish Milkmaid of 1996 (roughly comparable to a wine queen in Germany) and Olli-Pekka Heinonen, the acting Finnish Minister of Education. Elina Haavio-Mannila, the best-known sexologist in Finland, also joined in (and won the million rouble prize). Matti Pellonpää, who plays the main part in almost all Aki Kaurismäki films, was a studio guest in the last instalment. He died shortly after the filming, and this was his last appearance on television.

The *Kapusta* series was first transmitted in autumn 1995. The press wrote very positive reviews. Normally it is rather difficult to induce the newspapers to write anything at all about a language course on television. In this case, however, we had big headlines in almost all the major Finnish newspapers, such as, for example, 'Who's afraid of Russian?' or 'Flirting and cursing in Russian'.

As far as the television viewers are concerned, we have no reliable statistical information: we know how many viewers we have, but we do not know who they are. It can be conjectured, however, that it was particularly the younger members of the public who welcomed this series so positively. The traditional, somewhat older, language learning audience, who also attended the courses at the adult education centres, tended to reject it in some cases. Example: 'I don't learn enough from this course; it is too humorous for me and not educational enough.'

Our audience rating was around 150,000 viewers per instalment, which, with a total population of 5 million Fins, is really tremendous for a Russian television course.

The additional material we produced also sold very well. Some 5,000 Russian First-Aid Boxes containing the back-up books, the audio cassette and the computer game have been purchased. So that is one pack per thousand inhabitants in Finland. Over 1,000 CD-ROMs have been sold up to now.

Our own broadcasting corporation has also reacted very positively to this series. The team won Finnish Television's second prize for education, which is awarded by our company and the commercial competition. We have been given the go-ahead for the next 20 instalments and the chance to transmit an abridged version of the course (2 x 25 minutes) in the prime time as an entertainment programme.

The entire production, the 8 x 20 minutes of television, cost altogether only about US$ 200,000, including technical costs, wages and cash expenditure. Of course, in Helsinki, when it is a matter of Russian courses, we enjoy a geographical advantage – St Petersburg is only three hours away from us by car.

We hope that with our *Kapusta* series we have managed to eliminate prejudices and have prepared the ground for a revival of a broad knowledge of Russian in Finland, without political burdens from the past, but with a lot of irony and humour.

Roman Schatz, *born in Germany where he completed his studies and started his career as a TV and radio journalist, lives in Finland since 1986 and works as an executive producer at the Finnish Broadcasting Company YLE. He is author of several books, translator and language instructor, and has specialised in language education through electronic media.*

Success in cable networks:
The Discovery Channel

Joyce Taylor
Discovery Communications Europe, London

At one time in my career I spent 8 years as Producer/Director of Film and Video at a university. I made programmes about genetics and geology, management and microbiology, surgery and sewage. I also learnt to live with the fact that in many academic circles, books are respectable and television is not. I have sat at countless dinner parties and heard people tell each other that they rarely watch television and that they regard their children's interest in television as 'a bad thing'. This is sad because television and video offer so many opportunities. As a window on the world taking us to places or situations we would not otherwise encounter. As a provider of case study material it can give a general context, it can illustrate examples. It can demonstrate practical 'how to' skills.

Discovery Communications is a company dedicated to providing quality products and services designed to satisfy the curious mind. At the heart of Discovery is television in the form of The Discovery Channel and The Learning Channel. Discovery is distributed world-wide in 60 territories and in Europe it reaches over 11 million homes.

The Discovery Channel delivers high quality, accessible factual programming that is engaging, entertaining and stimulating. We invite our viewers to 'explore their world'. But the way we do so is taylored to each region. So in Europe only about 25 per cent of the programming is the same as in the Unites States. The programmes we transmit are not didactic, in the sense that they are not primarily intended to educate, but they can be and are being used as an educational tool, and we know from our research that our viewers expect to learn from watching.

Our sister channel in Europe is The Learning Channel (TLC). It is what we call 'really useful television'. Its core schedule is practical 'how to' programming: gardening, crafts, house decoration, cooking, fishing, travel. All these series invite the viewer to move 'from viewing to doing'. In Europe TLC broadcasts during daytime and Discovery in the evening. (I confess we use the term TLC wherever possible, because we found that the word 'learning' keeps the viewers away and does not reflect adequately the channel's focus.)

There has been a fear that the growing multiplicity of television channels would lead to the driving out of documentary programmes and we

would be awash in a sea of soap operas and game shows. Of course, increasing bandwidth has led to increasing entertainment but it has also allowed channels like ours to establish and grow. And that's because there is a real desire for our kind of programmes.

Last year Discovery and United Nations co-sponsored the largest piece of global research ever undertaken which was conducted by Roper Starch Worldwide.[1] The research covered a wide range of subjects and opinions but included some questions about television. People were asked about the most important attributes of television programmes they watched. 'Educational' was the second most important description after 'interesting'. Other attributes like 'relaxing' and 'exciting' came well down the list.

In categories of programmes that viewers would like to see more of, movies came first, but home-produced news and informational programming came second and third. There were some interesting regional variations which seemed to indicate that there was a sort of 'hierarchy of needs'.

In countries where there had been very limited availability of television there was the greatest desire for entertainment. However, in many of these countries informational programmes had a negative connotation because they were associated with dull state fare or propaganda films. In more mature markets there was a sense that the need for mindless entertainment was satisfied and there was a thirst for interesting and involving factual fare. In Italy for example 4 out of 5 respondents wanted more factual programmes. Unlike many other European countries Italy has a very low

---

1 The Roper Starch 1995 Global Consumer Survey. Ref. Tom Miller, Senior Vice President, Roper Starch Worldwide Inc.

proportion of documentaries on its broadcast channels. As we launched earlier this year in Italy we were gratified with this finding.

At Discovery we also track the viewers' image of The Channel at regular intervals. When asked to rate Discovery along with other cable and satellite channels, viewers consistently place Discovery at the top with nearly 50 per cent, rating it as excellent or very good. This is way ahead of the next two channels, both of which are entertainment and score only 25 per cent each. Discovery also heads in the category of channels which show programmes 'that make you feel involved' – even ahead of the broadcast channels in the UK.

Who is the Discovery viewer? The channel is targeted to adults, but we know we have plenty of enthusiastic young people who also watch. The advertising sales people would say that our audience is generally more upmarket, more educated, and orientated more towards men than women. But demographics is much too restricting a way to look at our audience, and we have tried other ways of looking at our viewers. We have called some of them adventurers – mainly men that are fascinated by the physical world, pragmatists – mainly women interested in the practical side of life, and humanists – both men and women interested in people, history and culture. Each group finds different parts of the Discovery schedule attractive. But just to add to the earlier debate about research: I think it is great at telling us where we have been, but not so good at saying where we should go.

Of course, at Discovery I represent commercial television rather than public service TV, and we have to offer the viewers what they want in two ways: first, the broad offer of the channel has to appeal enough to attract people to pay a subscription fee.

John Hendricks is the founder of Discovery in the United States. The other day he was asked as to when he knew that Discovery was going to be a success – because it really struggled to become established in the early years. He said that it was when he got a call from a large cable company telling him that since they had taken Discovery sales were reporting a 4 per cent lift in penetration amongst homes which had consistently refused to hook up to cable.

We also have to appeal to our audience in a more focused way through the performance of the schedule because we are measured by ratings. This means we have to produce programmes which entertain as well as inform and we have to package, market and promote these programmes in a way that helps viewers find what they are interested in.

We have to work very hard at promoting programmes for a number of reasons: first, because we have to help viewers find them; second, because we are competing with many channels; third, because we are competing with other media for part of the viewers' day.

We have just done some research among 18- to 24-year-old men who are increasingly spending time with their computers. What it showed was that in general they regard watching television as a passive and relaxing experience. At the other end of the scale computer usage was interactive and stimulating. However, watching Discovery came between both experiences. It was not as demanding as the computer, demanding full attention, but it was enjoyable because it was not entirely passive.

Some of the focus group quotes were 'It entertains while it informs'; 'Watching Discovery is time spent learning and enjoying it'; 'It's like school you enjoy'. I like that quote because just as students respond to the lecture by a good teacher, we have to find the right mix of presenter, script and visuals that will engage and entertain our viewers so that they keep coming back.

I mentioned at the start that the channels are at the heart of Discovery but we have also diversified into video and CD-ROM, and we have made a very large investment in a Web-Site which is full of information and activity including live interactive events and people reporting in from places round the world.

Discovery used to be called a niche channel but as bandwidth increases even further in the digital age, Discovery looks like a fairly wide genre of programming and the possibility of digital sub-channels emerges, covering subject areas like History, Science, Nature, Leisure, etc. In this way our target audience narrows into more focused interest groups, more like the magazine readers.

On TLC we have two types of viewers: those who watch to learn how to do something and those who just like to watch but have no intention of taking up painting, sewing or golf. We also recognise that we have many different audiences – the person interested in sewing is unlikely to be the same as the person who is fanatical about fishing. So what we want to do is to take these single audiences and put them in touch with other ways of following their interest, possibly through video, CD-ROM or the Internet.

I have said that Discovery is a commercial business, but in the United States, where it is now ten years old, they have many educational initiatives. *Assignment Discovery* is a two-hour daily block of programming without advertising which is distributed for schools. Discovery also produces an *EDUCATOR GUIDE to the schools* providing detailed information designed for teachers, on each programme. Once a week on Sunday there is *Teacher TV* – a joint initiative with the National Education Association which focuses on teachers and technology. Discovery also has subject area specialists who reversion documentaries for use in classrooms with additional information support and guidance.

Joyce Taylor *is Managing Director, Discovery Communications – Europe, since November 1995. Previously, she was Chief Executive Officer of United Artists Programming, which manages 13 cable and satellite channels. She began her career with the BBC and subsequently spent eight years in educational film and television. She is a graduate in Business Administration from Strathclyde University and is a Governor of the National Film and Television School in London.*

3: Television and Learning: Aspects of a Problematic Interrelation

Broadcasting and the adult learner

A review of current research and research needs

Naomi E. Sargant
Open University Visiting Professor, London

The changing environment

It is currently fashionable to ignore the educational potential of terrestrial broadcasting and to concentrate on the varied applications of newer technologies. It is also in the interests of broadcasting managers to reduce their commitment to educational programming since it will never become a major audience winner and they must compete with other channels in the ratings game. It is in the interest of software providers of new technologies to promote their products as more desirable, since they have a market they wish to exploit. It is in the interests of hardware manufacturers to promote such software applications to encourage the purchase of their new equipment. The ideology of the market-place has been dominant across Europe for many years now, and education is not structured or funded to play a dominant role in this market: its position is rather that of Cinderella.

Competition between the media is accompanied by deregulation, which in turn has been used to justify the removal of many public service requirements on broadcasting. For example, in the UK, the 1990 Broadcasting Act removed educational requirements from ITV, and the new Broadcasting Bill, currently going through Parliament, makes no new educational requirement at all of the future digital channels, which are to be given franchises for, at minimum, 12 years. The assumption is that the new choices to be provided by the expansion of digital channels will be allocated according to commercial criteria, and implicitly that education and training will only be provided for those who can afford to pay or for whom there is sponsorship.

As far as the BBC as the main UK public service broadcaster is concerned, it is true that its educational duty is maintained in its new Charter, however, education budgets are being moved over to other departments, production staff sacked and fewer education programmes are now scheduled for peak-time audiences. While its new *Learning Zone* is a welcome innovation, it should be a welcome addition to existing provision, and not a replacement for it. Ironically in the European Year of Lifelong Learning, the BBC will make no contribution to this year's Adult Learners' Week on television, limiting themselves to time on radio and to the night-time *Learning Zone*.

All the evidence points to the fact that educational broadcasting is only held in place on terrestrial television by regulatory fiat. However, regulation is against current trends both in the market-place and with changing technologies.

The importance of educational programmes on television and the current state of research

Why does any of this matter? Or why have we not noticed how the ground-rules have changed against us all? Television continues to be the most important medium for conveying information, news and culture in its broad sense. It is universal in its availability and it is still free at the point of use to its viewers. As Lady Plowden, a former Chair of the Independent Broadcasting Authority, said memorably: 'Broadcasting is democratic, there are no reserved seats'. For educators, it is particularly important since the production of one message can reach very many adults at the same cost and some target groups can only be reached cost-effectively in this way, as the advertising industry and the government are well aware. It is not just that broadcasting is democratic, it is nowadays a necessary prerequisite of an active democracy.

The brief for this paper is to review what research has to tell us about the changing needs of adult learners in relation to broadcast television. What is most striking is to discover how little research into the effectiveness of educational broadcasting, as such, now appears to be carried out. This cannot of course be because of lack of appropriate methodology. Advertising research using much of the same methodology continues as a major industry, with vast expenditures and continuing refinement of techniques. Many of these provide lessons for educational broadcasting and many of them are already affecting general programme-making. Telecommunications research is also advancing apace.

A simple explanation of the lack of interest in research into educational broadcasting could just be lack of resources. More cynically, it could stem from arrogance on behalf of educators who think they know best what to do, or arrogance on behalf of education producers who prefer their own 'creative imperative' to learning from what has worked for other producers or other audiences. A professional problem stems from the fact that few producers remake series on the same topic as before and indeed few series are themselves remade. This represents the major difference with advertising. The imperative to increase the effectiveness of the communication of Coca-Cola's advertising message and increase its market share by 1 per cent translates into millions of dollars. Neither the educator nor the education producer share this imperative.

And often there are perfectly good reasons for change. The curriculum may have changed or the knowledge become obsolescent. Before the arrival of video recorders, much television programming was thought of as 'disposable' and such was the pressure on schedule time, that it was not even often repeated. Increasingly as material is developed for dual-use on different media i.e. TV and video or TV and CD-Rom, durability of content should become a researchable issue as the life of a CD-Rom will be longer and the investment in it greater.

The use of television for education

It is instructive to review what research and policy analysis in the field of educational broadcasting is still being carried out, but it is first necessary to be reminded of the different ways in which television can be useful to educators and to learners. A basic distinction, found helpful since the start of the Open University, is between communicating with 'open' audiences to whom broadcasters speak directly, usually in their own homes, and 'closed' audiences which may be target groups of students registered with or attending an educational institution.

A second distinction which produces a two-way matrix of possibilities is whether or not learners are taught directly or whether the system is designed to offer some tutoring or other mediation between the broadcast and the learner. This second option may involve a systematic array of integrated learning support.

Educational effects of general output broadcasting

Before looking at these options in more detail, it is important to note that much general output broadcasting can have an educational effect, sometimes planned for and sometimes unplanned. The stories are legion, just one example comes from my boss at Channel 4, Jeremy Isaacs. He sat next to an Open University history student at a summer school he was addressing on War and Society who told him that her interest in history had been aroused by watching *The World at War*.

A US study of the incidental learning of aging adults via television in reviewing the research literature on the subject, noted that:

> ... not only can intentional learning occur from purposely watching educational programmes, but incidental learning can result from casual viewing of commercial television. Aging adults not only watch more television proportionately than their younger counterparts, but they also actively seek educational broadcasts. Little research, however, has been done on the amount that aging adults actually learn from commercial television. (Stokes & Pankowski,1988)

Barry Gunter, then Head of Research at the Independent Broadcasting Authority in the UK, in a paper *Learning from television* (Gunter, 1992) commented that:

64

... it is difficult to dispute one consistent and over-riding finding: viewers can and do learn from television. What is really intriguing, however, is how much and what kinds of things they learn while viewing, and whether they learn from television when they are expected or invited to do so. (Gunter,1992)

He went on to highlight two key issues. First that learning from television depends on the ability of viewers to follow and identify with programmes, and second, that viewers often learn from programmes not primarily intended to impart information, while at the same time failing to learn from programmes which are designed to inform. Focusing on learning from television news, he reported that political knowledge levels of young children and teenagers had been found to be positively associated with reported levels of television news watching. However, he went on to say:

Although with much of the evidence on this subject, it can be difficult to disentangle whether watching the news leads to better knowledge, or better knowledge leads to more news viewing, at least two studies have indicated that the influence flows primarily from television news viewing to enhanced political knowledge. (Gunter, 1992)

The positive association between political knowledge and levels of television news watching is reported in more detail by Lukesch (1992). He shows that boys watch more television news than girls and older boys watch more than younger ones. Boys have greater political knowledge than girls, and older boys more than younger ones. He suggests that information from the media carries more weight than personally communicated information.

Gunter records other factors which affect learning from the news:
- having a sound background knowledge about, say, politics or economics can significantly increase the extent to which news stories on those topics were understood;
- the production features, such as sequencing, packaging stories, use of pictures can affect learning;
- items with negative consequences for those involved were well remembered;
- the use of film footage can distract attention away from what the newscaster is saying. News pictures must be supportive of the narrative.

This last factor is also noted as important in a paper on experience in Sweden by Hoijer (1991) who comments that '... the correspondence between the verbal and the visual information is important as well as the tempo'. In her paper, she summarises research which is related to popular education as one of the main programming goals for Swedish public service television; the agreement is that 'the supply of programmes as a whole shall be characterised by an ambition to provide popular education'. She notes that:

Popular education may be related to current affairs programmes like news and news magazines as well as to factual or expository programmes or documentaries. The former usually reaches very high audience ratings while the latter categories usually have lower audience sizes. On the other hand they often receive high appreciation.

She provides summaries of some main findings of the research on news experiments, on analyses of the news and on studies of audience comprehension of expository programmes focusing on programme strategies such as repetitions and reformulations and visual illustration. Several findings match those referred to by Gunter: the need for adequate background information to the news, the need for a unifying theme, too many items presented too fast, texts devastated by irrelevant pictures. Her conclusion was that it was 'news for the initiated'.

Work on expository science programmes showed that viewers found abstract themes more difficult to understand than concrete ones, and that the viewers can relate concrete themes to their own life and experience. Viewers primarily assimilate or pay attention to themes or content which are psychologically close to them. They are helped by good verbal and visual presentation, with experts who use everyday language, and with mental time to interpret the visuals and relate them to the verbal information.

She concludes by noting that the audience is not of course homogeneous and that background knowledge is largely related to social position, and especially the level of formal education.

The segments among the citizens who have a long education have naturally received a broad background of knowledge which makes it easier to understand and assimilate information from media. ... For television with popular education as a programming goal, it is a big challenge to overcome this tendency and to catch sight of the perspectives of the ordinary, not so well-informed audience groups which, in fact, constitute the broad majority of the viewers. (Hoijer, op. cit.)

Hoijer also makes a vital research point, commenting on the combination of long-term research goals aiming at general knowledge with more short-term research goals of the evaluation of specific programmes and the need for such research to be undertaken within an overall theoretical perspective of cumulative knowledge about viewers' incidental learning processes.

While this section has focused on learning from news and factual programmes, learning from television drama and from performance is also particularly important, especially for those who are house-bound or who live in rural areas, and there are excellent examples of educational work building on major drama series and operas for this purpose.

The use of television for direct educational broadcasting

The classic educational strategy is to use the mass medium for mass popular broadcasting to speak to anyone in the community who is interested in watching. Such educational programmes may be on general or specialist topics and should be transmitted at accessible times for the general population. Such programmes are, however, in competition with general output for good slots, and decisions about their scheduling will not usually be in the hands of educational producers. Programmes for the disabled and foreign languages are two obvious examples.

More often education programmes are allocated slots at the edges of the schedule, for example, in the early morning, late at night or Sunday morning. By definition, these times are not attractive to the general public. Though such times are adequate for motivated target groups who know what they are interested in, they are unlikely to attract large audiences or to bring in newcomers to the subject area. Their subsequent low audiences are seen as a self-fulfilling prophecy, justifying even further cuts in budgets. Occasionally such slots can be turned to good account: for example scheduling *Years Ahead*, a magazine programme for over 60s, at 3:45 p.m. in the afternoon when a high proportion of the target group was available to view.

The research issues behind these strategies have less to do with the content of individual programmes and more to do with the overall pattern of audience behaviour and competition with other programmes. Educational programmes need to look as good as any other general output, or people will not bother to watch. To obtain information about the general audience it is necessary to have access to a large sample of people, probably requiring the collaboration of the national broadcasting research system. It is usually management, advertisers or regulators who own the relevant research and they may not be prepared to make it available, often as it involves information of competitive advantage.

For example, while quantitative audience ratings are publicly available in the UK, the qualitative measures of audience appreciation, often of more use to educators as Hojier noted, are not. An argument that is being pressed in the UK is that since the national broadcasting research organisation BARB is to a large extent funded from the licence fee, the public is entitled to have access to its findings.

Examples of research information which are relevant to the planning of educational output and which act as the frame within which the programme or series is viewed are:

- studies of the public's attitudes to types of programmes;
- research into people's use of time;

- profiles of audiences for different programme types;
- profiles of audiences for different time slots;
- the effect of using repeat programmes or series;
- the effect of changing schedule slots on the audience.

The crude measures of effects are provided by the audience ratings. Broadcasting management is unlikely to provide the resources for much ad hoc research on the effects of specific programmes or series, though several such surveys were carried out in the early years of Channel 4, and the BBC has conducted several programme-specific studies using their TOPS panel.

What has proved of increasing interest is the body of information arising from the provision of various forms of programme back-up and follow-up. While some producers are still taken unawares by the unexpected effects of programmes, in principle the idea that programmes can and should have an effect, and an afterlife, is now understood and accepted across a wide range of programmes and not just educational ones. The provision of telephone helplines, dial and listen advice lines and the provision of a wide variety of follow-up information provides informal feedback to programme-makers, which is in its turn becoming the subject of evaluation.

Who is in control?
So far the discussion has concentrated on educational programming and the educational effects of general output programming which is driven by broadcasters and not by educators. Broadcasters and their education producers are in the driving seat, make the judgments about needs and content and are responsible for follow-up arrangements. The key change, often to the other side of the matrix, comes when the broadcaster engages in a partnership or collaboration with the outside educator or even hands over control, lending or renting the space on the channel. In many countries institutions have been set up which use broadcasting basically as a cheap and effective delivery system to reach large and/or scattered populations through distance learning.

In a significant paper to an EDEN conference of distance educators, Walter Flemmer, then Vice-President of the EBU's Working Party for Educational Programmes, discussed whether broadcasting should or should not play a role in distance learning: how such a mass medium like television could serve special audiences and how the process of learning could be 'brought into a basket with news programmes, entertainment and culture, with a view to capturing the highest potential audience'.

Reminding his audience of the 30-year-long proud tradition of educational programmes on public television stations he questioned whether all these programmes were part of distance learning and whether or not distance learning was a contradiction compared to educational television:

So today we are sitting on different sides of one table. Maybe we are in strong competition. Or maybe we are working in quite the same, or in a comparable field. (Flemmer, 1994)

His useful review of the current state of educational broadcasting in Europe was not encouraging, though there were some bright points such as the guarantee of production in Sweden until 1998, and the maintenance of the educational mandate on the BBC and Channel 4 in the UK. Certainly times are harder, as educational television has to compete with commercial stations and is more confined to less good transmission times: early morning, afternoons and late at night, and now night-time.

Competition on the other side comes from the producers of new media and new delivery systems such as cable and satellite. And education producers have increasingly to maintain relationships and credibility with education institutions and national curriculum and qualification requirements. Flemmer concludes firmly:

... the role of broadcasting in distance learning must always be based on a journalistically structured open programme. It is not our duty to transmit lectures coming from universities or schools, but to organise and produce our own distance-learning programmes – they are, however, often based on cooperation with educational institutions. (Flemmer, 1994)

Cooperation and partnerships between educational broadcasters, educational institutions and ministries of education.

In the same paper, Flemmer identifies a number of strategies for organising and financing educational broadcasting, each of which can be found in many countries:

- the state or the education authorities can set up their own instructional television;
- the broadcasting institutions can put out instructional programmes without any liability;
- publishers and other private institutions can produce and distribute audio-visual teaching packages;
- state authorities and broadcasting institutions can cooperate with each other.

There are in existence already a number of proper partnerships between broadcasters and educational institutions, each of which would justify a research paper in itself. It is possible to suggest, as Flemmer does, that some belong more to broadcasting than to distance learning though for some the distinction may not be meaningful. He suggests that the success of the *Telekolleg* model, set up in 1967, resulted from the choice of cooperation between the broadcasting institutions organised under public law and the State.

This has ensured that the professional production of instructional programmes means that they are attractive 'beyond the narrow framework of the schools, to a wider interested public', but at the same time gives the programmes the same standing and certification as schools administered by the state.

> The decision … sprang from the reflection that broadcasting was an activity practised by society and that the provision of educational broadcasts was one of the tasks of broadcasting. (Flemmer, 1994.)

With the *Telekolleg*, the split of responsibility is interesting. Bavarian Broadcasting is in charge of the organisation and financing of the educational broadcasts and the supporting literature, while the State Ministry of Education is responsible for tutorial and learner support and for examinations.

The Open University in the UK (UKOU) provides a somewhat similar example, with a partnership agreement between the BBC and the Open University, a government-funded degree-granting institution. While decisions about academic content rest with the university, the content of the programmes is agreed by a course-team containing both sides, with the production responsibility resting firmly with the broadcasters.

The programmes are not designed for an open audience, but are planned top-down specifically to be integrated with the rest of the course materials. Despite this, they consistently attract quite large eavesdropper audiences, which new research indicates should not be ignored (Taylor, 1993). The OU/BBC partnership has also stood the test of time, though television is of course not the only medium now used, and its scheduling is under increasing pressure.

Such a partnership in the 1960s was quite new. Public service broadcasters have always been fiercely independent and reluctant to hand over control of their airtime or to accept money directly into programmes for fear of stepping over the dividing line into advertising and sponsorship.

Channels within channels

In the 1960s and 1970s many public service channels did not transmit all day long and certainly did not transmit programming at night-time. BBC2, for example, at the start of the Open University did not open up until the evening. Similarly Channel 4 at its inception did not open up until 5 p.m. There was no great problem involved, other than cost, in the idea of allowing education into the silent hours and indeed there was seen to be merit in not showing viewers a blank screen. With funding for programme production paid for by the educators or the tax-payers, both sides were happy. However, as competition for ratings has increased, channel controllers become more jealous of their schedule time even though they have increased financial problems in funding the programmes. These tensions have led to a number of compromises to the general benefit of educational television, though there is not yet enough research to demonstrate which solutions are most satisfactory.

The Open Secondary in Norway provides such an example, in which more control has been handed over to educators: the Open Secondary was launched by NKS Distance Education in September 1991 in cooperation with the Ministry of Education and the national television channel, NRK. The NRK set up a new Learning Channel on the same channel as other NRK programmes, transmitting its programmes on Saturday and Sunday mornings. More significantly, they were willing to try out new programme formats, and to accept low-cost production provided it met their technical standards (Blom,1994). The main media employed were television programmes and correspondence courses. Students were also offered learning support and a TV study guide, but sat public exams at their local secondary school. The programmes, she noted, also attracted an eavesdropper audience of ca. 50,000.

Blom (1994) describes what this meant for NKS Distance Education as educational leaders of the project:

> NRK was willing to try out new programme formats with an emphasis on the leading needs of the active, registered students rather than the wishes and tastes of the general public. This ... meant that it was no longer crucial to keep the delicate balance of education or entertainment for educational programmes. We could give priority to the educational aspect. For a public service channel it was necessary that such programmes of special interest to only a few were transmitted outside of prime viewing time. In other words, it was up to NKS to create the programmes with their own students as the main target group, but certainly with other groups in mind, such as regular students in secondary schools all over the country, their parents, teachers and adults who simply enjoyed watching the programmes.

In Blom's evaluation of the results, it is noted that the choice of television was important for the first objective, recruiting students: more than half said that they had first heard about the Open Secondary through television. While, disappointingly, the completion rate of students was the same as the year before with no television and the television programmes did not seem to have their intended pacing effect, research showed that among the active students it 'had been extremely important for their involvement' and that they preferred television to receiving video cassettes through the post. Despite this more than 40 per cent also recorded the programmes on video! The review article also provides useful information on programme content strategy, student reactions and learner support.

Another example of a channel within a channel is the UK United Artists The Learning Channel (TLC) which runs for three day-time hours on the same channel as the Discovery Channel and is delivered via both satellite and cable. Its early years were encouraging, with good audience reaction.[1] It participated actively in the UK Adult Learners' Week for some years and started commissioning its own new materials, rather than relying on other broadcasters' repeats. However, management has recently decided to reposition the channel, to stop using the word 'learning' and to use its initials TLC as a brand name, focusing on leisure and home skills programmes. This is not encouraging.

Night-time and down-loading

There is an increasing interest in the use of the night-time hours both for the general audience who is awake at that time and for down-loading on to video. Ownership of video recorders is now at a high level in many countries and night-time use is (being planned) in Sweden, France as well as the UK.

The BBC's experience with its use of the night-time hours is instructive, and its current project The Learning Zone is to be discussed in more detail later.[2] Its earlier version, BBC Select, was in effect an attempt to use the night-time hours as a cheap delivery system for video material. It was not successful for a variety of reasons, though some elements of that experiment have been incorporated into The Learning Zone (e.g. Focus).

BBC Select provides some interesting lessons for the future development of subscription services. It was originally planned to develop a range of specialist pay television services for niche markets to be down-loaded in night-time hours using new conditional access technology, and allowing for encryption.

Services were expected to include some education and training, professional and leisure interests as well as some services which were to be transmitted on open network. The analogy was the range of specialist leisure and technical magazines to be found in most news-agents.

The main advantage of this new service was to be that it built on the almost universally available BBC transmission system and would use people's existing television sets and videos. For services which were to be encrypted, however, new financial and technological barriers would be introduced, as indeed they will with the move to digital broadcasting. It was not designed for the purpose of transmitting the BBC's own material, but as with Norway's Open Secondary was to provide a distribution system for people outside the BBC who were prepared to pay both for the production and transmission of their own programmes.

While a number of specialist uses did develop e.g. a legal magazine, training programmes for nurses and programmes for the voluntary sector, issues emerged in relation to the requirement for the BBC to maintain editorial control and sponsorship rules which led to a decision to run the

---

1   Cf. Joyce Taylor's contribution to this volume, pp. 55–60.
2   Cf. Jenny King's contribution, pp. 79–85.

segment as an integral part of the education output under the Education Directorate, hence the development of The Learning Zone, which is now effectively another channel within a channel. The research issues raised by this experience go beyond those of educational broadcasting and access to its evaluation would be of interest to all engaged in the development of subscription and specialist services.

A side effect of this night-time use has been to use it for repeats of other educational material, particularly, in the UK, of BBC Schools and OU programmes. The OU has always taken seriously the value of the programmes being seen on the main BBC channels, as helping with its publicity and as intrinsically valuable to the general population. Being demoted to night-time in one sense cannot be easily objected to since such a large number of OU students already record and watch on time-shift. It is very bad news in terms of overall PR to be out of sight and out of mind, and if it is to become a test of the acceptability of pay television services, it is even worse. It is almost certainly the threat of being moved to night-time that has caused the OU itself to, belatedly, become actively interested in its eavesdropper audience!

A specialist channel?

Europe has not so far seen fit to support an entire specialist channel dedicated to education and training though there are a number of encouraging precedents in North America. Two projects are of interest here. Glikman (1994) describes extended research into the history of continuing education in France which became timely again as the country renewed its interest in the educational roles and functions that educational television could specifically fulfil.

In 1993, the French government decided to create, during the daytime, a terrestrial (Hertzian) learning channel on the fifth network on which ARTE, a French-German cultural channel, was already broadcasting during the evening. The issue was not to develop precise programmes, but to 'clarify the channel's global design, targets and purposes'.

Glikman proposes that significant differences are less between the styles of production, content and so on, but rather between the way the programmes are related to educational systems and in the underlying educational and social goals. She distinguishes three types of use of Hertzian educational television:

1. When television is used as a promotional tool for face-to-face educational systems, for example in relation to the BBC's Adult Literacy campaign in the 1970s. Its role is then to sensitise underprivileged groups and to encourage them to contact appropriate organisations. The recent BBC Family Literacy campaign which used short 'commercial-style' programmes devised with the assistance of an advertising agency is similar in its strategy.

2. Its oldest use, she describes, is using television at the centre of an open multi-media system, in which television is the driving force. Programmes, usually in series, may cover a range of topics and offer 'additional or deepened knowledge'. These series usually reach people who are already quite 'advantaged', but who are willing to learn more. They have, however, no impact on the general social situation.

3. The third type is as a component of a distance learning system in which television participates in a complete curricula supported by media and other resources and is supplied by educational organisations in partnership with broadcasting companies. These include the OU/UK, the *Telekolleg* in Germany and *A saber* in Spain. Since they allow people to obtain better qualifications, they contribute to a policy of ascending mobility.

Her paper is a strong restatement of the importance of terrestrial broadcasting, free at the point of use. Other media, either for individuals or in groups, can only reach already motivated audiences, ready to register for courses, prepared to go to resource centres or to buy necessary equipment.

> Only Hertzian television allows education to meet new popula-
> tions: those who are not spontaneously motivated by knowledge
> or willing to enter a learning process. Particularly being the main
> link of underprivileged people ... television is the best if not the
> only way to reach these groups, which spend more time looking
> at it than all others. Met by chance, in the flow of information or
> entertainment programmes, promotional programmes can break
> down psychological blocks and activate a demand for education.
> (Glikman, 1994)

A second important piece of policy research stems from the activities of the EBU itself. Following on a preliminary piece of research by Gwynne-Jones and Hasebrink (1995), a more detailed feasibility study has been carried out on the potential for a European Educational Television Channel. The study considered availability of programmes, distribution, the audience/market, other funding and proposed a short to medium way forward for the EBU members to pursue.

Such studies as these go well beyond the research normally carried out and described by educators and academics and have more to do with projects normally carried out by management consultants.

Servicing institutional needs

Glikman's third type, where television acts as one component of a distance learning system is of course an increasingly common model, and is more frequently the subject of academic research, as the educational institution has more interest in its monitoring and evaluation. An interesting case, where the partnership is between the US Public Broadcasting Service (PBS) and a wide range of American institutions of higher education, is the PBS Adult Learning Service, the first national effort to provide coordination and focus for adult learning via television. Brock's paper sets out an agenda of the research needs for adult learners via television, assuming that some learners must or wish to study for credit through such distance institutions of higher education (Brock, 1990).

What is helpful is that she assumes that 'television has proven itself as an important delivery mode to meet the educational needs of adult students at a distance'. Coming at it as a manager, she chooses to focus on research needed for 'pragmatic' purposes. She lists as topics: the awareness of the public of such opportunities, awareness with conventional campuses of such options, better and comparable profiles of current and future students, learning styles, student retention and comparisons with conventional students, student support services, counselling and access to library services, faculty training and the need for a national clearing-house for information about adult learning through television:

> ... since current research clearly demonstrates that television is an effective teaching/learning medium for a variety of adult learners, the main point ... is that a high priority should be given to research which serves the pragmatic purposes of supporting television course development, improved management of such courses and advocacy for their greater acceptance and use. (Brock, op. cit.)

Another writer in the field is less tolerant of what he variously describes as slick production, broadcast quality and interactivity. He is, however, a strong proponent of instructional television and its effectiveness. He has reviewed, he says, 44 studies and 21 research summaries and argues that there can be a high degree of confidence in such a number:

> No matter how it is produced, how it is delivered, whether or not it is interactive, low-tech or high-tech, students learn equally well with each technology and learn as well as their on-campus, face-to-face counterparts even though students would rather be on campus with the instructor if that were a real choice. (Russell, 1992)

Russell is a particular supporter of the VideoClass System, a variety of the candid or nowadays Virtual Classroom and argues that by heeding the research and down-sizing the technology it is possible to lower costs, increase course offerings and reach many more learners with confidence. He lists in the same paper a set of questions, too many for this paper, that researchers should consider, reminding us that 'the media are mere vehicles that deliver instruction but do not influence achievement ... it is only the content of the vehicle that can influence achievement'.

The message itself

Hence we return to the message itself. It is here that the research is thinnest. It depends, of course, on what one means by research and whether we are sticking with research into educational programmes on television. Is it research into the content of one individual programme, into the effectiveness of a series or the socio-economic benefits of a project?

As noted earlier, there is little new research at the macro-managerial broadcasting level, though there is some awareness of its desirability among educational producers. There are few institutes or academic departments, with the honourable exception of our hosts here, who have concentrated on research into educational broadcasting. Sadly, educational broadcasting is itself too narrowcast to be of interest to most mass-communications researchers.

Among educators and academic researchers interest has mainly moved to work on newer technologies. Even though the term educational television is still used, it is not used in the Hertzian sense (e.g. the UK *Journal of Educational Television* does not address itself to broadcasters, or even to distance educators, but mainly to people producing a variety of video and multi-media based materials for use inside institutions).

Perhaps the most interesting new research which links the task of the forms of Hertzian television with the new multi-media forms comes from Diana Laurillard's research project on multi-media, education and narrative organisation. Arguably, one of the most important characteristics of broadcast television has been its linear structure. The much vaunted benefit of the new media is their interactivity. Laurillard's proposal focuses on this difference:

> For interactive media, one of the key benefits is seen as being the *lack of imposed structure*, giving much greater freedom of control to the user. However, in the context of instruction this benefit runs counter to the learner's need to discern structure if there is a message to be understood.
> We have found from observation that learners working on interactive media with no clear narrative structure display learning behaviour that is generally unfocused and inconclusive. ... Thus one of the key benefits of interactive media, the greater learner control it offers, becomes pedagogically disadvantageous if it results in mere absence of structure. (Laurillard, 1995)

It is clear that the importance of educational programmes on television needs to be restated, to broadcasters, to educators and to the community, if broadcasting which is accessible to all, is not to be forgotten about in the rush to drive on the information superhighway. It is particularly necessary to ensure that educators look beyond the confines of their own and their institution's needs, and use and research into all the technologies both old and new which are at our disposal for the educational benefit of the whole community.

References

BBC (1995) Findings from the BBC Second Chance Panel 1994. BBC Education, London 1995.

Blom, D. (1994): The Open Secondary – Norway's biggest classroom. In: Human resources, human potentials, human development: the role of distance education. Proceedings of 1994 EDEN Conference. Tallinin, Estland. (EDEN Secreteriat Milton Keynes.).

Brock, D. (1990): Research needs for adult learners via television In: Moore, M. G.: *Contemporary issues in American Distance Education*; pp. 172-180.

Croft, M. (1986): WLU Telecollege: Distance Education by television. In: ICDE Bulletin, vol 11 May 1989. pp. 26-30; ICDE, Canada.

Flemmer, Walter (1992): The role of broadcasting in distance learning. Paper presented to 1992 EDEN Conference, Krakow, Poland (EDEN Secretariat, Milton Keynes).

Glikman, Viviane (1994): Research and policy: which design for the future French learning channel? Paper presented to the ETA conference on *Media and Learning: Designing for the 21st Century*, Bournemouth 1994.

Gunter, Berry (1992): Learning from television Paper presented at British Association Science Festival, 1992 (mimeograph). London: ITC 1992.

Gwynne Jones, Euffron; Hasebrink, Uwe (1995): European Educational Television: A feasibility study. Hamburg: Hans-Bredow-Institut 1995.

Heuvelman, Ard (1989): OFF SCREEN The influence of visualisation of educational programmes on cognitive processes in viewers. University of Twente/TELEAC 1989.

Holjer, Brigitta (1991): Research related to popular education for the Swedish Public Television Service. Sveriges Radio, Stockholm 1991.

King, Jenny (1995): The Learning Zone: Research on awareness and take-up of a new night-time educational service on BBC2. London: BBC Broadcasting Research 1995 (Internal Publication 95C309).

Laurillard, Diana et al. (1995): Multi-media, education and narrative organisation: description of and proposal for a ESRC-funded project (in mimeograph). Milton Keynes: The Open University 1995.

Lukesch, Herbert (1992): TV learning: incidental or a systematic process. In: *Communications* Vol. 17 No. 2 (1992), pp. 205-214.

Radcliffe, John (1991): Television and distance education in Europe: current roles and future challenges. In A.W. Bates (Ed.): *Media and Technology in European Distance Education*. Milton Keynes: Open University 1990; pp. 113-120.

Russell, T. L. (1992): Television's indelible impact on distance education: what we should have learned from comparative research. In: *Research in Distance Education*; Vol 4 (1992) No 4; Athabasca University, Alberta, Canada.

Stokes, L.; Pankowski, M.: Incidental learning of aging adults via television In: *Adult Education Quarterly* Vol 38 (1988), No 2 (Winter).

Taylor J. (1993): Final report on the Open University Drop-in Viewing Audience Survey PLUM No 40. Milton Keynes: Open University 1993.

Taylor J. (1996): What shall we do in The Learning Zone? Milton Keynes: The Open University (PLUM Paper 68).

Wearn, T.; Asquith, R. (1996): Are we running out of time? In: Market Research Society Conference Papers, Birmingham 1966.

Naomi E. Sargant *graduated in Sociology from Bedford College, London University and spent twelve years as a market and social researcher at the Gallup Poll before joining Enfield College of Technology. She then became a founder member of the Open University, running its Survey Research Department, and subsequently was Professor of Applied Social Research and Pro-Vice Chancellor in charge of Student Affairs. In 1981 she became the founding Senior Commissioning Editor for Educational Programming at Channel 4 for eight years. She has also been involved in setting up the Open College and the Open Polytechnic. She is at present Visiting Professor at the Open University. She also works as a consultant and has written widely on the education of adults, evaluation and the use of the media for education. Recent books are* Learning and 'leisure' *(NIACE 1991),* Adult learners, broadcasting and Channel 4 *(C4, 1992),* Learning for a purpose *(NIACE, 1993) and* The Learning Divide *(NIACE, 1996).*

The Learning Zone and its users

Jenny King
BBC Broadcasting Research, London

The BBC Broadcasting Research Department undertakes a wide range of both quantitative and qualitative research on educational programmes, whether they are designed for the specialist learner or the general viewing public. So, in effect, all this research is both viewer- and learner-orientated. We analyse viewing data provided by the Broadcasters' Audience Research Board (generally known as BARB) and audience reaction data obtained from a Television Opinion Panel (TOP) consisting of some 3,000 individuals; additionally we commission ad hoc research on specific series and individual programmes.

Rather than giving you a general overview of our work, however, I shall talk about a specific example of a major research project we undertook at the end of last year. This project was on a new night-time educational service launched in October 1995 – and is called *The Learning Zone* (TLZ).

I am going to present a brief outline of *The Learning Zone*: what it is, how it works and who the target audience are intended to be, and I will then outline research undertaken in the very early stages of *The Learning Zone* – and the fact that they were 'early stages' needs to be constantly re-emphasised – which was designed to assess the initial awareness of, interest in, and take-up of TLZ among the two principal target audiences.

The Learning Zone
Lord Reith, the first Chairman of the BBC in the early 1920s, set the well-known three key principles for the corporation: Educate – Entertain – Inform. While BBC1 is the channel of broad appeal, with popular programmes for a wide range of audiences, BBC2 provides output for a more specialist audience. This channel, which is now 32 years old, is well-known for its innovation, and *The Learning Zone* definitely is an innovation.

Broadcast in the night between 00:30 and 07:00 a.m. from Sunday to Thursday, it is divided into five distinct segments:

- Open University (transmitted 12:30–2:00 a.m., Tuesday–Friday) – aimed at OU students wishing to catch up and record for study purposes;
- FETV (2:00–4:00 a.m., Monday and Friday) – dedicated to further and adult education sectors, for use by both teachers and students;

- Nightschool (2:00–4:00 a.m., Tuesday, Wednesday, Thursday during the school term) – aimed at teachers and pupils in primary and secondary education;
- BBC Language (4:00–6:00 a.m., Monday) – entire language courses, repeated for anyone learning a foreign language or wishing to improve their skills;
- BBC Focus (4:00–6:00 a.m., Tuesday–Friday) Open Access television unit providing opportunity for any non-profitmaking organisation – such as the Royal College of Nursing – involved in communicating specialist information, education and training material. (BBC Focus has developed out of BBC Select.)

The trail that promoted the use of TLZ was shown some 70 times on BBC TV over a five-week period – including a slot immediately after *EastEnders*, a popular programme at 7.30 in the evening which attracts an average 15 million viewers. It was estimated that, in total, the trail would be seen by some 40 per cent of the population.

TLZ and the use of video recorders
All programmes broadcast in *The Learning Zone* are designed to be taped for play-back at a later date. The use of video recorders has increased in recent years: from 23 per cent of households in 1984 to 74 per cent of households ten years later, in 1994. However, our research has shown that a significant minority of people still have difficulty using the equipment.

Table 1: Ability to use a video recorder

	General population
"I find it easy to set the video recorder"	55%
"Someone else always sets the video recorder for me"	24%
"I usually push record button when programme starts"	15%
"I sometimes have difficulty setting timer on video"	11%

BBC Broadcasting Research; April 1996 (multiple coded)

As one knows, usually the person who does know how to set the video is a small child...!

The target audiences

The two target audiences which TLZ is intended and designed for are:

- *Motivated adult learners* – Open University students for example, or those choosing to learn a foreign language through watching BBC language output.
- *Educationalists* – teachers and students at Further Education colleges, for example.

In response to the trail, 55,000 individuals – later identified as 'motivated adult learners' – completed a call, requesting an information pack. In a postal survey of a sample of 1,000 of these motivated adult learners, it was generally agreed that the information pack was well-presented but some wanted more detailed information on the content of individual programmes.

It may be interesting to note at this point that 28 per cent of these motivated adult learners defined themselves as 'providing any kind of teaching or training, to adults or school children'. This is a very high proportion but, interestingly, almost a third of those who claimed to be teachers or trainers further defined themselves as teaching/training in the workplace – often irrespective of their actual job title. There is therefore a big market – a latent interest, in educational or training programmes and support material for these people.

A tracking study to monitor the build-up in awareness and interest in TLZ among the general viewing population was undertaken in three waves:
- wave 1: two weeks prior to the launch of the service;
- wave 2: two weeks after the launch;
- wave 3: six weeks after the launch.

Awareness

The survey, conducted by a face-to-face interview among 1,000 adults in each wave, found that there was a good level of awareness of TLZ.

Table 2: Awareness of *The Learning Zone*

%Adult Population

	2 weeks before launch	2 weeks after launch	6 weeks after launch
	15%	25%	23%

BBC Broadcasting Research; April 1996

81

Awareness built up over the campaign, from 15 per cent of adults among the general population two weeks before the launch to some 23 per cent of adults – equivalent to some 10 million individuals, six weeks after the start of transmission.

Interest

The tracking study also highlighted the good level of interest in TLZ among the general population. 28 per cent of the adult population said that they were very or fairly likely to use TLZ in future – this would equate to just under 12 million viewers.

Table 3: Potential Use of *The Learning Zone*

Percentage of adult population who have not yet used TLZ

BBC Broadcasting Research; April 1996

It is of course the top group – those who say that they are 'very likely' to use TLZ in future – who are the main potential target: those to be converted from potential to actual viewers. The decisive question was how many people would actually use *The Learning Zone*.

The take-up

We have seen that the campaign around its launch created a significant level of interest and that there was a good level of interest in using the service – but what was the actual take-up among the two target audiences?

Although TLZ is not ratings-led, viewing figures are nevertheless an important – and quantifiable – aspect of the research. Six weeks after the launch, 5 per cent of the general population – equivalent to some 2.2 million people – said that they had watched TLZ. Of these people, 3 out of 4 had watched the programmes live. Were they insomniacs or shift workers – or extremely motivated?

Eight weeks after the launch, 23 per cent of the motivated adult learners – those people who had responded to the TV trail and requested information, had watched programmes from TLZ. A further 30 per cent had taped programmes but not yet actually replayed the output.

What is more, following telephone interviews with a sample of 200 Further Education colleges, from a total 650 throughout the country, we know that 70 per cent of Further Education colleges had used – or intended to use – programmes from TLZ some 10 weeks after launch. These are clearly encouragingly high levels of take-up in what were the very early stages of the service.

Table 4: Programmes watched

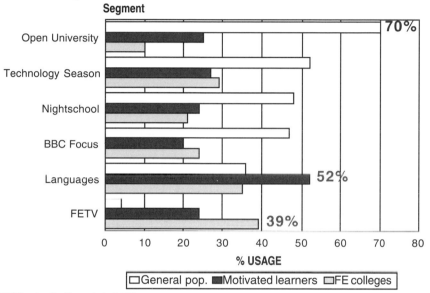

BBC Broadcasting Research; April 1996

As can be seen, BBC Languages is very popular. This is supported by a separate piece of research undertaken for the BBC which found that 36 per cent of adults in the general population were interested in learning a foreign language.

Normally, detailed audience data can be provided by analysis of BARB data. But this methodology, using metered television sets in 4,500 households throughout the United Kingdom, has limitations. It only monitors television viewing within private households – therefore excluding viewing in educational establishments. Additionally, the data only records taped viewing if the programme is recorded and played back on the same equipment and within a seven-day period. These limitations have a particular impact on viewing data for TLZ and will produce an underestimation of the true levels of take-up.

Bearing in mind these limitations, we come to the following picture: 200,000 viewers tuned in for at least 15 consecutive *The Learning Zone* in an average day whilst the weekly reach is 800,000 viewers (people watching at least 15 consecutive minutes in a week).

Table 5: Average audiences (12.30–06.00 a.m.) in multi-channel households

Viewers (Millions)

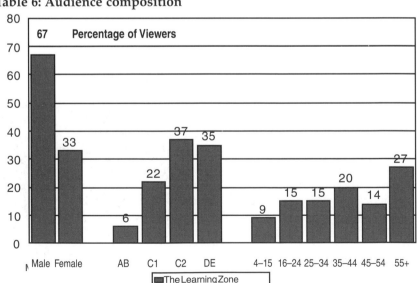

ITV LATE NIGHT MOVIES

BBC-1 MOVIES

SKY MOVIES – SATELLITE

GMTV:
starts at 6am

BBC-2 THE LEARNING ZONE

BBC Broadcasting Research; April 1996 (Based wks. 2–11, 1996)

Remember, however, that these viewers among the general viewing public are not a primary target audience; these people could however be converted to 'motivated adult learners'.

As can be seen, the commercial channel ITV attracts the greatest number of viewers to its late-night movies. All output suffers an understandable drop-off in the small hours of the night.

Table 6: Audience composition

Percentage of Viewers

The Learning Zone

BBC Broadcasting Research; April 1996 (Based on 4 week period: wks. 8–11, 1996)

Summary

We have seen that TLZ, launched in October 1995, is a great innovation, with its programmes designed to be taped and played back at a later date.

The five elements of the output appeal to two specific target audiences: motivated adult learners and educationalists. And there is some eavesdropping from the general viewing public.

And all the research, which was undertaken in the very early stages of TLZ, would seem to indicate a good level of awareness and interest in the service – and most importantly, there has been a healthy amount of use of the output. It is still early days – so watch this space!

More research is now needed to progress and develop *The Learning Zone* – in particular, to find out how the eavesdropping audience can be converted to Motivated Adult Learners, and what they need and want from the output.

Jenny King *is Senior Researcher at the BBC Broadcasting Research Department, being in charge of quantitative and qualitative research in connection with News, Current Affairs and the Education Group. She graduated with a BA (Hons) from Loughborough, England in 1984, worked for ten years in sport and leisure research for clients including the Sports Council (GB) and local government bodies throughout the UK and then moved into broadcasting research. Recent major ad hoc research projects have included several pieces of research of* The Learning Zone *and analysis on the wants and needs of deaf and hard-of-hearing viewers.*

Imagining learners: Changing expectations of educational television

John MacMahon

Radio Telefís Éireann (RTE), Dublin

Introduction

Why talk about imagining learners? Educational television has, after all, a long tradition of researching its audience and of developing suitable programmes in response to the findings of such research. Most people would argue that this should be sufficient to provide a more than adequate foundation for educational television. Why bring the imagination into it?

In this presentation I hope to show that the imagination has an important influence on how we, as programme-makers, approach our audiences, and on how we arrange and structure our communications and interactions with them.

Education and learning are now at the forefront of contemporary thinking and policy development. According to the recent European Commission White Paper on Education and Training 'education and training will increasingly become the main vehicles for self-awareness, belonging, advancement and self-fulfilment. Education and training ... is the key for everyone to controlling their future and their professional development.' (p.2) The concept of lifelong learning has taken hold and the European Union has designated 1996 as the Year of Lifelong Learning. Underlying this change in perceptions of education is a sense that education and learning are no longer concerned with learning facts and understanding the past.

It is clear to many people that if we can spend a considerable amount of energy and imagination in re-creating what we believe happened in the past, then we can equally apply such energy and imagination to visualising what the future might be like. In other words, we can envision the future. If we can envision the future then we can set about moving in the direction that will lead us to our goal. Such speculation about the future can of course lead to considerations of some unattainable utopia, or indeed of some futuristic technocracy.

These are issues for consideration in some wider forum. I intend to confine my focus here on television, and, in particular, on the utilisation of television for educational purposes. In exploring applications of the imagination to television I want to examine the use of educational television to enable people to move from what are largely passive learning patterns to a more active interaction with their environments.

As people become active, and take responsibility for creating their own futures, the social, cultural and political environments become more like effervescent mosaics of meanings with a greater degree of participation and involvement by many more people. These issues range far wider than this present paper permits me.

My focus here is on learning and television. The questions that interest me are those which challenge much of what we, as programme-maker, take for granted in our day to day production activities and decisions. What do we really know, or, more fundamentally, what can we know, about the interactions between individuals and the television images which they receive and which result in learning?

We certainly make assumptions about these matters and work on from there. We categorise our learning audience as schoolchildren or as adult learners. As we move towards an environment in which lifelong learning is essential we must become aware that our audience is everybody, it is no longer school pupils or adults, younger people or older people, it is everybody.

Much of what we define as learning, and recognise as valid learning, is based on concepts of schooling and on pedagogical techniques which have been developed in the context of formal education. Certain other approaches have emerged from the experience gained in the education of adults in particular environments. All these have given rise to 'mythologies' about learning and about how people learn – these constitute the cognitive frameworks within which we operate in the belief that they are the only reality which we can know. Before 'imagining' our learners of the future I would first like to examine four of the categorisations of learning at present.

Four learning mythologies
A mythology is a way of seeing and doing things, a definition of reality, which is used as a basis for beliefs and operations. In education various mythologies can be identified and here I will examine four of the more commonly encountered approaches (Fox, 1983), using some programme excerpts as examples:

- Transfer Theory,
- Shaping Theory,
- Travelling Theory,
- Growing Theory.

Each of these theories has had some significant influence on thinking and practice in the world of education. As educational television operates within the wider environment of the educational world we can accept that these theories have also influenced the ways in which we formulate and produce programmes. I would like to examine these four theories in some more detail.

Transfer Theory

This is one which is very familiar and which is probably the easiest, and least challenging, for television production. It is primarily concerned with the 'facts' of a situation and with the transfer of information, usually from an 'expert' to the students. In this theory delivery is a central concern, with considerable effort expended on preparing the material and on devising 'effective' methods of transfer. Whether or not the message is received or relevant is not a major concern.

Shaping Theory

This involves moulding the learner to a predetermined specification through demonstration and practice. On television this approach is regularly used since it is relatively easy to present demonstrations of certain types of behaviour which can be 'copied' by the viewer. Cookery programmes provide a popular example. While there are many positive examples of this approach it can also result it television being blamed for negative or destructive behaviour, particularly among young people.

Travelling Theory

In this theory learning is seen as a 'journey' of exploration with the teacher providing some level of local knowledge and resources, but aware that he or she is a fellow explorer who is also learning. The teacher, or presenter, knows the area and uses this knowledge to introduce others to it, while remaining open to new experiences and challenges which may emerge.

Growing Theory

This fourth theory is about developing and cultivating people and encouraging and enabling them to grow in their own unique ways. At various times different possible directions of development reveal themselves and the task of the teacher is to nourish and cultivate these, even if definite and precise ends are not evident. In television terms this theory is difficult to implement as it is essentially a process approach and involves personal change in which the driving force and the learning involved is internal and an aspect of one's growing personality.

The complexity of learning

Looking at these four theories suggests that different concepts of 'learning' require different responses and approaches. What do we mean when we talk about learning? The acquisition of factual information, and of ideas, is one definition, but does it cover all aspects of learning? Is there something deeper and more fundamental involved than the acquisition of information – some form of personal growth and development? Is learning about engaging with the outer, external world, or one's own inner, personal understandings?

I suggest that learning is about both, and that it is through engaging in the complex interactions between the external and the internal that we come to deeper and more mature understandings of ourselves and the worlds in which we live.

An understanding of this fundamental underlying external/internal duality provides a perspective on how we approach our task as educational broadcasters. If the 'external reality' dominates the emphasis will be on the mastery of a body of knowledge, or a skill. If the 'inner reality' is dominant then we are concerned with the growth, change and development of the learner as a person. In exploring this duality we can identify a difference between passive and active learning.

We each process information received from the external world and make our own sense of it. This is a passive view of learning – the learner is a container to be filled. Paulo Freire has labeled this the 'banking' theory of learning. In contrast an active view of learning puts the emphasis on the creating of meanings, the generation of new ways of seeing and the exploration of personal experiences.

Learning, viewed from this perspective, is about personal change and development. A significant question for all involved in educational broadcasting is: 'Can we create programmes which result in personal change through the use of the media or does the technology limit us to the delivery of information and ideas about external realities?'

I would now like to look again at the four models which I have already examined, this time in the context of concepts of active and passive learning. To do this I suggest that approaches to education can be classified along a continuum of answer types. At one end I would place closed answers, based on factual information. Basic mathematical and scientific concepts provide good examples of this. At the other end of this continuum I would postulate a more Socratic approach, one which is open-ended and raises further questions, rather than provides answers.

A second continuum provides a range of learning experiences which range from the practical, factual, informational, to a more emotive and holistic perspective involving personal understanding. Using these two continua I can now classify the four theories identified by Fox in relation to each other. The Transfer and Shaping theories suggest a high degree of convergence based on predetermined categories in which the 'right' answer or the 'right' way is the objective.

Travelling and Growing theories deal more with the person and thus tend towards a more active learning style. The travelling theory is more clearly based on the factual and what currently exists, while the growing theory is more expressive and creative. Both, however, imply a certain openness to new experiences rather than depend on preset answers.

The value of such a grid is that it can help to make explicit some of the assumptions which we make about learners. It is, however, important to keep in mind that any such classification is relative, and that other ways of looking at the situation are also possible. It is also necessary to ensure that there is a match between the programme-makers' perception of the learners and the learners expectations of the programme. Many learners will expect a 'Transfer' approach when the programme-makers may have adopted a 'Travelling' or a 'Growing' approach.

A recent response from a group of students provides a good illustration. The programme in question adopted an open and explorative approach to the topic of communications. A letter from the group of students stated that: 'We had hoped that the communications section of the programme would prove more 'instructional'. This, however, was not the case. Instead of appproaching communication in an actively informative way, the programme focused on individuals whose talents are developed in very specific areas....'

This comment illustrates the need to match programme-makers' images of the learners with learners' expectations of the programmes. I would suggest that it is part of the programme-makers' responsibility to extend the models of the learner that are available to the audience and to question the dominance of the 'transfer' model in particular. As producers of educational television we need to examine our views of the learners and the learners' views of us and our productions.

If learners expect to be taught in the traditional sense, and if producers want a more holistic approach to learning then the match is not there. Images and expectations need to be matched, but not just left there. I would argue that in any educational relationship, there is likely to be some developmental role in which the perceptions and understandings of both parties changes.

New images of learners
Changes in our understanding of what 'education' is about, changes in the technologies which are available, changes in the demands made by learners themselves, all challenge us to take a new and fresh look at our images of the learners. In the past we have been able to differentiate between students in schools and adult learners, home-based learners and course participants, and suchlike.

More recently market concepts of the learner have gained some currency, and now the image of the learner very often is that of a consumer. With the development of a strong market interest in educational media products, there is now some danger that the dominant new image of the learner will be that of the learner as consumer.

This image of learner as consumer is an attractive one for many of us. I believe that education involves something more than purchasing a product which is marketed as 'educational' in some way or other. The active involvement of the learning consumer may in fact be one way of identifying what is educational about new media products. However, a consumerist perspective on the learner is limited since the emphasis is ultimately on the product itself rather than on the learning processes which the product is intended to activate.

Two predominant metaphors for interaction between the viewer and television can be identified. The couch metaphor relates to television in general – passive, relaxed, undemanding. The desk metaphor comes from education – attentive, mentally active, involved. Educational television juggles with these two metaphors, trying to keep both in balance. Which is the more appropriate?

I would suggest that we need to look for alternative images and generate different metaphors for different purposes. One alternative is the workstation, another the playground. These are images that need to be developed and explored. I would, however, challenge the dualistic either/or conceptualisation of learners as couch or desk related. The learner is not always either passive or active, one style may be more appropriate at a particular time than another. A 'both/and' approach is required – both the couch and the desk, both the workstation and the playground.

There is a further consideration. Educational activities can be either individual or communal. Television and the PC are in many senses individualistic. Trends suggest, however, that television may have a more communal dimension in that people watch together and discuss issues related to the content. PC usage tends to be individual and does not generate the same amount of interaction as TV. In imagining our learners we need to imagine them working alone or in groups and ground their learning to the human interactions involved. Such concepts, however, remain within conventional viewpoints.

An alternative, more radical, view of the role which broadcasting can play places emphasis on the learner as creator of his or her own meanings, and the presentation of these through the use of television and more recently, multimedia technologies. Such a view involves the learner in the production process as well as at the receiving end of the programme – an emphasis on presentation rather than product. Most learners are not ready to adopt this new role and need to be encouraged towards it.

We need to cultivate learners as imaginers, so that they can imagine and conceive their own realities, their own futures. Learning, in the future, will be about stimulating and cultivating the imaginations of individuals, groups and even cultures. However, imagining is not even sufficient, the creations of the imaginations need to be translated into presentations. Such presentations can of course still be traded as commercial products, but they will have been produced with other purposes in mind, the trading value is a spin-off.

New partnerships in learning

This analysis helps to emphasise the role of the learner in educational television. The partnership between the programme-makers and the learners may be either passive or active. If it is seen as passive, then the programme-makers, and the audience, are likely to be working within a Transfer or Shaping theory. If active learning is to be cultivated, then

Travelling and Growing theories are required. Existing approaches to both broadcasting and to education tend to adopt passive approaches to learning.

Educational broadcasting has consistently led the way in developing interactions with its audience. In the past this has been achieved mainly through the provision of support material in print form. This approach has now become common among most broadcasters. As the technology for two-way communications with learners is now more easily available educational broadcasting can again be at the forefront in the development of new forms of interaction with the audience.

Educational broadcasting needs to continue to develop its interactions with its audience through the exploration of the possibilities presented by new communications technologies. To avail of this opportunity to the full we must first re-conceptualise our audience as active partners in the learning process.

In this context I find Enzensberger's distinction between repressive and emancipatory forms of broadcasting of relevance. Enzensberger argues that in its present form television does not serve communications, but prevents it since it allows no reciprocal action between transmitter and receiver. I believe that education is about enabling individuals, groups and communities to have a voice of their own and to express these voices.

This viewpoint has been expressed by Paulo Freire in his concept of education as conscientisation which is 'a critical self-insertion into reality'. Where Freire has used literacy as the means of achieving conscientisation I believe that in the developed world, media production presents a more likely means of achieving such conscientisation. This perspective is surprisingly close to post-modern theorists such as Lyotard who envisages an open culture based on a plurality of narratives: 'Such a social culture comprises a multifold history of narrative cultures – one where little stories are recounted, invented, heard, played out'.

Such a culture requires that each person has an opportunity to deploy her or his narrative imagination. It would be a culture in which the 'little narratives' overcome the power of the some unifying and pre-ordained 'Master Narrative'. (Kearney, 1991; pp.200–201)

In 'imagining' new possibilities and roles for educational broadcasting we must, I believe, consider the emerging partnership with learners so that we can join with them in exploring and communicating and listening to the multiplicity of 'little narratives' that can be brought into existence.

Looking ahead

One of my purposes in this presentation was to make our own concepts of learning problematic so that we can once again ask ourselves what we mean when we use terms such as 'education' and 'learning'. If we consciously adopt the transfer theory of learning then we have little difficulty in explaining what we, as educational broadcasters, intend to achieve through our programme making. If, however, we are dissatisfied with the 'transfer' theory then we need to explore other options.

In this paper I have identified some possible options, and in particular the option of assisting people to develop and grow. If we are to adopt such an approach then we need to enter new partnerships with our learning audience so that they become equal partners in the process of growth and development. While in the past the technology to permit a greater degree of participation may not have been readily available, developments over the past decade have resulted in much of the technology needed for production being available to more and more people.

As educators working with television we now have the ability to ensure that the 'little narratives' rather than the 'major narratives' are told. Such narratives can be creatively and entertainingly told only if we are bold enough to imagine our learners in a new and different way. This is, I believe, the major task which now challenges educational broadcasters. I hope that we can respond positively.

References

Enzensberger, Hans Magnus (1974): Constituents of a Theory of the Media. In: *The Consciousness Industry*, (trans. Stuart Hood), The Seabury Press, New York, pp. 95-128.

European Commission (1995): White Paper on Education and Training, European Commission, Brussels.

Fox, Dennis (1983): Personal Theories of Teaching. In: *Studies in Higher Education*, Vol. 8 No. 2, pp. 151–163.

Freire, Paulo (1972): *Cultural Action for Freedom*. Penguin, Harmondsworth.

Kearney, Richard (1991): *Poetics of Imagining*. Routledge, London.

MacMahon, John: The Rogue Learner – Human Responses to Educational Media. In: *Educational Media International*, 32/1995/3 (September), pp. 170-175.

John MacMahon, *Ph.D., is Editor, Educational Television at Radio Telfís Éireann and has extensive experience in educational broadcasting and in open and distance learning. Current programme responsibilities include LearnNet, a weekly live programme for adult learners and a European co-production about changing attitudes to older people. He obtained a Ph.D. from the University of Dublin in 1989 for his research on broadcast-based independent learning. His research interests centre on the interactions between human learning and electronic technologies and the relationship of traditional sources of knowledge to the electronic media environment. His most recent work examines the positive sides of the trickster rogue and suggests that this figure provides a model for creative lifelong learners in a multimedia society (see references).*

Addressing the do-it-yourself learner

Teleac's new conception and programming for multimedia adult education

Klaas Rodenburg

Teleac Research Department, Utrecht

Profile of the Educational Broadcasting System Teleac

- Teleac is an educational broadcasting organisation that is part of the public broadcasting system. Teleac is active in the field of education for adults.
- Teleac offers studying possibilities for adults by means of transmission of TV and radio programmes via the public network. 'Remote studies' are supported by books and other media.
- Teleac makes knowledge available and stimulates participation in educational activities. In doing so, Teleac lends valuable support to the permanent education of the entire population.
- Teleac's approach is multimedial by the combination of television, radio, textbooks, and other media. This approach encourages 'do-it-yourself' learning by participants.
- Teleac is part of the cooperative of educational broadcasting corporations 'Educom'. Teleac cooperates with partners in TV 2 and with foreign educational broadcasting institutions.
- Teleac strives to be the leading institution in the Dutch-speaking regions. Therefore Teleac wishes to characterise itself as an educational broadcasting corporation with a multi-media approach.

Teleac customers

Teleac's target group consists of persons who want to be kept informed in order to be oriented, to educate themselves or to keep track of developments. Teleac accommodates the studying requirements of as many adults and as many different target groups as possible.

Teleac customers spend their precious spare time and money on:

- personal development and widening of their horizon;
- advancement of their well-being and health;
- acquiring new skills;
- improvement of social position and career.

In view of these aims, customers expect from Teleac informative and instructive television and radio programmes, if necessary supported by didactically sound and structured accompanying material.

Teleac strategy

Since Teleac was founded, its right of existence has been embedded in the combination of adult education and public broadcasting system. This principle has not changed and is still the same in 1993. For the strategy, it is of essential importance that the educational broadcasting organisation Teleac has been acknowledged as a broadcasting licensee on the basis of the Media Act through the cooperative 'Educom'.

Assignment

From the principle of permanent education Teleac offers studying possibilities that answer the needs for education of as many adults as possible.

This assignment arises from the culture-political vision on education for adults.

The broadcasting media television and radio are the most suitable media for a contribution to the education of the entire population; this assignment has been laid down in the social function of the public broadcasting system.

Teleac's responsibility as an educational broadcasting organisation consists of production and transmission of programmes with an educational aim through the open network. Printed media and activities give essential support in this respect.

Identity

The remote media television, radio and book as well as the multimedia approach are excellently suited for furthering do-it-yourself learning. Teleac approaches individuals who are looking for information to get familiar with fields of knowledge, to receive education or to keep up-to-date. For this purpose, it offers programmes and materials that allow individuals to study individually and independently. Each participant can choose from the offers of possibilities for home study and follow his own learning path.

Teleac has a unique position both in the system of public broadcasting and in the field of education for adults: as a nationwide broadcasting organisation with educational responsibility, and as an educational institution that takes advantage of broadcasting corporations.

Teleac distinguishes itself from other broadcasting corporations by programme series with a high informative standard, a clear structure, great depth, and support (in writing or otherwise). The approach is innovative where contents, programmes and didactics are concerned.

For Teleac, developments in the field of leisure activities, education of adults and information supply are very important. Particular consideration must be given to the offer supplied by other organisations.

In the social field of force Teleac deals mainly with the public broadcasting corporations, with the national government and with organisations that are active in the social and educative fields. The government and social organisations are of indirect importance as well, because they have an influence on developments in society, which in turn influence Teleac's policy.

Chances

An organisation like Teleac is especially capable of stimulating education for people who have not (yet) participated or avail of little other possibilities to receive education. Particular chances are to be seen with the group of senior citizens, which is increasing in size. Moreover, new media can offer possibilities for the further development of remote education (offer, support, and distribution).

Where educative needs are concerned, Teleac has chances in the following areas:

- profession-specific orientation and education;
- developments in the field of science and technology;
- leisure activities;
- health education.

Choices will have to be made from the chances and possibilities available.

Challenges

On the one hand, Teleac is confronted with offers in the field of recreational activities and on the other hand with offers also aimed at satisfying studying and information needs. In the former case we are dealing with demands for time and attention, while the latter case concerns competition. Since participation in Teleac activities is primarily done in spare time, there will always be other offers regarding leisure activities.

Table 1: Information and education offered *

Offer	Spontaneous learning	Do-it-yourself learning	Supervised learning
— TV programmes	xxx	xx	x
— Radio programmes	xxx	xx	x
— Newspapers	xxx	x	
— Magazines	xxx	x	
— Hobby magazines	xxx	xx	
— Trade journals	x	xxx	
— Textbooks		xxx	xx
— Museums and the like	xxx	xx	x
— Public libraries	xxx	xxx	
— Clubs etc.	xx	xx	xx
— Company courses	x	xx	xxx
— Educational centres	x	xxx	xxx
— Schooling institutes	x	xx	xxx

*The number of crosses indicates the global size of competition.

In the educational market Teleac primarily deals with competition in the field of do-it-yourself learning. In the information supply market, developments regarding electronic media are of interest. Moreover, the further extension of the offer in television programmes and audio-visual services needs to be taken into account. These developments might be threatening in case Teleac maintains a passive attitude. For an active Teleac however, they constitute a challenge.

Public broadcasting system

The broadcasting system is of strategic importance, because Teleac's further existence as an educative broadcasting organisation depends on it. Also on a tactical level the partners in the public broadcasting system are of the utmost importance, because they determine the freedom of action Teleac will have. The position of educative broadcasting organisations and the educative programmes will have to be strengthened within the entity of public broadcasting.

Government

Teleac deals with the Government as a legislator and as a representative of social interests and needs. The importance of the Government as a legislator is related to the policy with respect to the public broadcasting system and grown-up education. The Government's role as a representative of public interest is related to the learning needs of large groups in society.

Social organisations

For three reasons, contacts with organisations in society are of outstanding importance:

* for the signalisation of learning needs.
* or creating a social basis.
* for setting up cooperation bodies.

Main outlines of policy

Aims

The main aim for the nineties is: satisfying the learning needs of as many adults as possible in a largest possible variety of audience groups. The better Teleac reaches this goal, the larger is its contribution to the work of public broadcasting corporations in the Netherlands. The total of programmes will have to reach a sufficiently large target group to maintain acces to the open network as an educative broadcasting institution in the long run.

Teleac strives to be the leading educative institution in the Dutch-speaking regions. Therefore Teleac will characterise itself more actively as an educational broadcasting institution with a multimedia approach. Within this framework, Teleac also participates actively in the exploration of technological innovations in the field of remote education.

Location

To reach this goal, a good relationship with the partners in public broadcasting corporations is of vital importance.

A broadcasting organisation such as Teleac, which is aimed at target groups, is strongly dependent on the cooperation of other broadcasting organisations with respect to broadcasting times and programme structure.

Therefore, the long-term policy of public broadcasting corporations needs to be taken into consideration. It will increasingly be determined by weighing the range, cost and income, which will have consequences for the total offer of public broadcasting corporations and the programmes for each channel.

To fill in its educational function in society, Teleac needs to maintain an active policy with respect to the establishing and maintaining of contacts with the Government, social organisations and educational institutions. The cooperation criterion is the extent to which the services can contribute to an adequate realisation of the job. By cooperation, learning needs can better be answered and social effects can be reinforced.

Programme policy

The major criterion for compilation of the offer is the extent to which Teleac can answer educational needs that are not or not sufficiently provided for otherwise.

The policy of offering an extensive and varied assortment of programmes and materials, is to be continued. Moreover, it will be attempted to answer the demand more rapidly and to address new target groups. The programme package needs to be characterised by pluriformity, recognisability, originality, innovative spirit and attractiveness for a wide audience.

To realise this policy, scarce TV and radio broadcasting time has to be used as effectively as possible. Furthermore, multimedia approach will be more varied, whereby the specific possibilities of the medium radio are to be utilised optimally.

Knowledge, learning and education

What is knowledge? Can knowledge exist outside of the human being? How do people acquire knowledge? Experiences in everyday life and general human values and needs determine the importance of learning for the individual. Learning needs are related to information, knowledge, insight, general education, and skills. Learning processes can be directed towards orientation, acquiring knowledge and insight, and towards instruction and training.

Usually three basic ways of acquiring knowledge are discerned: The first and still the most important is through personal experience (called experiential learning or learning by experience). The second is achieved by means of communication, i.e. learning and acquiring knowledge from other people (social learning). In modern society social networks are becoming more and more important for learning and acquiring knowledge. The third is attained by processing information from data carriers, by learning from the media (cognitive learning).

If we apply this to television, we have to ask ourselves the following questions: What goes on while someone is watching television and what goes on when he has switched the television set off? Maybe learning starts after watching, but little is known about this process. Research into this therefore has to be carried out.

We at Teleac distinguish three kinds of learning processes with regard to televiewing:

- *Spontaneous learning:*
  Spontaneous learning occurs when a person learns something without any intention (non-intentional learning).
- *Do-it-yourself learning:*
  The person himself or herself organizes activities with the purpose of learning something (intentional).
- *Supervised or guided learning:*
  The person participates in educational activities organised and tutored by an institution (individually or in groups).

The first, spontaneous or non-intentional learning is still the most important. These are normal everyday learning processes, and most of the time one realises only afterwards that one has learnt something. There is a mass of literature on what is called the socialisation process.

According to our conception the learner is an individual, but not isolated from his social environment or social networks. Intentional learning comes about when the learner undertakes all kinds of activities to acquire information. There is a lot of literature in adult education on the concept of self-directed learning. It is almost the same as the concept of autonomous learning, and we use the term 'do-it-yourself' learning. This expresses an active attitude also during television viewing.

The third mode of learning is supervised or guided learning. This way of learning is mostly associated with schools, and even in adult education it is still a predominant mode of learning. There are also some combinations between do-it-yourself learning and guided learning called guided self-study, as practised at the Open University.

In terms of the three aforementioned kinds of learning processes, participation in educative projects by Teleac can be described as follows:

Learning process	Participant
Spontaneous learning	– incidental viewer / listener
Do-it-yourself learning	– regular viewer / listener
	– student A (looking / listening / reading / practising)
Supervised learning	– student B (like A + contact)

99

Learning projects

Most research about what people do if they want to learn something has been done in the United States, in Canada and in the UK. This research has not yet been replicated in the Netherlands nor in any other continental European country. This applies to educational broadcasters as well as to everyone who is active in the field of adults' learning.

The Canadian Allen Tough coined the term 'learning projects' which is a very broad conception of learning. Someone preparing for responsibility like becoming a father or a mother, is engaging in a learning process. Although most of them will not view it as learning, many people start looking for information, they begin talking to different people within their social networks about a certain problem, they may even attend meetings on the subject or follow a structured course at an institution. Tough found out that most of these activities can be identified as learning projects, which he defined as processes of intentional learning organised by a person him- or herself. Very often these learning projects are not taken up for reasons of personal development, they prefer to deal with practical problems like gardening or child rearing, or they result in do-it-yourself work at home. Quite a lot of these learning projects also have something to do with a person's world of work.

Unfortunately, no research has been carried out since 1979 on the sources of information that people use. If we were to carry out a similar study today here in Europe, the figures would be different, and maybe even the order would be different.

Social contacts and social networks are the most important factors in learning processes, and people use all kinds of different sources of information.

The role of educational institutions is only a minor one. The mass media of television and radio will continue to be very important, while books will not be number one on the list as in 1979. In 1996 the personal computer and other new media will play an increasingly important role.

Brookfield (1986) said in his book *Understanding and facilitating adult learning*: 'With the development of microcomputers and various forms of interactive technologies, we can expect a corresponding increase in demand and variety of networking activities'. By networking, he does not mean computer networking but social networks.

For Teleac, learning and education have a dynamic meaning because learning is established by adequate information processing. Whether learning processes actually take place depends on the intention of the person and not on the intention of the offering side. However, an efficient way of offering the information is a necessary prerequisite. The intention of participants in Teleac programmes is diverse. It may vary from the introduction into a subject to the achievement of insight and improvement of professional skills.

Recent Teleac research

De belangstelling voor cursussen en het imago van Teleac (*The interest in courses and the image of Teleac*); Rapport Afdeling Onderzoek (Feb. 1990)

Teleac en de markt van volwasseneneducatie (*Teleac and the market of adult education*). Rapport AGB Qualitatief (April 1991).

Kiezen voor Teleac. Resultaten van de cursistenmonitor. (*Deciding for Teleac. Results of the students' monitor*). Rapport Stafbureau Onderzoek & Beleidsvoorbereiding (Nov. 1991).

Behoeftestructuren met betrekking tot onderwijs en vorming bij volwassenen. (*Requirement structures regarding instruction and education for adults*). Rapport Censydiam (April 1992).

Kijkers naar Teleac. Omvang, samenstelling en gedrag (*Teleac-viewers. Numbers, composition, and behaviour*). Rapport Stafbureau Onderzoek & Beleidsvoorbereiding (June 1992).

Klaas Rodenburg, *Ph.D., has been Head of Department of Research and Policy Planning, Educational Broadcasting Corporation Teleac, Netherlands, since 1979. Trained in Social Psychology at the University of Utrecht, he has carried out research and published works on conflict studies, adult education, mass communication, political psychology, distance education, and learning from television. His special interests are telelearning, lifelong learning, technology for education. Presently, he is working on Learning 2000 (research), public broadcasting after 2000 (research and policy) and new media (research and development).*

4: Viewers' Interests
and Expectations

The viewers' interests and their expectations from educational television programmes

Peter Diem

Head, ORF Media Research, Vienna

My paper is built up as follows: I should first like to present the general programme interest in educational broadcasts, then briefly take a look at the actual use of educational broadcasts and finally say something about the general attitude towards education provided by various media. In doing so I shall draw upon a qualitative study which was carried out specially for this event.

I shall play a short demo tape on this with excerpts lasting one minute each from six different educational programmes. These six minutes are then followed by a five-minute section from a group discussion on the excerpts from educational programmes shown on the demo tape.

Programme interest in educational broadcasts

Table 1 shows a ranking list in which the 'absolute programme interest' in certain programme categories is reproduced, as measured by Austrian Television every year. This 'absolute programme interest' indicates what percentage of the Austrian television audience that is prepared to watch television wants to see a certain type of programme 'in any event'.

There are some 200 programme categories to choose from in these surveys. It is not difficult to see that educational programmes do not necessarily have to be among those broadcasts which arouse no interest at all; they can even be among those programme categories which arouse great interest, although we include far more things than just education and school television in the educational area.

For us at the ORF it was first extremely surprising to find out that after the evening news, the weather forecast and the local news the category 'expeditions, foreign countries' ranked fifth with a programme interest of 39. This includes programmes in which such different things as volcanoes, brown bears and ethnography are dealt with. It concerns the series *Universum*, which can be seen on the ORF on Tuesday evenings.

The 'animal broadcasts' came ninth. This high ranking can certainly be explained by the fact that these broadcasts not only combine education, culture, information and entertainment, but are also of practical use for many people.

Table 1: Programme interest in 1996 – ranking list

The 'absolute programme interest' indicates what percentage of the Austrian viewing public prepared to watch television wants to see a certain type of programme 'in any event'.

%	Title	%	Title
63	Zeit im Bild 1 (news)		...
53	Weather report	7	Broadcast of church services
48	Bundesland heute (regional)	7	Classical concert
44	Österreich heute (national)	7	Contemporary TV film
39	Expedition, foreign countries	7	Modern comedy
39	Sport report skiing	7	Classical musical show
36	Election broadcast	7	Film for children and young people
35	Österreich Bild (Sun., holidays)	6	Vocational training course
35	Animal broadcast	6	Programme on an issue
33	Entertaining	6	Discussion on religious subjects
30	Zeit im Bild 2 (news)	6	Chansons
30	Short news	6	Folk, foreign folk music
30	Big entertainment show	5	Breakfast television
29	Sports news	5	Text aktuell in the morning
29	TV crime thriller	5	Archaeology magazine
28	Traditional Austrian folk music	5	Programme for ethnic groups
27	Consumers' programmes	5	Computer magazine
27	Sport studio	5	Television sermon
27	Sport broadcast, general	5	Religious meditation (evening)
27	Carnival broadcast	5	Religious help for life
26	Lottery	4	Language course
25	Magazine (Report, Thema)	4	Parent'/adults' school
25	Sport broadcast car racing	4	Customers' programme
25	With a hidden camera	4	Advertising
24	Contemporary history	4	Gymnastic porgramme/sports course
24	Wochenschau (news of the week)	4	General culture mag (10 _)
24	Broadcasts of major events	4	Portrait of an artist
24	Science documentation	4	Modern ballet
24	Sport broadcast football	4	Avant-garde/experimental film
24	Spy film/agent thriller	4	Puppet animated film
24	Entertainment series	3	Literature programme
23	Short show with game of chance	3	Book programme
23	Hits show	3	Programme for children up to 7 years
	...	3	Programme for primary school children
17	Adventure film	3	Programme for children from 8 to 12
17	Work from film history	3	Young people's magazine
16	Presse Stunde (discussion)	3	Jazz
16	Science magazine	2	School television
16	Operetta	2	ORF promotion/ORF products
16	Classical comedy	2	Readings
16	Nonsense broadcast	2	Modern light music
16	Youth series	2	Modern opera
15	Business magazine	2	Music experiment

The categories 'contemporary documentary' and 'science documentary' (both mentioned in 24 per cent of the responses) ranked fairly high; the science magazines came somewhere in the middle, being mentioned by 16 per cent of the adult population.

Only at the end of the interest scale do we find the further vocational training course, the computer magazine, the language course, the general culture magazine, the book broadcast and – right at the end – school television.

On the demographic structure of the interest

Each of these individual programme categories can be broken down into the percentage share of each demographic group with the help of our data (see Table 2 opposite). I should now like to illustrate that by giving some examples, but I must stress once again: these conclusions relate to opinions on what the programme offers, to potential use therefore, and not to their actual use.

School television: I shall start with the category at the bottom of the table, school television. Here we encounter – over quite a broad spectrum – little interest: men of 60 or more are a bit more interested and can thus perhaps deal with it a little better. Graduates and viewers with *Abitur* (the school-leaving certificate qualifying for university entrance) do not think much of it; they have apparently heard that it has been taken off the programme.

Book broadcasts: The next one is the book broadcasts. Here a certain emphasis of interest can be recognised among older viewers and also among university graduates and those with *Abitur*.

General culture magazine: When you then take the general culture magazine you can see a big increase among the graduates. It may be a question here of socially desired answers, but it is after all extremely interesting that older people are clearly more interested in magazines than young viewers, although the producers of culture magazines do everything imaginable to spoil older people's enjoyment in viewing them: *de facto* no classic culture is dealt with, but usually only fringe culture or avant-garde. Why older people like that is a mystery to me; probably they actually wish to see a different culture magazine, and they look at each one in the hope they will be offered something different.

Language course: Next is the language course. It meets with little interest among the young people, but finds more favour among the older viewers. There will certainly be a lot of philosophising about that; I personally believe that it is here a question of the effect that something is accepted because it seems to make sense – although it is not really needed.

Computer magazine: The computer magazine, previously mentioned by Erik Nordahl, is an interesting case. Although it is as a rule not well done, it does appear to be a programme that might accompany us for some time to come. Eleven per cent of the youngsters, the teenagers, are very interested in it; that the older viewers do not think so highly of it is

Table 2: Programme interest – Demographic structure

	School Television	Book Programme	General Culture Magazine	Language Course	Computer Course	Archaeology Magazine	Training Course, Vocational	Science Magazine	Science Documentary	Contemporary Documentary	Animal Programme	Expedition, Foreign Countries	
	%	%	%	%	%	%	%	%	%	%	%	%	Basis
ADULTS (> 12 years)	2	3	4	4	5	5	6	16	24	24	35	39	1609
AGE													
12–19 years	2	3	1	2	11	2	4	7	6	4	13	12	179
20–29 years	1	2	3	3	9	4	6	16	16	16	18	23	312
30–39 years	3	2	2	4	4	6	6	20	21	21	28	38	285
40 49 years	2	3	3	3	3	5	7	17	24	20	38	44	239
50–59 years	2	3	3	3	2	6	6	16	32	34	45	57	217
60–74 years	2	6	9	4	2	8	7	16	35	38	54	56	315
>75 years	4	7	15	8	4	8	6	12	32	43	64	52	62
Men 18–59 years	2	2	3	2	7	7	6	19	25	26	28	38	550
Men >60 years	4	3	5	4	4	8	8	16	37	46	52	56	146
Women 18–59 years	1	3	3	5	3	3	6	15	19	16	33	37	540
Women >60 years	2	7	12	5	1	8	7	15	34	35	58	54	231
12–29 years	1	2	2	3	10	3	6	13	13	11	16	19	491
12–49 years	2	3	3	3	7	4	6	10	18	16	25	30	1015
>50 years	2	5	7	4	2	7	7	16	34	37	52	56	594
RESPONDENT'S WORK													
Self-employed	–	–	6	6	8	2	6	26	32	30	36	50	61
Employed	1	4	3	3	7	7	6	19	26	25	28	41	421
Worker	3	1	1	3	5	5	8	12	15	16	30	34	351
Farmer	–	–	2	–	–	3	9	13	7	14	18	19	49
LIFE CYCLE													
12–39 years	2	3	3	4	11	5	6	18	18	17	22	28	440
Men/women with child	4	3	5	4	–	2	4	14	14	13	17	15	65
Men/women no child	1	–	4	4	–	2	5	17	26	12	42	56	60
Men/women job child	1	2	2	3	4	4	6	16	19	19	26	31	121
Men/women job no child	1	2	3	6	2	4	5	16	21	18	38	45	145
EDUCATION													
Prim./elementary school	3	2	4	2	4	2	6	9	17	16	34	34	487
Vocational/techn. school	2	3	3	4	4	6	7	18	26	25	39	45	827
University/Matura	1	5	8	6	7	10	3	21	27	34	25	34	295
Matura	–	5	6	6	8	7	3	22	27	31	24	32	243
University	3	6	18	4	3	20	–	15	25	48	28	42	52

understandable. (I myself didn't become a computer freak until the tender age of 52; it's never too late!). Women over 60, however, have problems with this subject: their interest in the computer magazine drops to 1 per cent. Sixth formers are, on the other hand, far more interested than children at primary school.

Archaeology magazine: Now the programmes are getting more and more exciting. Table 7 shows the potential interest in an archaeology magazine, though as a rule there is no such thing. The ORF put one on in the afternoon which was given fantastic marks. It was a magazine about Austrian, about European, finds; it showed very interesting things. But as it never came into the prime time, it always had an audience of only 1–2 per cent, so it never became a highflyer. There is something lying dormant in this category which the TV stations could discover. 10 per cent of those with *Abitur* showed an interest in principle.

Further vocational training course: Prestige answers are likely to have played a part in the answers on the further vocational training course. Those with *Abitur* or a degree do not think much of it, while those with lower educational qualifications do; there are no differences between the age groups.

Science magazine: In the case of the science magazine and the short scientific reports we have now reached an interest level of 16 per cent, i.e. one in six is interested in short scientific reports. Here the emphasis is on short. If there is a report on science it should be kept short. We have had very good experience with *Wissen aktuell*, that is, with five-minute scientific reports and science news in the early evening. The figures for the interest are especially high in the case of graduates and those with *Abitur*, namely 21 per cent. The same applies to science documentaries, which, however, are more widely accepted, even by those with only a middle school education.

Contemporary documentaries: High figures resulted for contemporary documentaries. Contemporary history is found to be interesting, but it should not be too recent. When I have already experienced things – I think, for example, of the course of contemporary history since Adenauer – then perhaps it becomes a little uninteresting for many viewers, because they have personally experienced the events themselves and there is not yet enough distance for them to be felt again as part of their own experience. Everything is interesting that has something to do with major world events, including wars and international affairs.

Animal broadcasts: There cannot be enough animal broadcasts, it seems. They are among the most exciting programmes offered by television today. Here we are naturally talking about well-made documentaries from all continents, especially those dealing with local wild animals, not just, for example, the films about the mating habits of baboons that are often referred to. Here we have the rare combination of entertainment, information and practical use in one programme – perhaps even a certain cultural value as well.

Expeditions, broadcasts on foreign countries and peoples: The figures for the programme category expeditions, broadcasts on foreign countries and peoples reflect the longing to travel to remote places. It can be said without exaggeration that this is the typical case of a programme which rises up into unexpectedly high spheres of interest. When you see that up to 57 per cent of the older television viewers say they are interested in broadcasts about foreign countries and peoples you can understand why these broadcasts are becoming increasingly popular.

The use of television broadcasts

The figures given so far related to the pure, abstract interest of the viewers as we have regularly ascertained it with the help of the programme categories given above. When the results of such surveys are presented one repeatedly hears that it is more a question of prestige answers, only reflecting what is socially desirable, and it is socially desirable to watch educational broadcasts and to be informed about culture.

But what about the actual use of the individual programmes?

The meter measuring, that is measuring with the help of audience measuring devices ('people meters'), shows that viewers' behaviour does indeed differ according to the target groups.[1]

Table 3 shows as an example the data on use for the ORF culture magazine, which is transmitted on Mondays at 10.30 p.m., so admittedly very late: 8.3 per cent of the viewers were found to be 'interested in the subject', but altogether only 2.3 per cent of the adults actually watched it.

Table 3: Cultural Magazine '10½' (Mondays; 10.30 p.m.)

Average age: 50.6	Viewers in %	Grade 0-5	Loyalty index
Adults (12 years and older)	2.3	3.8	43
Interested in the subject	8.3	4.3	55
12–19 years	0.6	3.5	50
20–29 years	0.9	3.9	34
30–39 years	2.6	3.6	47
40–49 years	3.2	3.9	49
50–59 years	2.9	3.7	44
60–74 years	3.4	3.8	40
75 years and older	2.7	4.0	40
Abitur/university	4.4	4.0	53
cable/sat. reception	1.7	3.7	37

1 Cf. Erik Nordahl Svendsen´s paper, this volume, pp 114–120.

However, patience seems to run short in the case of a culture magazine. The figures in the third column indicate the 'fidelity index'. It tells us what percentage of a broadcast was taken in. You can see for example that the viewers with *Abitur* make far more intensive use than the total population, i.e. that they also hold out much longer with a programme (fidelity index = 53 per cent). The older viewers (with a fidelity index of 43 per cent) did not stick it out for so long, and those in their twenties the shortest time of all (34 per cent).

Table 4 shows a second example, namely the figures for the series *Universum* with its programmes on animals and foreign countries and peoples. The data reflect the previously mentioned widespread interest in this series. 23 per cent are generally interested in the subject; the use by the total adult population is 15 per cent. The fidelity index is 72, an extremely high figure, and it increases with age.

Table 4: Documentation (Foreign Countries, Animals) UNIVERSUM (Tuesdays; 8.15 p.m.)

Average age: 53.2			
	Viewers in %	Grade 0-5	Loyalty index
Adults (12 years and older)	15.0	4.6	68
Interested in the subject	23.0	4.6	72
12–19 years	5.6	4.5	58
20–29 years	4.8	4.4	52
30–39 years	13.1	4.6	64
40–49 years	12.4	4.5	65
50–59 years	21.7	4.5	72
60–74 years	26.6	4.7	71
75 years and older	29.7	4.7	77
Abitur/university	13.8	4.6	68
cable/sat. reception	12.4	4.6	65

The appreciation of the programme is also extraordinarily positive and increases with age. This assessment, or grading, which in Anglo-Saxon countries is known as the appreciation index, is carried out by us in Austria using a scale ranging from 0 to 5. The figures given here of 4.6 on average (with a maximum of 4.7 for the seniors) can be regarded as well-nigh ideal.

So with the help of quantitative audience research for all demographic groups and for the programme categories we have drawn up we can demonstrate the interest and also the actual use. Now what about the qualitative aspect of audience research?

The group discussion – an example of practice-related qualitative research

I shall now report on the results of a study carried out specially for this conference in which we obtained informative data from a group discussion. I should also like to demonstrate by this that with relatively simple means – for a price of about DM 5,000 – you can find out the attitude of the audience to a broadcast or to a certain programme area. We all know the objections that are raised to the group discussion, to the qualitative approach with a so-called focus group. Of course, twelve test subjects cannot possibly make representative statements, but they can provide us with certain insights, as I shall show.

Our study was carried out with a group of 12 persons, six men and six women. One subject of our interests was the attitude towards individual media as vehicles of education, in other words the question concerning the competence of media and socialisation institutions to impart knowledge and education. Added to this were questions concerning actual broadcasts offered by the television programme.

Measurements were taken using an index with values between 0 and 10. This is a scale which is very suitable for such purposes and which in general I can strongly recommend – not least because people understand it very well and it is easy to make international comparisons.

Table 5: Who/what imparts education/knowledge?

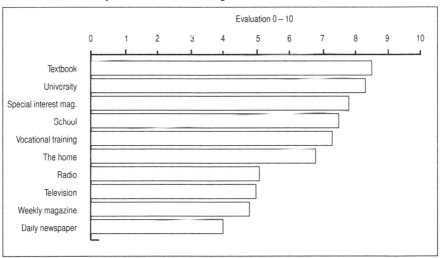

As far as the competence for imparting knowledge is concerned the institutions 'text book' and 'university' come first with figures of 8.4 and 8.3. This was not unexpected. The specialised journals are apparently given a high priority: when you go to a kiosk these days you can find a special interest periodical on every area of life, whether it is a magazine about yachting or old clocks, the computer or golf. So the specialised journal as an educational medium attains a figure of 7.8; the school 7.5, which is not bad, the family only 6.5.

We know from international comparisons that a figure of 6.5 on the scale of 0–10 is a kind of quality threshold. It is the value above which something is successful. Be it a question of whether a programme is good enough to be transmitted, or of assessing a presenter, you can say: the arithmetic mean of 5 is only average, success, life, does not begin until 6.5. Thus sound radio (5.0) and television (4.9) do not quite make the grade: the figures for the 'educational function' are clearly below average, as are the weekly magazine and the daily newspaper.

Now let us turn to what we showed this group. We presented altogether six productions, four from Austria and two from Germany.

What do we hope to achieve with video tests of this kind, with filmed group discussions? We want to present the programme-makers with their audience, we want to show them how people react to various programmes.

The report on the discussion, the evaluation of the participants' remarks, is finished in one day. The original recording of the group discussion is shown to the programme-makers and they see their audience – sometimes for the very first time. Expressed rather vividly: for the first time they can see the whites of their eyes. For once they have to remain seated for 60 minutes and watch, so they have to do what they are incessantly demanding of their audience. A hard job!

Summary

For imparting knowledge television – from the viewpoint of an interested audience – ranks before the daily newspaper, but well behind special interest journals. It is the duty of television to give people an appetite for different specialised areas and themes.

The quality of knowledge broadcasts is obviously of fundamental importance for a fastidious television audience and is judged with great discrimination. If educational television today is not made lavishly, well and excitingly, i.e. with outstanding direction and camera work, it does not go down with its audience. Thus decisive importance attaches to presentation in a manner suitable for the media, and is in fact a prerequisite for acceptance. Only when the formal requirements are met does personal interest in the subject dealt with define the attractiveness and assessment of the individual programmes. It must not be forgotten that nowadays a ten- or eleven-year-old has more than seven years of television experience. The present generation of television viewers has become hard to please as far as form and content are concerned.

What people enjoy are lavish presentations which make use of the original stylistic means of television and display an effort which corresponds to that of other forms of broadcasting. Thus *de facto* all other subjects would be suitable for television treatment, perhaps even numismatics. Each of us is interested in something different; it is only a question of defining the target groups. And there are, of course, a lot of these. The distinctions possible today between various lifestyles are steadily increasing.

What is rejected are 'unspecific pictures' – that is a nice euphemism for miserable films – long interviews with experts, especially in a foreign language – and studio discussions, the 'scientific talkshow', so to speak. It should also be borne in mind that the people in the German-speaking countries are spoilt; unlike, for example, Scandinavia and some western European countries, we have practically no sub-titles, because everything is dubbed.

In the last few years a clear change in the content and also in the stylistic means in knowledge programmes has been observed. The typical illustrated school television broadcast has disappeared – maybe to the regret of some older viewers and much to the pleasure of the younger test subjects.

Very important, however, is the fact that, especially in the case of older target groups, forms of editing with rapid changes of picture, that is with a high cutting speed or rapid sequences of cut-ins, are to be avoided. That should give us food for thought in view of the average age for such television programmes, which as a rule ranges from 48 to 52.

Many of the people hear badly anyway, and, as if to punish them, the pictures are also quickly snatched away in front of their eyes. So a large part of the television audience is, as a rule, being treated wrongly. What is needed is calm, is clarity, to also give viewers, especially older ones, a chance to think things through. Thus it is to be recommended, for example, that maps are shown on the screen when subjects from other parts of the world are being dealt with.

At the moment the audience (still) feels there is a lack of reports on foreign countries and civilisations. Apparently television does, after all, serve not only to provide people with entertainment and information, but it is also a window on the world, and if it fulfils this function, if it succeeds in being both the hearth at home and a window on the world at the same time, 'messenger on horseback' and 'teller of fairytales', then probably good use is being made of it.

Peter Diem, *Ph.D., studied jurisprudence and political science at Vienna and in the USA., graduated as an academic translator for English and received a Master of Science from Southern Illinois University. After working as head of the Basic Research Department with the ÖVP (Austrian People's Party) and the Book Market Research Department at the Fritz Molden Publishing House in Vienna, he became the head of the Media Research Department with the Austrian Broadcasting Corporation ORF in 1979. He has published numerous works on political science themes and on questions of methodology in media research. He is also a lecturer at the universities of Vienna and Salzburg.*

Television for education:
Subject interest and media suitability
Some results of a Danish Survey

Erik Nordahl Svendsen
Head of Audience Research, Danmarks Radio, Copenhagen

The assessment of a need for education on television

If there is a need for educational programmes on television – how can we assess it? The means are generally the same as for any other programme area: we can ask questions about interests, and we can measure viewing behaviour. Moreover, different kinds of qualitative studies (like focus groups, etc.) or big scale surveys can be used if the necessary finance is available, but as this is seldom the case I will not go into this.

This paper is based on a special survey made for this conference, as we had very little general knowledge about the interests of the Danish viewers with regards to educational television programmes.

The use of television for learning purposes however differs from most other uses of the TV set. The viewer may often pick up something new from any programme, learning by accident. But the idea of educational programmes is that he or she purposely learns about a particular subject, more or less as from any course offered that is embedded in a curriculum. This definition has three simple but important consequences:

- *The viewer's interest depends highly on the subject.*
  We come closer to a true picture when we ask about interest in specific subjects rather than a general need for education. This holds true in spite of the fact that people having a higher level of education generally profess more interest in more subjects than people having a low level of or no education after school. The St. Matthew effect – those who have been given much shall have even more – holds true although it is clearer in humanities than in practical or commercial subjects.
- *Television has its strengths and its limits as a medium, and these must be individually considered for each subject.*
  Subjects are to a varying degree visual, or they demand a certain amount of interaction with, if not instruction from, a live teacher. According to a survey carried out by our department this year people judge the ability of television as an educational medium strongly related to the individual subject. Those interested in the subject tend to be a little more positive towards television as the educational medium.

But there is no general correlation: The number of subject-interests or factors such as age or educational level have a very low correlation with an aggregated belief in television's being suitable for education. The basic, subjective needs for education from television should therefore be measured both as the stated interest in learning about the subject and, even more, as the proportion of those interested who believe that television is a suitable medium for just this subject. Results from the Danish survey, which I shall talk about later, illustrate this point.

- *Measuring viewing behaviour in small people-meter panels becomes a real challenge.*
  This is a another consequence of defining educational programmes in this demanding way, as a curriculum. I must admit that we are far beyond save statistics when we get down to small numbers.

What can be learned from the analysis of TV Meter data?
As a rule we do not expect high ratings for education, even if many people claimed an interest in the subject when asked. But we do expect an educational programme to be more frequently used by interested or relevant target groups than by others. The panel is in principle an asset to the educational programme producer in this analysis because we are versed in the interests and activities of the panel members, which would be very costly to collect in ad hoc surveys.

When the producer of educational programmes defines a target group in the meter panel, we use some of the standard concepts or calculations for a series of programmes to assess the programmes' relationship with its audience. The uncertainty in a small sample warns us against looking too firmly at the rating for a single programme. But for a series we can use measures like:

1. *reach and frequency*
   How many have seen at least one programme in the series? What is the number of programmes watched in average? Has the series reached the target, and do they follow it regularly – as may be assumed from the curriculum plan?
2. *average rating index*
   What is the average rating in target, in relation to average total rating?
3. *share in target group*
   Does the target group select the programme more than the general audience, given that they watch television at that time?
4. *fidelity of target group* (net fraction, 'Treue-Index')
   Does the target group watch more of the single programme than the average viewer? Has the series appealed to the target group?

Two examples are given below. *The Computer School*, a series about the new IBM operating system OS/2 and the software Perfect Office, and

Science or God?, a series of lectures from the Niels Bohr Institute for Theoretical Physics at the University of Copenhagen. Both series were scheduled on Sunday around noon.

The data in the following two tables are not taken from a special survey, but they are based on a secondary analysis of standard data gained from our TV meter system. The question is whether the TV Meter data, in spite of ratings of 1–2 per cent, indicate any special interest in the programmes in well-defined target groups. The importance does not lie in the details, but in the general interpretation.

Table 1: Educational series *The Computer School* (8 programmes)

		Target groups		
	12+ yrs	Quite/very interested in computers	Very interested in computers	Use computer at home (not games)
Universe (1000)	4,483	1,062	404	1,160
Reach (1 min)	11%	15%	13%	12%
Frequency (of 8)	1.3	1.3	1.3	1.2
Rating Index	100	156	191	100
Avg. share of viewing	15%	41%	38%	25%
Avg. fidelity of programme	42	51	75	41

Those interested in computers were clearly more attracted to *The Computer School* than the general audience (rating index, share, fidelity), and they were a little more interested than those using computers already. Perhaps the introduction was too elementary for them. But loyalty to the series is low in all targets (frequency), so a progression in the curriculum will be a problem.

Table 2: Series *Science or God?* (14 programmes)

		Target groups		
	12+ yrs	Quite/very interested in religion	Quite/very interested in science	Quite/very interested in religion and science
Universe (1000)	4.483	1.164	1.635	665
Reach (1 min)	14%	16%	18%	18%
Frequency (of 14)	1.3	1.3	1.2	1.3
Rating Index	100	167	136	208
Avg. share of viewing	9%	17%	13%	22%
Avg. fidelity of programme	27	26	48	43

Here the relevant target groups are those who are interested in religion, or those who are interested in science, or those who are interested in both. Viewers interested in both religion and in science watched the programmes more frequently than the others did. The group combining the two interests was the most enthusiastic (rating index, share), a scientific interest perhaps proving the most important (fidelity). Were the religious people enstranged by the physics? Loyalty to the series is again rather low in this case, as it was in all target groups.

The two examples demonstrate that even small numbers may give relevant information from a TV-meter system, when detailed and relevant target groups are analysed. And the results could well lead on to focus groups if time and money allow, in order to acquire better founded knowledge about the quality or problems of the series. So far, we can only say that very specific educational series on television attracted audiences of the relevant kind.

The Danish survey

In weeks 9-12, 1996, a survey among the Danish population (aged 13+) covering 1.011 interviews was carried out by Danish Gallup in the form of personal interviews in the home (CAPI technique). The interviewees were shown a list with sixteen different subjects for possible educational programmes on television. This list was taken from the actual repertoire of DR-TV's TV-Open this spring. The main question was:

'Now, about your interest in education. Many people feel a need to learn something new: work-related, general knowledge or perhaps some practical skills. One way of learning is to select educational programmes from television. I will now read a list of subjects, and in each case ask you about your interest in learning more about them. My question is

(a) whether you are interested in learning more about the subject, and
(b) whether you believe that education on television could be a suitable way of learning about that subject?

Take your time to consider your interest, and whether you believe television to be suitable.'

The answers are accumulated in Table 3 (p. 118). Here are some comments on the results.

Interest in general

Almost everybody stated some interest in learning more through television. Only six per cent showed no interest at all in any of the sixteen subjects. Television was accepted as a suitable medium for at least one subject by even more people (98 per cent). On the general level a weak, positive correlation was found.

It is important to note, however, that many people accept television as a suitable medium without sharing any interest in many of the specific subjects, and vice versa: not all fans of a subject think of television as being a medium suited to their needs.

Table 3: Interest in learning more / Suitability of TV (numbers indicate answers in per cent)

	Interested in learning more about the subject			TV is suitable	
	Yes	Maybe	No	All persons	'Yes' persons
History of Middle East	28	19	52	71	84
Geography; Nature of Siberia	22	19	58	78	88
Philosophy: Science and God	24	13	63	47	67
Foreign languages	50	14	35	59	63
Humanities (None*)			17		
Playing guitar or piano	18	8	74	19	27
Gymnastics	38	14	47	60	68
DIY	46	17	36	71	84
Camping	21	9	69	44	49
Drawing	22	9	69	40	50
Hunting	10	4	86	30	60
Practical skills (None*)			15		
Agricultural affairs	14	10	75	67	89
Economics via the computer	29	13	58	42	51
Computers in general	49	10	40	51	58
Accounting	27	15	58	43	51
Starting own business	16	11	72	42	55
Environment on the job	34	22	43	61	69
Job/business (None*)			21		
All subjects (None*)			6		2

* 'None' indicates 'not interested' in any ot the mentioned subjects (in per cent).

The subjects are categorised under three headings: Humanities, Practical Skills or Leisure, and Job/Business.

Humanities (4 topics or series)
83 per cent showed an interest in at least one subject in this group, foreign languages being the clear leader. On the other hand, some doubt was expressed concerning the ability of the television medium to cater for the highly verbal subjects (Language and Philosophy) whereas History and Geography were judged to be more visual subjects, being well-known as a result of documentaries on television. People having a higher level of education and young people showed more interest in the humanistic subjects.

Practical Skills or Leisure (6 topics or series)
Practical skills or leisure activities attracted considerable interest from 85 per cent, with Do-it-Yourself heading the field (especially among men), also in terms of TV suitability. Gymnastics came second (first among women), also awarded a high level of TV suitability.

Two minority subjects – playing an instrument or hunting – demonstrate the importance of TV suitability: the musicians did not deem television to be a very useful medium for learning their skills whereas the hunters did, the latter contrasting with the opinion held by the general public.

Interest in learning these practical skills was broader among people with no or only some further education, and, to the greatest extent, among people under 60. So the audience for practical skills courses are generally heavy users of television.

Job/Business (6 topics or series, concentrating on computers and economy)

The series mentioned here caught the interest of 79 per cent, learning about computers in general being the key subject. But of those professing an interest in these subjects only about half thought that television was most suitable for learning about them. Environmental issues at work are the exception, with a high result for television as a suitable medium.

The groups most interested in learning about business and job are men, people under 40 years and those with some or higher education. These target groups are generally light viewers of television.

Table 4 demonstrates the connection between interest in a subject (horizontal axis) and the percentage of those interested who think that the subject would be well suited for presentation on television. We can note, for example, in the upper right corner that 'Do-it-Yourself' courses arouse a broad interest and are thought of as well suited for television,

Table 4: interest in a subject/suitability TV presentation

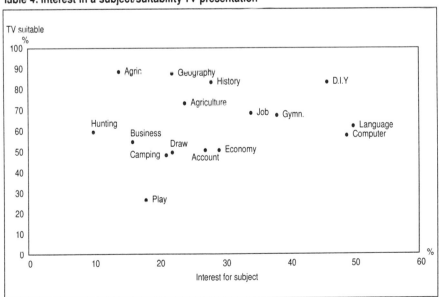

and so are programmes about Agriculture, Geography or History, subjects which are very close to those presented in general television output.

At the bottom we find 'Play', and if we would relate this result to the course 'How to play the piano' mentioned by Mogens Arngot, for example, we would conclude that only few of those interested in learning to play the piano believe that television would be a suitable medium for it.

We have also asked people if they are at the moment actively engaged in some kind of education. About 15 per cent of the Danes seemed to be receiving full-time education; roughly another 15 per cent are engaged in some kind of part-time education. Then we asked them if they could think that some part of the education they were undergoing at present could in principle be received via television. And as many as 25 per cent accepted the idea that television could be used as an educational medium in the kind of education that they are actively engaged in for the moment. This at least demonstrates an openness towards using television as an educational medium.

Erik Nordahl Svendsen, *who holds a MA in Political Science, is head of the Audience Research Department of Danmarks Radio since 1984. He has written books on journalism and is editor of the Yearly Report on Audience Studies in DR. In 1994 he has been elected Vice-chairman of the Group of European Audience Researchers (GEAR).*

Educational programmes and people's viewing behaviour in the Netherlands

Ard Heuvelman
Audience Research, Netherlands Broadcasting Corporation (NOS),
Hilversum

With the rise of commercial broadcasters public service broadcasting has had to review its strategies in many European countries. A more market-oriented approach with a market-conscious programme production has become a necessity (Diem, 1993). In this severe competition for the audience, programmes with low ratings have come under pressure.

An example of the influence of competition from the Netherlands: The Dutch educational broadcaster Teleac's first series of programmes (called *Accidents in and around the house*) were watched in 1965 by an average of 1.4 million people. Over the last year (April 1995–April 1996) Teleac programmes were watched by 140,000 viewers per programme on average. It could be argued that, from an educational point of view, a host of classrooms could be filled with this amount of students. On the other hand, perhaps television's effectiveness as an educational medium should also be called into question.

In this paper I will address the question: Is television still used as a medium to learn from? And if so, what makes television attractive as an educational medium. The answers I will come up with are partly based on research, but will necessarily also contain some speculation. Furthermore, I will not consider specific programme contents, as this matter is dealt with adequately in Holland by Teleac's research department.[1] The main issues in this paper are:

- research on motives to watch television;
- research on 'need for cognition';
- the audience for educational programmes in Holland;
- research consequences for educational programme formats.

Research on motives to watch television
Research on viewers' motives to watch television started within the 'uses and gratifications' approach of mass communication studies. A study by Rubin (1983) was replicated for the Dutch situation by Vierkant (1987). He presented 29 statements about television viewing to a representative

---

1   Cf. Klaas Rodenburg's contribution, this volume pp. 94–101.

sample of the Dutch population. Factor analyses revealed six main motives for watching television:

1. Watching television to relax (television as entertainer).
2. Watching television for information (television as an information provider).
3. Watching television out of loneliness (television as a companion).
4. Watching television to pass the time.
5. Watching television to escape, to forget about daily problems.
6. Watching television for social reasons (to share experiences).

Of course, different people have different motives. Frissen (1992) studied the behaviour and motives of heavy users of television in the Netherlands (Average viewing time in the Netherlands was 169 minutes per day in March, 1996). Heavy viewers in the Netherlands are often the elderly, the less educated, people with lower incomes, the unemployed and the disabled (Frissen, 1992). She found that heavy viewers use television less as a source of information, but more to relax, out of loneliness, to pass the time or to escape.

People who use television for information and education have less 'television-affinity' than heavy users do, i.e. they attach less value to the medium. This does not mean that more heavy television users do not watch educational programmes or that 'lighter' users do not watch television for reasons other than for information purposes. However, in general, the audience for educational programmes in the Netherlands will continue to be relatively small as long as no motives other than the viewers' 'information motive' can be satisfied.

Research on 'need for cognition'
What exactly do we mean by 'watching television for information'? Or, what is this need for information? When we try to define this need for information independently of the use of television – in order to avoid tautologies – it appears rather difficult to demonstrate a clear connection with actual viewing behaviour. It seems that we must not place too much emphasis on a goal-oriented search for specific information when it concerns television viewing (Peeters, 1991).

Why would anyone watch, for instance, a documentary about recent political developments in Albania, a programme about giant tortoises on the Galapagos Islands or a current affairs programme treating topics unknown before viewing? Sometimes a specific interest or a specific need for information will play a part, but most of the time the viewing motive will be more general. When we look at viewers' motives for watching informative and educational programmes we find, in general, that viewers are driven by a more general curiosity, by an intrinsic need for cognitive activity, and not so much by a need to reduce uncertainty through information or to solve a problem. This is what the social psychologists

Cacioppo and Petty (1982) called the 'need for cognition', i.e. need for and enjoyment in mental effort.

Peeters (1991) performed research with a representative sample of the Dutch population of television viewers, and found that entertainment programmes such as game shows and light music are particularly popular with people having a low need for cognition. Television news and current affairs programmes, on the other hand, are very popular with people with a high need for cognition. A remarkable result of Peeters' study was that the category 'other informative programmes', including educational programmes and with the exception of art programmes, was not highly appreciated by people with a high need for cognition.

The audience for Teleac programmes in Holland

Who watched Teleac's educational programmes in the Netherlands during the last 12 months (April 1995 to April 1996)? I used the people's meter results to analyse the Teleac audience during the last year. On average 140,000 people watched the programmes (rating score 1.0) with a share of 6 per cent of the Dutch television market, and an average appreciation score of 7.1 on a scale from 1 (lowest) to 10 (highest).

Table 1 contains results of a breakdown in sex, age, and education of the viewers and a comparison of the Teleac audience profile with the Dutch population.

Table 1: Teleac Audience from April 1995 to April 1996 (secondary analysis of TV Meter data)

Teleac Audience Characteristics	Average Rating	Number Viewers	Average Appreciation	Profile Teleac	Dutch Population
Sex					
– male	1.2	75,000	7.1	54	49
– female	1.0	60,000	7.0	46	51
Age					
– 6-19 years	0.4	10,000	7.5	7	18
– 20-34 years	0.8	30,000	7.1	22	27
– 35-49 years	1.0	35,000	7.1	26	25
– 50 years & over	1.5	60,000	7.1	45	30
Education					
– lower	1.5	20,000	7.2	16	12
– lower vocational	1.1	35,000	7.1	25	24
– secondary	1.0	45,000	7.0	85	87
– higher/academic	0.9	35,000	7.2	24	28

The above table shows an overrepresentation of male viewers, people older than 50, and the lower educated. Viewers of the age up to 34, women and the higher educated are underrepresented as compared to the Dutch population. Some other results (not shown in the table) illustrate that in terms of social economic status there are no differences between the Teleac audience and the Dutch population, and that Teleac viewers have a higher 'cultural affinity' than the average Dutch citizen. As regards the type of household, it appears that families with young children (up to the age of 17) tend to watch Teleac less than other households do.

Teleac aims at different markets, which can in general be defined as an educational market and a broadcast market. Programmes for these different markets differ not only in teaching goals and subject matter, but also in format. Programmes for the educational market tend to have a clearer didactic structure (with a central presenter, structured interviews etc.) than programmes for the broadcast market. Analyses of viewing behaviour reveal that programmes for the broadcast market have not only higher ratings than the educational market programmes, but also have a more loyal audience (people watch more programmes in the same series) and fewer 'zappers' during the programme.

Speculations about consequences of research for educational programme formats

What can we conclude after this short excursion through people's viewing motives and viewing behaviour for educational programme production? First, I think that the audience for educational programmes will remain relatively small as long as no viewing motives other than the information motive can be satisfied with these programmes. Second, that people with a higher need for cognition – a main target group for educational television! – tend not to appreciate the existing educational programmes very much.

In my view the development of new programme formats should have a high priority: formats with which we can keep the interest and attention of viewers at a more optimal level than we are able to at present. That does not mean that we should indiscriminately imitate formats of entertainment programmes, reality TV, investigate journalism or whatever, but that we should at least try to find out which aspects of such formats can be used successfully in educational programmes. Development of new formats demands close co-operation between programme makers and members of the audience, with researchers in the role of intermediaries.

One of the problems with qualitative research is that people tend to give socially desirable answers, especially when it concerns informative programmes. In a pre-test of an educational programme, for example, subjects who were not told who produced it found the programme to be 'a bit boring' and that they 'would switch it off after five minutes.' But when they found out that it was an educational programme they said that it was 'allright'. There are obviously other standards for educational programmes.

And to make things even more complicated, when people evaluate a programme as 'interesting' or 'informative', this does not necessarily mean that they have actually picked up much information from the programme. So, new formats must be suited for specific learning goals.

Many people assume that there has to be a significant correlation between appreciation and comprehension. But unfortunately, this is not the case, as several studies indicate (Heuvelman, 1994). Consequently, it will remain necessary to find out if people actually learn anything, particularly as far as aspects of visualisation (Heuvelman, 1996) or other format matters are concerned.

References

Cacioppo, J. & Petty, R. (1982) The need for cognition. *Journal of Personality and Social Psychology*, 42, pp. 116–131.

Diem, P. (1993) Finding out who, what, how, and how many. *Diffusion EBU*, autumn 1993, pp. 45–52.

Heuvelman, A. (1994) Some thoughts about cognitive and affective processes in the reception of informative television programmes. Paper presented at the seminar 'Understanding and understandability in the media', University of Copenhagen, Dept. of Nordic Philology, May 9–11, 1994.

Heuvelman, A. (1996) Realistic and schematic visuals. *Journal of Educational Media*, vol. 22 (2), pp. 87–95.

Frissen, V. (1992) *Veelkijken als sociaal handelen. Een empirisch onderzoek naar het verschijnsel veel televisiekijken in Nederland* (Heavy viewing as social action. An empirical study of heavy television viewing in the Netherlands) Dissertation. Catholic University of Nijmegen.

Peeters, A. (1991) *Televisiekijken en plezier in mentale inspanning: need for cognition in het Continue Kijkonderzoek?* (Television viewing and the pleasure of mental effort: need for cognition in the continuous audience research?) in: H. Bouwman, P. Nelissen & M. Vooijs: *Tussen vraag en aanbod*. Amsterdam: Otto Cramwinckel.

Rubin, A.M. (1983) Television uses and gratifications: the interactions of viewing patterns and motivations. *Journal of Broadcasting*, 27(1), pp. 37–51.

Vierkant, P. (1987) *Televisiekijkers in Nederland. Een onderzoek naar het televisiekijkgedrag van de Nederlandse Bevolking* (Television viewers in the Netherlands. A research into the television viewing behaviour of the Dutch population). Dissertation. State University of Groningen.

Ard Heuvelman, *Ph.D., studied Experimental and Social Psychology at the State University of Utrecht. Subsequently he worked as a researcher for the Teleac foundation (1980–1989) and conducted experiments on the relationship between visual formats of educational television programmes and their cognitive and affective effects. Since 1990 he has lectured at the University of Twente, and is also Research Manager at the Audience Research Department of the Netherlands Broadcasting Corporation. His special interests are the cognitive and affective effects of informative and educational television.*

As THEY like it!

Viewer types and their media menus

Uwe Hasebrink
Hans-Bredow-Institut, Hamburg

Why the search for viewer types?

Television does not tell us, the viewers, what we should do with it. It offers us something, it invites us, it promises us attractions – whether they be informative, entertaining, educational or all of these at the same time. That makes things easy for us. With our programme guides and remote control we taste what is offered and then make up our own personal television menu. As we like it.

This picture is not quite correct. In the meantime there are, it is true, numerous channels which transmit their programmes around the clock. Yet we still too often have the impression that precisely what we would like to see most at this moment is not being offered. It is here that the visions of the television future that is opening up now promise a remedy: one of the principal ideas in connection with the term information society consists in each one of us being able to pick out precisely the media offer we want at any place and any time.

Even if many of the visions promised in this connection are at present a long way from being realised or even capable of being realised, it can be regarded as certain that the future development of television will follow the above-mentioned model and try to increase the potential technical availability of audio-visual products as far as possible.

In the course of this development, any lasting impression of the structures of what is offered and the programming schedules will continue to decline; for if in principle everything is available, the actual use will be characterised to an increasing extent by the individual, social and economic prerequisites of the viewers. Thus although many programmes will technically be available, they can only be used under complicated and, for private households, costly conditions or on payment of an additional fee. The future use of television will have to be characterised as follows: As we like it – and as we can afford it.

All this results in differences between various forms of television use and between various groups of viewers being increased. Whereas there has up to now been something approaching consensus on what is meant by the statement 'The mean daily viewing time is three hours', in future this will hardly be possible. Whereas it is up to now still accepted that all the minutes spent watching television by members of the population (or of the random sample examined) – independent of the channel and the genre, independent of the viewer, independent of the social constellation and the motivation for watching television – are brought together to form the so-called 'viewer market' for which the various companies and corporations are competing, the growing differentiation of the programmes and the differentiation of the forms of use that goes with it will call for new approaches in market and viewer research.

This is the background against which I would like to speak at this point on the types of viewers and their media menus. Educational programmes, too, are being integrated into individual patterns of handling television, they are being placed in the context of various media menus and accordingly have different significance for particular viewers. I should like to begin by considering which criteria can be used to distinguish between different types of viewers.

Approaches for distinguishing between the types of viewers

The question as to how far groups of viewers can be identified who differ in the way they deal with television has tradition. It has various theoretical and practical origins, and each of the types is accordingly defined in the light of various criteria.

The typologies with the greatest significance are those which are constructed on the basis of non-media-related features: the simplest represent the usual target group definitions of applied media research, in which the audience is divided into different age, educational or income groups, and then an examination is made to find out which media they use.

Lifestyle studies proceed more ambitiously, differentiating between different lifestyles on the basis of a number of features such as education, work, income, marital status as well as values, political attitudes, consumption and leisure behaviour, and their use of the media and/or television is then examined. (e.g. Frank/Greenberg, 1980; Donohew et al., 1987; Krotz, 1991)

Another group of typologies proceeds from the attitudes, expectations or interests with regard to television (Espe et al., 1986; Frank, 1975). It was on such a basis that Rubin (1983, 1984) also developed his distinction between ritual and habitual use of television – although data on the use of certain programme types was also included.

Only very few typologies were developed on the basis of actual viewing behaviour. The distinction between heavy and light viewers has become prominent (e.g. Buß, 1985), as it has a decisive position in the framework of cultivation research. In more recent times, over and beyond this simple indicator Greenberg et al. (1988), Weimann et al. (1992) and Hawkins et al. (1991; Pingree et al., 1991) have presented analyses in which viewers were distinguished according to several aspects of their viewing behaviour. Weimann et al. (1992) took into account the mean viewing time and the attachment to certain programme types as the distinguishing criteria. Very many more criteria on the levels of exposure, programme selection and consistency of use are applied in the other two studies named.

My considerations begin with the last mentioned studies. The question posed is how viewers differ in their actual use behaviour and which varying patterns of use or television menus can be observed.

Levels of individual television use
Individual television use can be described on the following levels:

- Television use involves *exposure to the medium* at a certain time for a certain period.
- Television use takes place in certain *social constellations*.
- Television use is tied up with the *selection of certain channels*.
- Television use involves the *selection of certain programmes* of a certain genre with certain presenters, actors and directors.
- Television use comprises the *reception and/or the interpretation* of the programmes or parts of the programmes selected.

In view of these different aspects which are necessarily bound up with any use of television and which, in addition, are interconnected in a variety of ways which change in the course of time, it is obvious that 'television use' cannot be recorded on the basis of a single feature alone, such as the daily viewing time: there are all kinds of ways of watching television, and we have to proceed from different ways of handling the medium which we refer to as individual patterns of viewing.

Now viewer types can be defined on different levels of viewing behaviour – which criteria are applied in each case depends on the interest in the content. In the following examples I restrict myself to the use levels which can (at least partly) be recorded by means of telemetric audience measurements; I shall not therefore go into the fifth level, the reception processes in the narrower sense.

The database of the following exemplary evaluations presented is made up of people meter data from 410 households (West Germany) with a total of 941 people over a period of two fortnights in the spring of 1992. By linking up with the broadcasting files also made available by the market research institute GfK it was possible to reconstruct to which individual transmission of which genre the use in each case applied. Moreover, sociodemographic data on the households and the people were also available. The first evaluation was published in Hasebrink/Krotz (1993).

Patterns of exposure
I first want to illustrate the basic idea in the study of individual use patterns on the level of the exposure behaviour. This level which has been the most important in research up to now is connected with the fact that

watching television needs time and has to be integrated into the course of the day in some way. In the vast majority of cases the exposure behaviour is defined as the viewing time per day. But this definition does not take into account that the television use on a certain day can consist of a connected use phase or of several phases distributed over the day. We call these phases 'periods of exposure'.

This distinction plays an important part for the discussion about the future of television. We used to imagine that television use was a strongly habitualised behaviour, and the television evening, with the family gathered round the set to watch for about three hours, seemed to us to be typical. It has, however, been argued in more recent times that television is used more and more as a stop-gap to fill in gaps in time which are left over in the individual planning of the day. Accordingly the classic 'couch potato' evening was supposed to be losing its importance in favour of shorter exposure periods scattered throughout the day.

We took this consideration as the starting point for forming viewer types who differ in their exposure behaviour. In the 914 people in the random sample we examined we observed an average of 1.6 exposure periods per day and person which lasted on average 1:56 hours. The finding that hardly any connection exists between the number and the length of these periods ($r = -0.14$) is interesting; that means that all combinations of the two features can be observed: viewers who watch television often and for long periods, as well as viewers who seldom and briefly, seldom and for long periods, or often and briefly watch television.

Using the medians of the two values, we defined four groups of viewers, each making up about a quarter of the random sample. Figure 1 shows how many exposure periods of what duration make up the viewing time of the four groups of viewers observed over four weeks.

The difference between the first group with a few short exposure periods and the fourth group with many long periods reflects the well-known striking difference between heavy and light viewers. While almost one quarter of the population watches television for less than one hour a day, another almost one quarter watches a good five and a half hours. Although the second and third groups are very similar with regard to their average viewing time of about three hours, the latter is very differently constituted. The second group shows a strongly habitualised use behaviour: the television is used once almost daily for about three hours. This corresponds to the above-mentioned classic idea of the television evening. Group 3, however, switches on several times a day and then watches on average for only one hour. This is an indication of the new way sketched above of incorporating television viewing into everyday life.

Although this typology is based on a very simple definition of use patterns, the differences illustrated here between the groups do emphasise the importance of the perspective such an analysis provides. From our viewpoint the patterns described also point out qualitative differences in

Figure 1: Viewer types according to number and duration of periods of exposure (number and average duration of exposure in 4 weeks)

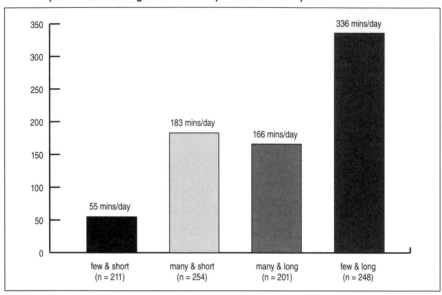

Source: Gfk 1992

handling television and the importance which this medium has in the everyday life of different groups of viewers.

Viewer types according to social constellations

The second example of a viewer typology has its origin in the statement above that watching television takes place in social constellations. It can be seen from the telemetric measurements whether someone watches television together with other members of the household or guests. For the evaluation we have distinguished between three kinds of constellation: situations with one, with two and with more than two persons. We broke down the sample into five groups by the proportions of viewing time accounted for by the three constellations; Figure 2 shows how the viewing time of each of these groups is made up.

The major feature for this differentiation is, of course, the size and structure of the household. Apart from the plausible observation that in one-person households television is watched alone in most cases, the finding that especially in two-person households television is rarely watched by one person but usually by two is interesting. In larger households, on the other hand, television is watched alone comparatively rather more frequently – here the constellation of two is the least frequent. This may be connected with the fact that in larger households there are also more television sets. The study according to age groups illustrates the family or household structures which as a rule accompany them: among the younger people there are many who frequently watch television in groups of three, while in the case of the adults in the family phase the mixed pattern predominates. Persons between 50 and 60 mostly watch television in pairs,

Figure 2: Viewer types according to social constellations (constellations in per cent of total viewing time)

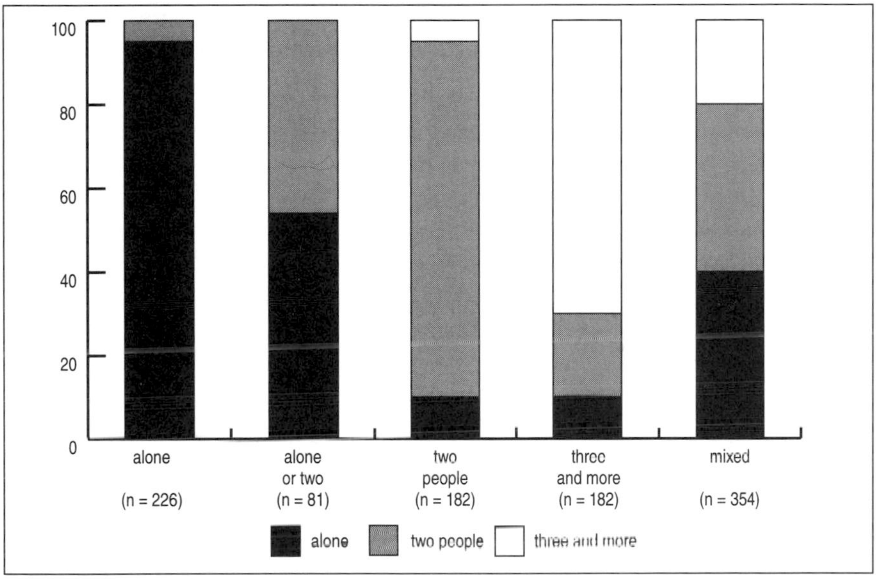

Source: Gfk 1992

while in the case of the over 70-year-olds it emerges that television is often watched alone, as a consequence, for example, of the loss of their partner.

These differences strongly indicate that in considering the social and communicative functions of television the different social constellations of watching television have to be taken into account.

Patterns of channel use

A further level of examination emerges from the fact that television use is always related to certain channels. As the most obvious change for the viewer in the television landscape in the last ten years has been the drastic increase in the available channels, it is only plausible that the clearest shifts in use behaviour were to be recorded on this level. This can first be made clear by the proportion which individual programmes account for in the overall television use, and the following illustration provides an overview of the development in the old States in the Federal Republic of Germany since 1985.

In 1985 the picture was almost exclusively dominated by ARD, ZDF and one of the Third Programmes in each region (96 per cent of television use). In the years that followed television use was distributed over a grow-

131

ing number of programmes; and for some years now no single programme has achieved more than a share of at least one-fifth of the total use.

The aggregated findings on the shares of individual programmes in the total use do not mean that all viewers divide up their use accordingly. But they are based on varying reactions by the viewers to the increased number of channels. In this connection previous studies have usually asked the question as to how far the duality 'public service versus private-commercial' existing on the broadcaster's side is expressed in the use. In theory there are at least two reaction patterns to be distinguished here:

- Groups of viewers are formed who for the most part use either public service or private programmes; in this case we could talk of a 'dual audience'.
- The viewers put together for themselves a certain mixture made up of public service and private channels and thus show a 'dual use behaviour'.

In the meantime numerous findings have been presented which tend to indicate a 'dual audience', in that clear differences were worked out between viewers preferring either public service or commercial channels (e.g. Berg/Kiefer, 1992, pp. 267-268; Landwehrmann/Jäckel, 1991, p. 92). The results of the long-term mass communication study in particular indicate that two groups form here with quite diverse expectations not only with regard to television: viewers preferring public service programmes use television as they do other media for information purposes to a greater extent; they have higher educational qualifications on average and are more interested in politics and culture (Berg/Kiefer, 1992, p. 267; Kiefer, 1994, p. A125).

Figure 3: Changes in use of individual programmes by adults in Germany (West)

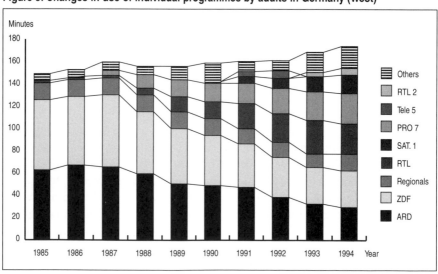

Source: Gfk 1992

The results of our evaluations of individual use behaviour also indicate this kind of 'dual audience': the viewing time given to ARD correlates closely with that for ZDF and the Third Programmes, while there is little correlation with the other channels. The viewing time devoted to RTL correlates most closely by far with that for SAT.1, that of 3Sat most closely with that of Eins plus (i.e. the then two public service satellite channels for cultural porgrammes). In in-depth analyses for persons in cabled households only (where all programmes examined can be received), three channel groups emerged:

(a) commercial programmes (RTL, SAT.1, PRO 7, Tele 5);
(b) the main public service programmes (ARD, ZDF); and
(c) public service cultural programmes (3Sat, Eins plus, the ARD Third Channels).

These findings indicate that the preference for public service or commercial programmes is a revealing feature for distinguishing viewer groups. In view of the close connection between subject interests, preferences for certain programme genres and programme choice behaviour, on the one hand, and the various programmes offered by the public service and private operators, on the other, 'circular processes in the direction of a consolidation of interests and in the end a narrowing of interests seem to be setting in'. (Kiefer, 1994, A126) In the light of this relatively clear trend, it still also has to be taken into account, however, that most viewers use both public service and private programmes – the exact patterns of this 'dual use behaviour' have so far hardly been examined. (s. Hasebrink/Krotz, 1996)

In addition to the shares of different programmes, we also asked to what extent the viewers use the increased number of channels anyway. It emerged that in 1992 people in cabled households switched on 14.1 different channels on average at least once in the course of four weeks (even if only for a few seconds), and persons in the other households 5.6 channels. In cabled households on average 6.0 channels were used per television day, and in non-cabled households it was 3.4. (Hasebrink/Krotz, 1993, p. 521)

Since purely 'accidental switchings' are considered in this evaluation, any statement on the number of channels used regularly and on which at least 5 per cent of one person's viewing time is spent is certainly more significant: in the case of persons in households without cable TV this was usually three or four channels, and in households with cable most frequently four to six and at most nine channels (ibid.). In view of the fact that in cabled households 20 or more channels can be received on average (Kiefer, 1994) and as many as 14 are switched on at least occasionally, this is a clear expression of the fact that even with this expanded reception potential only very few channels meet with any particular interest. This is in keeping with international experience, according to which 'as the number of channels available increases, proportionately fewer and fewer are actually used'. (Winterhoff-Spurk, 1991, p. 165)

The extent to which the increased number of channels has led to viewers actually using more channels is inevitably bound up with the fact that it has become more common to switch from one channel to the other. In the public discussion in the last few years this switching behaviour has – apart from the shift of market shares for individual programmes – attracted the greatest attention; reports of trends in television use have raised 'zapping' to a national sport and even proclaimed the age of *Homo zappens*. (e.g. FAZ of 25.5.1992; cf. also Jäckel, 1993, p. 5)

The trend described in this way is, on the one hand, perceived with the greatest concern: advertisers fear their commercials are not reaching a large enough audience, programme producers and planners see the coordination of their broadcasts and programme schemes violated and some worried voices diagnose the frequent zapping as a reduced power of concentration and frustration tolerance on the part of the viewers. On the other hand, the zappers are celebrated as the epitome of the active viewer who has freed himself from the confines of the programme and thus opened up for himself completely new opportunities for experience. (cf. Winkler, 1991)

So far the debate on this phenomenon has been able to contribute little to its clarification, and more and more new 'typologies' and new terms for the subforms of this switching behaviour have tended to cause confusion. Only in recent times have the first studies been carried out to obtain more precise information on different forms of 'channel surfing'.

Even though figures from previous years are not available for direct comparison, it can be assumed that the absolute frequency of switching has increased in the last ten years. What is decisive here is, first, the increase in television sets with remote control (1980: 40 per cent of the households in the old Federal States, 1990: 87 per cent; cf. Berg/Kiefer, 1992, p. 21); studies from other countries confirm the plausible assumption that remote control leads to more frequent zapping. (Chabrol/Perin, 1991, p. 94; Heeter/Greenberg, 1988; Stipp, 1989)

Added to this is the growing number of channels, which has its own effect on the frequency of switching channels (e.g. Chabrol/Perin, 1991, p. 93); persons in cabled households switch over more often than persons in households without cable television. (e.g. Hasebrink/Krotz, 1993, p. 522; Schmidt, 1989, p. 50) It has been unanimously established that men and younger people switch more frequently; it can also be observed that in situations in which one person watches television alone channels are switched far more often than in situations with two or more persons, in which there is a need to reach agreement on switching the channel. (Hasebrink/Krotz, 1993, p. 522)

For my considerations today two comments are of importance in this connection. Firstly, it emerges that the frequency of switching channels is also a major feature of individual use behaviour in which various groups of viewers in some cases clearly differ. Secondly, I am anxious to make one point clear: by the discussion about switching channels concentrating chiefly on its mere occurrence and the (increased) frequency of changing the channel, it has been possible for the impression to arise that acts of violence against any coordinated conception are strewn at will by the audience over the programme – an impression which quickly leads to the demise of the medium of television. On this note it was, for example, pointed out that only comparatively few of the viewers of a broadcast actually watch it in its entirety; the probability that viewers watch two complete consecutive broadcasts and thus follow the programme structure provided is correspondingly even more remote. (cf. Buß, 1991)

These findings naturally constitute a great challenge for the programme-makers, as a consequence of which all planning is increasingly aimed as far as possible at avoiding any cause to switch off and, following the development on the radio, at creating a programme designed for continuous viewing. The impression of the use behaviour thus produced is, however, only partly correct. Empirical and theoretical studies on switching channels show that the switching behaviour is by no means dependent on the programme provided and that viewers are still guided by individual broadcasts and the structures of the programmes provided as to their use of television. So it is still worthwhile (and more than ever) making programmes which are thought through in their arrangement.

Patterns of genre use

The next step in describing individual use behaviour asks how the television menu of different groups of viewers is composed of different programme genres. The programme genres differentiated below were defined on the basis of the viewing time allocated to them individually. Figure 4 shows how the daily viewing time averaged over all the viewers and in different population groups is distributed to the genres. (Total: information 21 per cent, action 20 per cent, sport 10 per cent, non-fictional entertainment 17 per cent, fictional entertainment 12 per cent, children's programmes 6 per cent, humour/satire 3 per cent; the other shares are allocated to miscellaneous genres not included in the analysis of the factors and non-coded programme constituents.)

In the light of these data the question is to be dealt with below as to which viewers choose more or less information broadcasts – among which educational programmes were also included – and how the use of these programmes is connected with other features of television use.

The first approach to the question as to the status of information broadcasts in individual television menus takes as its criterion the proportion of information use in the total viewing time. It is plausible to assume that information broadcasts have a higher priority for the viewers the more strongly they are represented in a purely quantitative sense in the television menu. It can be supposed that here considerable differences emerge between various groups of the population.

Figure 4 was based on a differentiation of seven socio-demographic groups each of which corresponds to a certain combination of the features age, education and work:

1. Viewers under 14 (N = 116);
2. Young people and young adults still being trained or educated (N=103);
3. People employed full-time with an education after the age of 16 (N=131);
4. People employed full-time with an education up to the age of 16 (N=182);
5. People under the age of 60 who do not work (N=103);
6. People who work part-time and pensioners under 60 (N=89);
7. Pensioners and people who do not work over 60 (N=185).

On average 37 minutes are spent every day watching information broadcasts on television; in the youngest age group it is 9 minutes, and for the pensioners it is 70 minutes. The differences reflect above all the marked difference in the extent of television use. Expressed in percentages of the use as a whole, it ranges from 12 per cent in the youngest group to 26 per cent in each of the groups of the working people with a higher formal education and the pensioners. There are only minimum differences between men and women on this level.

What is the connection between the share of information use dealt with and the other features of television use? There is virtually no connection with the viewing time (r = 0.07); as other studies have shown before, 'light viewing' cannot therefore be simply equated with 'selective information viewing'. On account of the specific programme structures the close posi-

Figure 4: Duration of the genre viewing by different groups of viewers

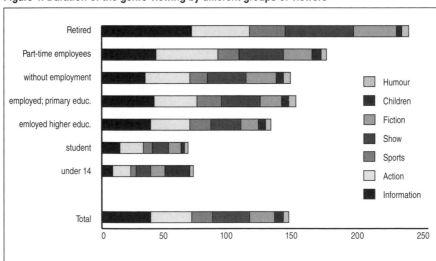

Source: Gfk 1992

136

tive connection between the information share and the proportion of use allocated to public service programmes (r = 0.45) is to be expected, and it is contrasted accordingly with a negative connection with the proportion of private programmes (r= –0.44). No connection can be established with the frequency of switching over channels, although there is definitely one with the length of time devoted to information broadcasts: viewers with a higher proportion of information broadcasts watch these on average in longer uninterrupted pieces.

The results presented so far are still aggregated to a great extent. In each of the groups examined very different ways of handling television can still be observed. That is why a different approach should be adopted here by first identifying different use patterns, which are then examined to find out in which groups they can be observed with particular frequency.

The starting point for identifying such patterns is two features of individual television use: the proportion of information broadcasts in the overall use already dealt with here and the time spent viewing every day. The latter constitutes, on the one hand, a simple and often used indicator of television use, on the other hand, it turned out that there is no linear connection between these two features (see above) – so the two features record statistically independent aspects of television use.

The entire sample was broken down on the basis of these two features into three equally large groups for each one. The two times three groups that resulted produced nine possible combinations, of which here the extreme ones only are presented:

1. Light viewers with a small information share (N = 126);
2. Heavy viewers with a small information share (N = 81);
3. Light viewers with a large information share (N = 88);
4. Heavy viewers with a large information share (N = 113).

Figure 5 shows the radically different television menus of these four groups of viewers. The two groups of heavy viewers, altogether a good 20 per cent of the entire sample, watch television on average for a good five and half hours every day, but the other two groups for less than one hour. In the case of the two groups with a preference for information this programme genre accounts for about one-third of their viewing time (37 and 33 per cent respectively), while for the other two groups it is only nine and ten per cent. In what other ways do these groups differ in their dealings with television?

1. The group of *light viewers with a low proportion of information* comprises almost exclusively children and young people. Almost a quarter of the just under one hour of viewing time is devoted to action programmes, and the broadcasts that can be described as children's programmes are also given high priority. These viewers watch television together with several persons more frequently than the others, and on average they switch channels most frequently.

Figure 5: Genre viewing for viewer types according to watching information programmes

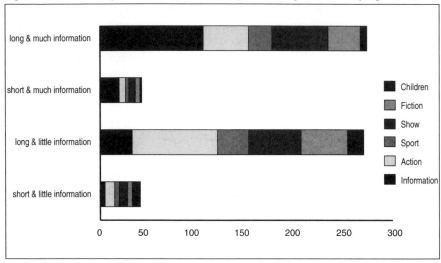

Source: Gfk 1992

2. The group of the *heavy viewers with a small information share* is made up of elderly people with less formal education. The daily use of television usually begins already before 5 p.m., and television is watched alone more than in the other groups. Channels are switched rather rarely, although altogether many channels are used. Commercial programmes and both action- and entertainment-orientated fictional programmes are preferred.

3. In the group of the *light viewers with a large share of information* young people and young adults as well as those who work and have a higher education are overrepresented. They seldom start watching television before 5 p.m. Channels are switched relatively often, even though only a few channels are used. Here three-quarters of the use are devoted to public service programmes. Besides the by far predominant use of information programmes, all the other programme genres represent relatively small proportions.

4. More than half of the *heavy viewers with a large information share* are pensioners and those who do not work over 60 years of age. Their television use is characterised by frequently watching with someone else as well as the long viewing time. They show a preference for public service programmes. The intensive use of information is supplemented by the also slightly over-average use of show entertainment in particular.

Résumé

I have tried to demonstrate how very much the viewers differ in what they do with television. Frequency and the length of exposure to the medium, the social constellation when watching it, the channel repertoire, channel switching behaviour and preference for certain genres and programme types turn out to be quite different – depending on what the viewers like and how their time budget and other demands of everyday life allow.

What conclusion can be drawn from this for the future of educational programmes on television? In reply I should like to formulate the following theses:

1. Television is a medium which offers the viewers very different programmes each of which promises very different gratifications. Accordingly very diverse things can be done with television. The hitherto usual practice of bringing together all television-related acts of uses to form an overall viewer market on which the individual channels or broadcasts achieve a certain market share will become obsolete as the differentiation of the programmes continues. For educational programmes this will have the advantage that to judge their success they will in fact be measured against what is comparable and not always be looked upon as 'rating killers'.

2. The reverse side of this differentiation of programmes will be that there will also be groups of viewers who will be more difficult to reach with educational programmes.

3. Viewers differ considerably in their television menus. More precise knowledge of these menus can provide a better impression of the context into which the viewers will place these educational programmes. From this, on the other hand, clear objectives can be derived for the planning of educational programmes: within the framework of which television menus of which groups of viewers is a certain programme to have which priority?

A concrete lesson from the description of television menus is that the often quoted distinction between 'selective light viewers with a preference for information' and 'entertainment-orientated heavy viewers' does not get us very far. Among the heavy viewers there is also a great interest in informative and educational programmes.

References

Berg, Klaus/Kiefer, Marie-Luise (1992): *Massenkommunikation IV. Eine Langzeitstudie zur Mediennutzung und Medienbewertung 1964-1990*. Baden-Baden: Nomos (Schriftenreihe Media Perspektiven; 12).

Buß, Michael (1985): *Die Vielseher. Fernsehzuschauerforschung in Deutschland. Theorie, Praxis, Ergebnisse*. Frankfurt/M.: Alfred Metzner Verlag

Buß, Michael (1991): 'Formen der Programmnutzung: Läßt sich das Publikum verplanen?' In: Ralph Weiß (Ed.): *Aufgaben und Perspektiven des öffentlich-rechtlichen Fernsehens*. Baden-Baden/Hamburg: Nomos (Symposien des Hans-Bredow-Instituts; 12), pp. 144-154.

Chabrol, Jean-Louis/Perin, Pascal (1991): *Le Zapping*. Paris: CNET.

Donohew, Lewis/Palmgreen, Philip/Rayburn, J.D. II. (1987): 'Social and psychological origins of media use: a lifestyle analysis'. In: *Journal of Broadcasting and Electronic Media 31*, 3, pp. 255-278

Espe, Hartmut/Seiwert, Margarete (1986): 'European television-viewer types: a six-nation classification by programme interests'. In: *European Journal of Communication 1*, 3, pp. 301-325

Frank, Bernward (1975): 'Programminteressen-Typologie der Fernsehzuschauer'. In: *Rundfunk und Fernsehen 22*, Heft 1/2, pp. 39-56

Frank, Ronald E./Greenberg, Marshall G. (1980): *The public's use of television. Who watches and why*. Beverly Hills et al.: Sage

Greenberg, Bradley S./Heeter, Carrie/Sipes, Sherry (1988): 'Viewing context and style with electronic assessment of viewing behavior'. In: Carrie Heeter/Bradley S. Greenberg (Eds.): *Cableviewing*. Norwood, N.J.: Ablex, pp. 123-139

Hasebrink, Uwe/Krotz, Friedrich (1993): 'Wie nutzen Zuschauer das Fernsehen? Konzept zur Analyse individuellen Nutzungsverhaltens anhand telemetrischer Daten'. In: *Media Perspektiven*, 11-12/93, pp. 515-527

Hasebrink, U.; Krotz, F. (1996): 'Fernsehnutzung im dualen System: duales Publikum und duales Nutzungsverhalten'. In: H. Pürer; W. Hömberg (Hrsg.): *Medien-Transformation. Zehn Jahre dualer Rundfunk in Deutschland*. Konstanz: UVK Medien (Schriftenreihe der DGPuK; Bd. 22), pp. 359-373

Hawkins, Robert P./Reynolds, Nancy/Pingree, Suzanne (1991): 'In search of television viewing styles'. In: *Journal of Broadcasting and Electronic Media 35*, 3, pp. 375-383

Heeter, Carrie/D'Alessio, David/Greenberg, B.S./McVoy, D. Stevens (1988): 'Cableviewing behaviors: An electronic assessment'. In: Carrie Heeter/Bradley S. Greenberg (Eds.): *Cableviewing*. Norwood, N.J.: Ablex, pp. 51-66

Heeter, Carrie/Greenberg, Bradley S. (1988): 'Profiling the Zappers'. In: Carrie Heeter/Bradley S. Greenberg (Eds.): *Cableviewing*. Norwood, N.J.: Ablex, pp. 67-73

Jäckel, Michael (1993): *Fernsehwanderungen. Eine empirische Untersuchung zum Zapping*. München: Reinhard Fischer (Medien-Skripten; 18)

Kiefer, Marie-Luise (1994): 'Mediennutzung in der Bundesrepublik'. In: Hans-Bredow-Institut (Eds.): *Internationales Handbuch für Hörfunk und Fernsehen 94/95*. Baden-Baden/Hamburg: Nomos, pp. A116-A131

Krotz, Friedrich (1991): 'Lebensstile, Lebenswelten und Medien: Zur Theorie und Empirie individuenbezogener Forschungsansätze des Mediengebrauchs'. In: *Rundfunk und Fernsehen 39*, Heft 3/1991, pp. 317-342

Landwehrmann, Friedrich/Jäckel, Michael (1991): *Kabelfernsehen – von der Skepsis zur Akzeptanz. Das erweiterte Programmangebot im Urteil der Zuschauer*. München: Reinhard Fischer (Schriftenreihe der Stiftung zur Förderung gemeinnützigen Rundfunks in Rheinland-Pfalz; 1)

Pingree, Suzanne/Hawkins, Robert P./Johnsson-Smaragdi, Ulla/Rosengren, Karl Erik/Reynolds, Nancy (1991): 'Audience flow and individual shifts: a Swedish-American comparison'. In: *European Journal of Communication 6*, 4, pp. 417-440

Rubin, Alan M. (1984): 'Ritualized and instrumental television viewing'. In: *Journal of Communication*, 34, pp. 67-77

Rubin, Alan M. (1983): 'Television uses and gratifications: the interactions of viewing patterns and motivations'. In: *Journal of Broadcasting 27*, 1, pp. 37-51

Schmidt, Claudia (1989): 'Kabelfernsehen: Nutzung, Funktionen und Bedeutung'. In: Claudia Schmidt/Christoph Bruns/Christiane Schöwer/Christoph Seeger (Eds.): *Endstation Seh-Sucht? Kommunikationsverhalten und neue Medientechniken. Ergebnisse der Begleitforschung der Evangelischen Kirche zum Kabelpilotprojekt Berlin.* Stuttgart: J. F. Steinkopf (GEP-Medien-Dokumentationen), pp. 43-139

Stipp, Horst (1989): 'Neue Techniken, neue Zuschauer? Zum Einfluß von Fernbedienung und Programmangebot auf das Zuschauerverhalten'. In: *Media Perspektiven*, 3/89, pp. 164-167

Weimann, Gabriel/Brosius, Hans-Bernd and Wober, Mallory (1992): 'TV diets: towards a typology of TV viewership'. In: *European Journal of Communication 7*, pp. 491-515

Winkler, Hartmut (1991): *Switching, Zapping: ein Text zum Thema und ein parallellaufendes Unterhaltungsprogramm.* Darmstadt: Häusser

Winterhoff-Spurk, Peter (1991): 'Wer die Wahl hat ... – Medienpsychologische Aspekte der Fernsehprogrammvermehrung'. In: Michael Jäckel/Michael Schenk (Eds.): *Kabelfernsehen in Deutschland. Pilotprojekte, Programmvermehrung, private Konkurrenz. Ergebnisse und Perspektiven.* München: Reinhard Fischer (Medien-Skripten; 11), pp. 159-180

Uwe Hasebrink, *Dr. phil., studied Psychology and German Philology in Hamburg. From 1983 he was a scientific collaborator at the* Institut für Sozialpsychologie *of the University of Hamburg; since 1986 he has been Departmental Head of the Hans-Bredow-Institut in Hamburg, and since 1988 Managing Director. He has carried out research and published works especially on television viewers' individual utilisation patterns, on listener types and their everyday media life as well as media use in Europe and the development of a European educational television channel.*

THE HANS BREDOW INSTITUTE

The Hans Bredow Institute is an independent research and services facility which continuously observes the rapid development of the media. By means of its own research and its services provided to the public, media policies and media practice, its aim is to contribute towards a better understanding of trends and the options open to the development of the media. This work is also supported by the Institute's specialised publications, first and foremost among them being the 'International Handbook for Radio and Television', which comes out every two years, and the journal for media and communication science entitled 'Radio and Television'.

The Institute is at present concentrating its research on prospects for the so-called information society. Thus in recent times there have been projects and events on providing public service broadcasting resulting from the change in telecommunications, on regulating multimedia, on checking concentration and on the structures of the programme industry. Further points of emphasis concern the individual use behaviour of television viewers and radio listeners and the debate about the quality of what the media offer.

With regard to educational programmes the Institute is currently studying the way in which school children deal with the interactive learning network which is being tested in Berlin within the framework of the COMENIUS Project. And for some years now the Institute has been looking into what cross-border European educational television might look like. In 1995 the Institute submitted a draft study on this, commissioned by the German Ministry of Education and the European Broadcasting Union, in which a four-phase concept has been developed for gradually building up European education television.

It was proposed as a first step that would be essential for any further development that a clearing house should be set up for European educational programmes. Its aim is to improve the situation of information on available audio-visual educational programmes, promote their distribution throughout Europe, also in view of the new digital media, and stimulate the (co-)production of suitable new programmes. The EBU has in the meantime taken up this proposal. The clearing house began its work in Geneva in October 1996.[1]

Address: Hans-Bredow-Institut für Rundfunk und Fernsehen, Heimhuder Str. 21, D-20148 Hamburg.

---

[1] See Chris Jelley's contribution on pp. 235–243.

Who are the viewers of ARTE?

Michael Schroeder
ARTE, Strasbourg

Some fundamentals

The European cultural channel ARTE celebrated its fourth anniversary in May 1996. Set up as the result of a Franco-German initiative which was mainly politically motivated, in the meantime ARTE has proved that it is not only viable as an institution but has also won the popularity and respect of the public.

ARTE's programme philosophy was deliberately given a European orientation. The agreements on which the European Economic Community of Interests ARTE is based (memorandum of association in conjunction with an interstate treaty) lays down the remit quite clearly; section 2 of the articles of association of ARTE G.E.I.E. states: 'The object of the association is to conceive television programmes, ... which are of a cultural and international character in a comprehensive sense and are suitable for the promotion of understanding and rapprochement between the peoples of Europe.' This also results in an educational remit for ARTE which is geared in particular towards imparting other cultures, points of view and languages.

ARTE's programmes are of a very special kind. With their diversity and originality they provide what is often a new angle for seeing connections. The programme pattern is characterised by the so-called theme evenings, which examine different aspects of a theme three times a week using a variety of programme formats. The theme evenings have developed into a trade mark and are not seldom among the programmes watched most frequently. The theme evenings account for 26 per cent of the entire programme time.

Another cornerstone are the numerous documentaries, which in the meantime have disappeared from the prime time of many stations, even public service stations. The documentaries make up 20 per cent of the programmes shown on ARTE. The third cornerstone are the cinema and television films, which are enjoying a growing popularity in Germany and France. The feature that distinguishes ARTE from other stations is not only the quality of the productions shown, but many of them are broadcast in the original with subtitles.

ARTE is transmitted simultaneously to many countries, and at present versions in French and German are available, which cable subscribers can even choose between. Versions in other languages are planned.

In addition to an increasingly international transmission range (cf. Figure 1), ARTE has also intensified its relations to other European stations by means of partnerships. Belgian television RTBF is connected to ARTE by an association contract. With Spanish and Swiss television there is cooperation which is primarily directed towards programme exchange. Negotiations with Swedish and Polish television are about to be concluded.

Whether and how the cultural remit and the international orientation are accepted by the viewers will be shown by the comments that follow. In this connection special attention has been paid to the description of the ARTE viewers with their specific viewing habits. In conclusion some of the challenges will be described which ARTE has to tackle in the future, especially against the background of an expanded audience.

Acceptance and range

The technical reach of ARTE has increased considerably in Europe in the last few years. While in 1993 it was possible to reach altogether only about 30 million households in Europe, by the beginning of 1996 this figure was already 45 million. Of these, 18.5 million households in France can receive ARTE via the house aerial; in Germany, according to the cable television company GfK, 21.5 million households were reached via cable or satellite at the beginning of 1996. At present 3.7 million households in Belgium contribute to ARTE's reception potential. In addition it can also be received by a further 1.5 million households in Austria, Switzerland and Luxembourg. As the broadcasting signal is transmitted over several satellites (ASTRA, EUTELSAT, TDF, Kopernikus) the station can be received to an increasing extent in the whole of Europe and even in North Africa and Israel.

Figure 1: Technical reach and regular ARTE viewers[1]

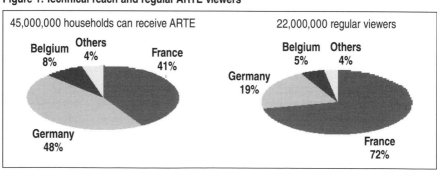

1   Sources: technical range:GfK, Médiamétrie, RTBF, SRG, April 1996; regular viewers are those who say they watch ARTE at least once a week; figures come from representative surveys by INRA in Germany (February 1996), IPSOS MEDIAS in France (February 1996), ISOPUBLIC in Switzerland (November 1995) and DIMARSO in Belgium (November 1995); the remaining figures are estimates.

If not only the technical reception but also the acceptance situation is examined we are faced with a rather different picture. Of the no fewer than 22 million European viewers who watch ARTE at least once a week, France accounts for by far the largest market. Almost threequarters of all weekly ARTE viewers are to be found here.

Table 1: ARTE's top audience ratings in Germany and France[2]

FRANCE			GERMANY		
Title	Market share	Audience	Title	Market share	Audience
Galère des femmes	10.0	2,150,000	Die Blechtrommel	4.0	1,015,000
Coeur sur la main	9.0	1,877,000	Allein unter Frauen	4.1	975,000
Mouton à cinq pattes	8.4	1,721,000	Im Reich der Sinne	5.9	671,000
L'amour	6.3	1,390,000	Herbstmilch	2.4	670,000
L'empire des sens	12.3	1,389,000	James Dean	2.2	510,000

ARTE also scores successes in the audiences regularly measured by the GfK in Germany and Médiamétrie in France. In 1996 more than 2 million viewers watched one broadcast in France for the first time. In Germany ARTE crossed the magic mark of 1 million viewers in the same year.

ARTE, however, is not only proud of itself as far as quantity is concerned. Surveys conducted regularly in the base countries Germany and France have produced excellent image figures, which it would be difficult for a television programme to exceed. Thus 85 per cent of the ARTE viewers in Germany and as many as 89 per cent in France have a high opinion

Table 2: Image elements of ARTE in Germany and France in 1996[3]

	ARTE France Regular and occasional viewers		ARTE Germany Regular and occasional viewers	
1. ARTE offers a different viewpoint from the other stations.	94	(91)	83	(83)
2. ARTE offers high-quality programmes.	89	(85)	85	(84)
3. ARTE is above all a European station.	80	(76)	76	(74)
4. ARTE makes an active contribution to international understanding.	65	(64)	76	(73)
5. ARTE is a station with a future.	80	(70)	68	(70)
6. ARTE is good for providing information on Europe.	69		71	

2 Source: Médiamétrie, GfK 1996; target group: 15 years and older in France, 14 years and older in Germany, German market shares relate to households with cable or satellite, french Market shares to all households with television.

3 The percentages relate to the answers 'agree completely', 'agree more or less'. Basis: representative survey by IPSOS and GFM-GETAS in March 1995 in Germany and France; the figures given in brackets refer to the previous year's survey; regular viewers are those who watch ARTE at least once a week, the occasional viewers watch an ARTE programme once to three times a month; all figures in percentages.

of the quality of ARTE programmes. The different angle as well as the European orientation are other image factors. Almost threequarters of the respondents give ARTE good chances for the future. Regarding ARTE as a means of international understanding is yet another weighty argument for its political legitimacy.

It is noticeable that the assessments for almost all of the image components have improved compared with the previous year. But the above results also show something else: both countries believe that there is a positive basis for European and cross-border television.

And finally, numerous prizes awarded in Europe show that ARTE has firmly established itself in the media world. Thus in 1994 ARTE received the *Adolf-Grimme-Preis* for the most original station design and in 1995 even the *Goldene Kamera* for its programmes. In addition there were also prizes for ARTE productions in Germany and abroad (e.g. *Goldenes Kabel*, *Prix César*). Even the popular German newspaper *Bild* referred to ARTE some months ago as 'the Rolls-Royce among the television stations'.

Profile of the ARTE viewers in Germany and France
What has been said above indicates that ARTE viewers are distinguished by a specific profile. A closer analysis will now be given on several levels, the sociodemographic one, the level of attitudes and behaviour patterns and the level of typologies, which ascertain coherent viewer types and profiles.

The sociodemographic approach
According to available studies in France and Germany ARTE viewers are to be categorised as belonging to the more highly educated and professional classes. Viewers over the age of 35 are also over-represented. It is therefore not likely to be surprising that ARTE viewers are to be found to a greater extent in the higher income brackets. Figure 2 shows the income distribution of the ARTE viewers in both countries.

Figure 2: Income distributions of ARTE viewers[4]

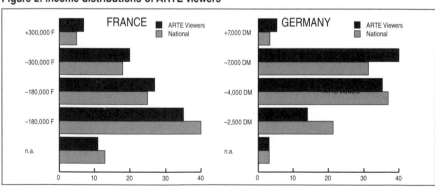

4   Source: IPSOS MEDIAS - INRA, representative survey of 3000 people in Germany and 1000 in France in February 1996; all data in percentages, ARTE viewers here means regular ARTE viewers.

It already emerges from these data, only briefly outlined here, that ARTE is watched for the most part by a certain group of viewers. This profile clearly distinguishes ARTE from those full national programmes which tend to be under-represented in the above-mentioned target groups.

ARTE viewers' attitudes and behaviour patterns

A closer look at the behaviour patterns and attitudes of the ARTE viewers seems to be more productive than an analysis of the sociodemographic data.

Table 3 gives an excerpt of items which are regularly measured in viewers and the population in France and Germany. It is noticeable that in some cases the figures for French and German ARTE viewers deviate considerably from the national average.

Table 3: Profile of the ARTE viewers in 1996 compared with the national average

	France		Germany	
	National average	Viewers of ARTE	National average	Viewers of ARTE
I. Geographical mobility				
1. Abroad more than three times a year	9	14	7	17
2. Never been abroad	67	56	49	32
II. Knowledge of languages				
English	37	45	45	67
French/German	11	13	13	28
No foreign language	48	39	49	26
III. Cultural behaviour[5]				
1. Go to the theatre or opera	11	18	18	33
2. Go to the cinema	43	55	30	40
3. Visit museums and exhibitions	38	48	24	51
4. Go to concerts	23	30	32	55
5. Read books	56	71	60	81
IV. Attitudes to Europe[6]				
1. A united Europe more important than national interests	43	49	44	61
2. Franco-German friendship motor of European understanding	71	77	59	65
3. TV plays an important role in the rapprochement of the European nations	69	71	59	54

5   Replies 'regularly' and 'occasionally' combined for I and II; all figures in percentages.

6   Replies 'agree completely' and 'agree more or less' combined; source: representative survey, February 1996, of 1000 people in France and 3000 in Germany, carried out by INRA and IPSOS MEDIAS; all figures in percentages.

Thus they are far more frequently abroad and have a considerably better knowledge of foreign languages. A third finding is also of importance: ARTE viewers are especially keen on culture; they go to the opera and theatre much more often and visit museums, exhibitions and concerts more frequently. Moreover, they are avid readers: 81 per cent of the German ARTE viewers read books in comparison to 60 per cent in the population as a whole. In France the proportion is 71 per cent to 56 per cent.

And finally, ARTE viewers are extremely pro-European. The statement: 'A united Europe is more important than national interests' is agreed to by the majority of ARTE viewers. On the national average this idea tends to be rejected. The necessity of the Franco-German motor for Europe was also seen far more clearly by ARTE viewers.

The multi-cultural programme conception and deliberate use of several languages on ARTE thus contribute towards a stronger European awareness in the population, as they seek to break up viewpoints from a national standpoint. ARTE's remit, quoted at the beginning – to contribute to international understanding in Europe – is thus perceived and completely shared by the viewers.

Ascertaining viewer typologies

ARTE viewers can also be classified by typologies. Specifically, they are divided up into regular viewers, that is those who watch at least once a week, occasional viewers, who watch once to three times a month, infrequent viewers, who watch ARTE less than once a month, and finally non-viewers, who turn their back on ARTE. According to these classification criteria, even so 48 per cent of the French and 15 per cent of the German television viewers who can technically receive ARTE are in the group of regular viewers. But from Figure 3 it can again be seen how Germany and France clearly differ, which was mentioned earlier.

Figure 3: Typologisation of ARTE viewers by viewing frequency[7]

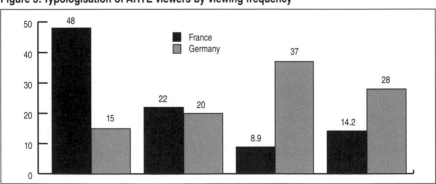

7   Source: IPSOS MEDIAS - INRA, representative survey of 3000 people in Germany and 1000 in France in February 1996. Regular viewers watch at least one programme a week, occasional viewers at least once a month, infrequent viewers less than once a month, all data in percentages, the percentages relate to the households that can receive ARTE.

But viewing frequency is only one criterion of differentiation. Figure 4 shows in an exemplary way how some structural features and attitudes can be assigned to the typologies. It emerges that for each typology there are specific constellations of replies, which, incidentally, also have an effect on other areas, such as, for example, reading behaviour. ARTE viewers read the print media to an above-average extent, such as the *FAZ, ZEIT* and *SPIEGEL* in Germany and *TELERAMA* in France.

Figure 4: Connection between the viewing frequency of ARTE viewers and structural features/attitudes.[8]

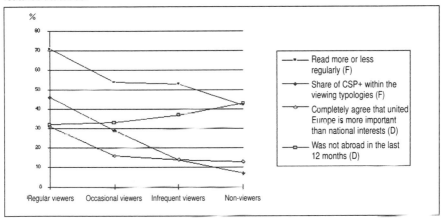

Viewing behaviour and programme preference

Over and beyond the approaches mentioned above, ARTE researched the viewing behaviour in depth. Two hypotheses may serve as a basis for discussion for the verification of which observations and research findings will be drawn on as examples.

Hypothesis 1: Great attention paid to ARTE programmes

A study carried out by IPSOS and GFM-GETAS on the use and acceptance of early evening programmes on ARTE showed that ARTE broadcasts are watched with a high degree of attention. Some ARTE programmes are, according to the findings, watched almost as intensively as *Tagesschau*, the 8 o'clock news of the ARD (cf. Table 4). Other findings of the same study confirm that programmes on ARTE are hardly ever watched as a result of random zapping, but of deliberate selection.

---

8   Source: IPSOS MEDIAS - INRA, representative survey of 3000 people in Germany and 1000 in France in February 1996. Regular viewers watch at least one programme a week, occasional viewers at least once a month, infrequent viewers less than once a month, all data in percentages.

Table 4: Degree of attention for some early evening programmes[9]

Germany	Figures in %	France	Figures in %
Tagesschau (news)	74.2	ARTE documentaries	67
ARTE documentaries	71.4	Regional news F3	63
Heute (news)	65.5	ARTE news	60
Sportschau	52.9	8 o'clock news (F2)	53
RTL series	34.1	8 o'clock news (TF1)	50
ARD early evening programmes	29.0	Coucou c'est nous (entertainment)	18

The same trend also emerges from the stability index for individual broadcasts – in France – regularly ascertained by ARTE Media Research. It indicates how many viewers saw at least 50 per cent, 75 per cent or 90 per cent of one broadcast. The figures for ARTE are regularly higher than for other comparable stations.

ARTE is not daily television. This kind of viewing behaviour also shows that the classical, purely broadcast-related analyses of audience ratings or even of average daily or weekly ratings only take this fact into consideration to a very limited extent. ARTE's success with the viewers can thus not be defined by the individual results of broadcasts alone, but also by the accumulative weekly audiences. The decisive question here is, rather, how many viewers are reached at the most by the ARTE programme.

Hypothesis 2: ARTE helps to impart knowledge
For the regular ARTE viewers, i.e. those who watch the ARTE programmes at least once a week, ARTE is in the top group of those stations in Germany and France from which they can learn most (cf. Table 5). Especially in

Table 5: Which television programme can you learn most from?[10]

	France			Germany		
	Average	ARTE viewers		Average	ARTE viewers	
TF 1	17	5	ARD	29	35	
F 2	10	6	ZDF	18	18	
F 3	15	7	RTL	16	5	
Canal +	4	3	SAT 1	9	5	
Cinquième	19	25	3SAT	5	7	
ARTE	22	46	ARTE	5	35	

9 Source: public opinion poll of 300 people in Germany and France who watch ARTE at least once a month, IPSOS-GfM, August 1993; the data relate to the following question: 'How attentively do you follow regularly seen early evening programmes?'; the percentages in the table relate to the reply: 'Attention was very strong'.

10 Source: IPSOS MEDIAS - INRA, representative survey of 3000 people in Germany and 1000 in France in February 1996. Regular viewers watch at least one programme a week, occasional viewers at least once a month, infrequent viewers less than once a month, all data in percentages, in Germany 10 stations were given to choose from.

France, the good results compared with national stations, even with *La Cinquieme*, are impressive. It is precisely the latter that set out to provide viewers with educational programmes. Thus television, in its function of imparting knowledge, has found a convincing representative in ARTE.

That ARTE viewers attach special importance to knowledge being transferred in the ARTE programmes also emerges from the programme preferences which were asked for. Documentaries come first in both countries. The history broadcasts, too, enjoy great popularity in France and Germany. Noticeable as well is the positioning of the theme evenings, which, of course, constitute a new programme genre and attach particular importance to being comprehensive.

Table 6: ARTE programme preferences[11]

Germany		France	
Documentaries (nature, discovery)	79	Documentaries (nature, discovery)	73
Films	78	Historical broadcasts	64
Historical broadcasts	64	Films	58
News broadcasts	63	Theme evenings	60
Art and cultural broadcasts	57	News broadcasts	52
Theme evenings	56	Art and cultural broadcasts	50
Humorous broadcasts	49	Humorous broadcasts	27
Musical broadcasts	38	Musical broadcasts	24
Animated films	31	Animated films	23

In summary, ARTE enjoys an interested and open-minded audience across borders, which on account of its attitudes and behaviour patterns is especially suited to programmes with an educational character.

Special challenges facing an international programme
In view of its international orientation ARTE is faced with great challenges if it wants to expand its audience significantly. Anyone making programmes of a high standard for several countries at the same time has to tackle language barriers and cultural differences in viewing habits. In particular four fields can be identified in which ARTE has to become more active.

Nationally characterised viewing habits
Unfortunately certain predetermined patterns of the national television markets also apply to ARTE. An especially telling example is the switching

11 Source: IPSOS MEDIAS - INRA, representative survey of 3000 people in Germany and 1000 in France in February 1996; all data in percentages; question: 'Which broadcasts do you watch regularly on ARTE?' The answers 'regularly' and 'occasionally' have been combined.

over times, or prime time, in the evening. In Germany the latter begins on almost all (national) stations at 8.15 p.m. It should be mentioned in this connection that the broadcasts in Germany almost always begin punctually at 8.15. In France, on the other hand, the evening programme does not begin until about 8.40 or 8.50 for all six national stations. But our French neighbours are not so particular about punctuality. The prime-time programme starting times announced in the TV guides are hardly adhered to any more. In the meantime 'delays' of up to 15 minutes are no longer unusual; so many programmes do not actually begin until around 9 o'clock.

ARTE might possibly manage, by means of appropriate programme formats, to take into account both the French and the German prime times.

National versus international orientation of programme content

ARTE programmes must not be tailored to only either the French or the German viewers. A transnational station also requires a certain percentage of programmes which can find the same degree of acceptance in several countries, i.e. which is suitable for transnational audiences. Programmes of this kind contribute considerably towards stabilising the station in both countries.

It can thus be observed that certain documentaries or films, but also theme evenings produce a good response on this and the other side of the Rhine. They are either programmes which communicate for the most part through pictures (e.g. animal or discovery documentaries) or programmes with a strongly narrative character (e.g. historical documentaries).

Precisely such criteria should play a bigger part in the selection of programmes. Here, too, media research can provide important help.

Multilingualism

Multilingual programmes are unfortunately not only a positive distinguishing feature, especially for those who are gifted at languages. The former also largely exclude certain groups of viewers. The consequence may be demotivation. This is also confirmed by the survey already referred to several times, according to which programmes in the original with subtitles are for many the main reason for not watching ARTE. (cf. Table 7)

Maybe state-of-the-art technology will soon make it possible to offer several language versions throughout Europe by means of data compression via satellite. This would be certain to have a positive effect on the acceptance of ARTE in Europe.

Broadcast formats which work with studio discussions or presenters will, however, continue to cause considerable difficulties. The available techniques, especially interpreting, cannot, for the time being, be replaced in such cases.

Table 7: The most frequent reasons for not watching ARTE[12]

Germany	
Inadequate breadth of the programmes	74
Subtitles, national language imposed on the original	66
France	
Subtitles, national language imposed on the original	31
Inconvenient transmission times	24

Different basic motivation

The Germans and the French actually live in a completely different communication culture, which also has an impact on the medium of television. A particularly striking example that illustrates this is provided by the style and content of news broadcasts in both countries.

A comparison was carried out taking the example of the German *Tagesschau* and the French *TF1 Journal*. Both these news programmes are 'market leaders' in their country and can certainly be regarded as characteristic of each country.[13] To make it easier to compare them, the information content was arranged into various categories. Table 8 shows the average percentage proportions of the individual categories in the entire news broadcast.

Table 8: Proportion of the various categories in the whole of main news broadcasts *Tagesschau* and *TF1 Journal*[14]

Categories	Tagesschau	TF1 Journal
Miscellaneous (faits divers)	16	47
Foreign affairs	47	39
Domestic politics	33	11
Economics, business	3	4

It is noticeable that according to this classification the category 'Miscellaneous', which includes mainly stories about people but also sport, has the lion's share in France, while in Germany political affairs are clearly dominant. On closer examination of the style and presentation form of the news, the prominent position of the French presenter is also evident. The French presenter is far more than just someone providing information, but he establishes a direct contact with the viewer by allusions and directly addressing him. His main function is to select and edit the news so that

---

12 Source: representative survey, February 1966, of 1000 people in France and 3000 in Germany, carried out by INRA and IPSOS, all figures in percentages. The replies relate to those viewers who watch ARTE rarely or hardly ever; the percentages comprise the answers 'agree'.

13 Cf. Darschin, Wolfgang; Frank, Bernward: 'Tendenzen im Zuschauerverhalten', in: Media Perspektiven No. 4, 1995, pp. 154-165, p. 161 et seq.; also: N.N.: 'Audience nationale des journaux télévisés', in: *Mediamétrie-Hébdo* 1994, Paris, 1995.

14 Source: Schroeder, Michael: Frankreich – Deutschland: zwei unterschiedliche Auffassungen von Kommunikation', in: Deutsch-Französische Medienbilder, (Eds.) Koch, Ursula, Schröter, Detlef, Albert, Pierre, publ. by Verlag Reinhard Fischer, Munich, 1993; duration of study: 14 days.

the viewers stay with him and do not switch to another programme. In the meantime the presenters have developed into stars whose price in the media is traded as on the stock exchange.[15]

One could go even further and advance the hypothesis that the basic motivation for using television to be informed about current events is not so pronounced as in Germany. Added to this is the fact that the French hardly distinguish between news and commentary, both areas merging into one another. In the German news broadcasts this principle of the separation of both areas is largely upheld (*Tagesschau, Tagesthemen, heute, heute journal*).[16]

In view of this initial situation, ARTE has to develop new programme formats and presentation forms. Two attempts have already been made, firstly, with the news broadcast '8½' without a presenter, and, secondly, with the new magazine programme '7½', which by its original way of giving priority to certain points of content offers an additional encouragement to both audiences compared with the respective national stations.

Michael Schroeder *studied Marketing and International Business at Münster University and holds a Ph.D. from Saarbrücken University, where he graduated in 1993 with a thesis on 'International Market and Management Strategies for the Print Media'. Before that he spent two years at an elite French business school in Paris. Since 1994 he has been working in Strasbourg for ARTE. Until April 1996 he was in charge of media research and sponsoring; he is now the personal adviser to the future president of ARTE. Michael Schroeder has published numerous articles in Germany and France on the subject of intercultural communication and the media.*

15 Cf. o.V.: 'Les schizos de l'info', in: *Télérama*, No. 2370, 14.7.1995, pp. 74–78.

16 Cf. Schroeder, Michael: 'Frankreich – Deutschland: zwei unterschiedliche Auffassungen von Kommunikation', op.cit., pp. 24–25.

5: Science and Technology as the Subject of Popular Programmes

Scientific Mysteries of the Universe

A television series with the Nobel laureate Professor Gerd Binnig

Ulrike Emrich Head of Main Department Science and Education
Reinhold Gruber Producer Sciences and Technology,
Bayerischer Rundfunk, Munich

A look forward into the 21st century is not reassuring: the momentum of new scientific knowledge and technologies can change every area of life. From politics we expect the solution to societal problems, from science further progress in conserving the ecosystem Earth. Science itself is still characterised by the belief that, in spite of everything, there is a hopeful future, that destructive forces will be mastered from outside and inside and that we shall be able to organise ourselves in this world in a humane way. In the media the term scientific and technical progress has often lost its once positive connotation, and the outcome of the increase in knowledge occasionally turns out to be negative.

Do we know more and more about less and less? Have we turned into 'information giants and knowledge dwarfs', as the philosopher Professor Mittelstrass put it? But the need to find our bearings in the information labyrinth and the data jungle is indeed growing. The viewer has a right to comprehensive information on the findings and trends in German and international science.

The Bavarian Broadcasting Corporation (BR) is the only television station in the ARD to have a Main Department for Science and Education and thus to take account of the importance of Germany as a location for research and science: with a regular science slot in its television evening programme and about eight broadcasts a year in the ARD science magazine *Globus – Forschung und Technik* (Globe – Research and Technology).

The existing science broadcasts are based above all on the principle of 'Explain the World to Me'. The aim of the new series *Welträtsel der Wissenschaft* (scientific mysteries of the universe) is to impart science as an experience and to address the viewer emotionally. People are meant to have the feeling that it also concerns them. We have managed to gain the services of the Nobel Prize Winner for Physics in 1986 as the presenter. Professor Gerd Binnig from Munich is the only German Nobel laureate to present a series on the ARD.

Scientific mysteries of the universe
This is the report of a project in progress. We shall give a brief outline of the project; whether it will turn out to be a popular programme, has still to be decided by the viewers.

The title

The main title of the series indicates that it is less a matter of answers than of question. Professor Hans-Peter Dürr, Director of the Max Planck Institute for Physics once said:

> In my experience, what interests the broad public (in micro-physics) is generally not so much certain facts as fundamental and philosophical questions.

The aim of our new series is not to cast a mysterious veil over the attempts by the natural sciences to bring clarity to an understanding of the world. But the naive belief in progress, which in principle does not recognise anything that is mysterious, which only sees momentary limits to knowledge, this naive belief is not meant to be a matter for the series. We tried out the term 'scientific', although it is clear to us that science certainly puts many people off.

The presenter

The results of public opinion surveys lead us to suppose that viewers by no means prefer programmes with a presenter to programmes without one. What is important to them are the topics and the way the programmes are made. What is to be concluded from this?

Professor Binnig is not meant to be a presenter who only bridges sections or is given a chance to say in the link-up text what the programme itself did not manage to achieve or what is left over to mention to make the programme more topical. Gerd Binnig will be presenting the programmes, together with a youthful female partner. So his presence will always be felt, even though he will not be on screen all the time. His partner will put the questions. Asking questions is the beginning of all science.

It will be an experiment to have a physics Nobel laureate make a programme together with an actress. But something playful can result from this and it is by playing that we want to take our viewers through the universe's mysteries of knowledge. It is a risk for both sides, for the producers and for the Nobel laureate. After all, scientific prominence and a sympathetic, unpretentious manner are by no means tantamount to a good effect on television. On the other hand, the 'height of fall' is, of course, great for a Nobel laureate. He will be exposed to the criticism of his colleagues when he crosses borders while ranging over the diverse themes that are planned.

The makers of the programmes

The project was set off by Professor Binnig during a conversation with Reiner Korbmann, Editor-in-Chief of the science magazine *Bild der Wissenschaft* (Image of Science). Mr Korbmann approached Mrs Ulrike Emrich, Head of the Programme Area Science and Education at Bavarian Television, and Dr Andreas von Ferenczy of Ferenczy Media. From this meeting emerged the will to implement the project under the aegis of the Bavarian Broadcasting Corporation. Thomas Deicke from Munich, a

successful science author, was engaged as script writer. The director is John Delbridge from Hamburg. He has produced important broadcasts in the area of entertaining educational television. Sets will be designed by Eckhard Rocholl, whose major achievement will be the creation of the virtual reality studio.

Ferenczy TV (Ferenczy Media) in Grünwald near Munich has been commissioned with the production. Bavarian Television has overall responsibility for the series.

The style of the broadcast

In a dialogue with a youthful woman partner Gerd Binnig discusses exciting questions in the various subject areas. In a modern 'Fun Vehicle' the protagonists repeatedly travel to important scenes of research and science: science as an experience, research as an adventure trip. By means of computer animation and virtual reality studio technology, the internal world of the studio and the external world of real life merge to a large extent.

The traditional pattern of 'studio – insert film – studio' is broken through. A great measure of movement in themes and styles is intended to make the viewers curious and receptive to 'Science as a World of Experience' – a world which strongly influences their familiar world, today more than ever.

Titles and themes for 1996

'Gulliver's New Travels – Gerd Binnig in the world of atoms'
The first instalment deals with Professor Binnig's very own field, the nanoworld. In 1986 he shared the Nobel Prize for Physics with Heinrich Rohrer for the invention of the scanning tunnelling microscope.

On a trip through the dimensions of the macro-, micro- and nanoworlds the viewer learns the significance of atoms and atomic structures for the world generally and for the future of our technical civilisation.

But can there be an answer to the riddle: An atom – what actually is that?

'The Secret of Life – The long path to Homo sapiens'
In the second broadcast the two travellers in the matter of *Scientific Mysteries of the Universe* make a great leap to life and consciousness – and yet they come back to the subject of atoms and physics, as the models provided by natural science to explain the univers provoke by the statement that in the end man, too, in all his complexity is only the product of a development of atomic and molecular structures over billions of years – a product of evolution on the basis of physical laws. Nevertheless, human life and consciousness are still the classic scientific mysteries of the universe.

Themes planned for 1997

- The Fate of the Universe – where it comes from, where it is going.
- Forwards into Infinity: The secret of time.

- After Us the Robots? Our future in cyberspace.
- Responsibility for the Earth: Between chaos and creativity – Visions of science.

The programme environment of the broadcasts

We have understood the message of private television: Television takes place in a market which is increasingly determined by supply and demand. Our programme remit inside a public service corporation cannot, indeed must not, prevent us from attracting audiences. We do not want an area of grace for educational programmes, what we do want is an audience, and if possible a young one.

The Bavarian Broadcasting Corporation is, it is true, not a private company that sells advertising time by means of television programmes. Our product is, as it always has been, the programme itself.

Nevertheless, the broadcasts should be put on the market by an event management. This will comprise essentially being accompanied by special articles in *Bild der Wissenschaft*, a periodical presenting science issues in a popular way, through its emphasis on particular themes in each issue. In addition, the broadcasts are to be made available as videos and CD-ROMs.

But this, too, is certainly an event: the first and only science broadcast on German television to be presented by a Nobel laureate.

Ulrike Emrich *became the Head of the Programme Area 'Science and Society' at Bavarian Television in October 1991. This was reorganised in October 1995 as 'Science and Education' and contains now the departments 'Humanities', 'Science and Technology', 'Medicine', 'Languages' and 'Education and Training'. Previously she had been working in the Press Office of the Max Planck Society.*

Reinhold Gruber *studied German Language and Discipline of Theatre at Munich University. After two years of service in the German Army he studied Journalism at the Academy of Film and Television in Munich. In 1969 he began to work as a free-lancer for the Schools and Family Department at Bavarian Television. Since 1976 he has been an editor in the Department of Natural Sciences and Technology at Bavarian Television.*

How do you chain people to educational programmes?

Pál Sipos, Péter Stodulka
Magyar TV, Budapest

Only a few people legitimately regard themselves as experts on *Magyar TV* (MTV), the Hungarian broadcasting corporation. Consequently, in order to understand the scientific and educational programme situation in Hungarian Television, we have to consider a number of really important facts.

Fact no. 1: For just over 30 years Hungarian Television occupied a monopoly position in the Hungarian media market. During that period it obediently fulfilled the expectations of the Hungarian Socialist Workers' Party, the ruling communist organisation in Hungary. A look back from today's situation of 'We don't have money for this and that' - combined with a slightly ironic twist - shows that it played a highly significant role in spreading real-value culture among its audience, deploying its special means to educate generations of Hungarians. For a long while this meant that the programmes broadcast by Hungarian Television were genuine public service productions produced either at home or abroad, with a positive conservative approach to cultural values.

Documentaries on technological innovations and the results of scientific research, on nature and history were extremely popular, as they satisfied both people's curiosity and their need for visual information. Even entertainment programmes had educative aims, and the audience, as it had no other television programme available, contented itself with this sort of Hungarian television.

Fact no. 2: The political changes of the late 1980's, on the one hand, and the country's gradual opening to all sorts of information collected from satellite television channels for example, on the other, obliged Hungarian Television producers and policy makers to face the challenges of the 1990's. When the few Hungarian commercial cable channels and European and American satellite television programmes appeared on the scene, a model was evidently swept away whose message always seemed to be: 'Good television knows your needs, takes care of you and supplies you with high culture and education - so don't ask any questions!' Something new had to be introduced.

This 'something new' may at last be launched at the beginning of 1997. The six years from 1989 to 1995 were overshadowed by the ex-lex situation of Hungarian Television and the so-called media war deriving from it, resulting in a continuous feeling of insecurity among the employees of MTV. With the passing of the Media Law 'the rules of the game' have been openly declared, and by the end of 1996 the state-owned public service television and one or two commercial channels will be ready to commence a new phase in the history of the Hungarian media market.

Fact no. 3: Mostly in the 1960's and 1970's, school television had quite a history and considerable influence in Hungary. But to tell the truth, its programmes were obediently watched by classes supervised by their teachers, as this was part of a centrally initiated project. As soon as it turned out to be not 'so important', they returned to the normal 'chalk and talk' of education: the teachers taught, the students learned, the television collected dust in the cupboard.

The advantage of these programmes lay not in the introduction of a 'second teacher', a rival to the established teacher of the class, - such examples of alternativity were not really welcomed by the socialist system, anyway - but in the fact that physics or chemistry experiments and demonstrations, for example, were shown on television, thus enabling the kids to understand physical and chemical processes better. As school television programmes were needed neither by the teachers nor by the kids, they were kept alive only by tradition and by the fact that some people were fanatics in this field, doing their very best but without any real success.

Fact no. 4: The Hungarian Television Corporation is a public service institution, owned and controlled by the state. It is financed partly by the budget, mainly by licence fees and to a remarkable extent by commercial advertising revenues. At present Hungarian Television has all the disadvantages of this sort of finance-mix: first, it seeks to satisfy with its programming policy political expectations (due to the budget allowance), second, the needs of the general audience (due to licence fees) and third, the demands of the advertising agencies (due to commercial advertising revenues). In order to 'translate' these criteria, the preferences of the programming department are now prescribed by the above-mentioned financial considerations. Hence, the ranking observed is 1. political and news programmes, 2. television series and feature films, 3. entertainment and sports programmes.

And now back to the question we posed in the title of this chapter: How do you chain people to educational programmes?

To begin with, a word of explanation: Hungarian people like scientific, educative and all sorts of programmes that supply them with information on their history, the nature around them, the life and history of other people, etc. This was revealed by a survey conducted in the summer of 1995 by a public opinion research institute on the programme preferences of the Hungarian audience. Much to the amazement of many media experts, it showed that for the Hungarians the third most popular type of programme was the scientific and educative documentary, which came after television series and feature films, beating entertainment programmes, sports and talk shows.

That means we have our audience willing to watch either Hungarian or foreign scientific and educative documentaries. If these programmes arouse the natural curiosity and interest of our audience and satisfy their visual and dramatic expectations, they will be watched. Since easily understandable, even entertaining narration and high-quality camera work are basic requirements in these films, our audience would even enjoy watching them.

So the problem is not to be found in our viewers: we do not really need to chain them to the television to make them watch our programmes. Do we need chains at all? Yes, we do, because admittedly, although the audience would watch scientific and educative programmes, they are not able to, as they do not find these programmes in easily accessible slots.

The problem derives from the previously mentioned financial orientation of the programming department: they reserve the early prime time and prime-time slots for television series, feature films, entertainment and sports programmes, arguing that this is what the audience and the advertising agencies need. In a country like Hungary, where rapid social, economic and political transitions and changes are taking place side by side, where the market economy and political democracy have just been introduced to the general public, which also has to face radical personal cuts in finance, the programming department of a television company has a three-fold responsibility. It should consider the public-service programming policy and the philosophy of the institution in harmony with its legal foundation; it should take the expectations of the audience into account; finally, it should serve, inform and influence the advertising agencies.

If the programming department reserves time slots for scientific and educative programmes in the 'grave-yard slots' such as the early and late hours of weekday afternoons or the (early or late) morning hours on weekends, audience ratings will clearly show that there is no need for such programmes or that only a very small segment of the audience is really interested in such matters. Most advertising agencies are interested in acquiring only prime-time advertisement slots, as the ratings show high figures there. They have no intention to invest money in the grave-yard slots, although they are full of interesting and high-value scientific and educative programmes, thus inducing the often repeated statement: producing such programmes is a waste of money, as no-one watches them and no advertisement revenue can be acquired as a result.

Paradoxically, we therefore had to fight for better time slots in order to demonstrate that our programmes can attract as many viewers as any other prime-time programmes. At the beginning of this year, we obtained an early prime-time slot for the weekly 30-minute programme *Scientific News*, and once a month a real prime-time slot for nature films. The audience ratings clearly corroborated our hypothesis: *Scientific News* has an average 15 per cent rating, meaning that 1.2 million people watch it regularly. The programmes broadcast in the prime-time slot attracted almost the same number of people as any of the other entertainment programmes shown during the other weeks: 37 to 43 per cent, meaning 2.9 to almost 3.5 million people. Even the advertisement slots were sold. So we did in fact need a chain, which proved to be more effective when used to blackmail, frighten and coax our colleagues in the programming department into granting us access to our audience.

Taking into consideration audience needs, not only in the media or television sense, may lead to successful television programmes. In the light of the continuous economic decline of the 1980's and 1990's, it became quite obvious by 1994 that very few Hungarian families could afford special after-school preparatory courses for their kids attending secondary education and striving for further education at college or university. These courses, usually extremely expensive, are still vital for teenagers, as in Hungary there is a compulsory entrance examination at colleges and universities with only the cream being admitted. This public need - sadly, we cannot talk in terms of public demand - was met with a daily educational programme, called *Repeta* in Hungarian, derived from the German word 'repetieren' (meaning 'to repeat or revise'), covering the subjects of Literature, History, Maths, Physics and Biology.

These 40-minute programmes, broadcast from Monday to Thursday at 3.20 p.m., have received high critical acclaim and very positive feedback from the audience, from both kids and teachers. What is more, previously the programmes broadcast in these slots attracted the interest of very few people. When *Repeta* was launched, within a few months the ratings showed a gradual increase in these slots, now reaching an average of 5 per cent, i.e. 400,000 people daily.

Repeta assists those who cannot afford the expensive after-school courses to help them prepare for the university entrance examination. So, in a way, the aim of this programme is to ensure equality of opportunity. Péter Stodulka, the producer of the programmes and one of the 'founding fathers' of the whole project *Repeta*, will give you further details in the following contribution.

If we were to make a programme, however, only for the above-mentioned groups, our task would be more than easy to fulfil - they would watch us in any case, as they comprise our motivated audience. In this event we would have been content with a 2 per cent audience share, the usual rate in this time slot previously. However, *Repeta* is not only meant for young people seeking entrance to university education. The programmes were also targeted at those who had studied the given subjects before and just wanted to brush up their knowledge, as well as at teachers and all those interested in science generally.

Our aims were higher. We thought we could attract a group of viewers larger than all secondary school students and those who have completed their secondary studies, already in possession of the basic knowledge necessary to understand our examples. Mathematics sounds frightening for a lot of people, although there are many ways to induce them to watch the programme.

Our trick, albeit simple, proved to be effective: each episode contains an extra topic which can be anything besides maths. So far we have already shown sports events (snowboard races, bike exhibitions) and fashion shows; we have dealt with the topics of AIDS and drug awareness; we have also introduced young bands, broadcast news on coming events, useful information for the summer holidays as well as on technical innovations and Internet. We present topics that are interesting for all young people, and since these topics are inserted in between the examples from the subjects, those only interested in the extra topics have also had to listen to mathematics, for example.

As the contents of the subject areas are already given, we only have to find a form that is 'easily digestible'. If we want to compete with the music channels MTV or VIVA we have to present something similar. We do not need to undertake market research to measure the needs of the young: you have to make the style and the studio set attractive and colourful, the prerecorded segments in the same style as video clips (edited to music, fast and spectacular). The segments should be no longer than 2 to 3 minutes, the mathematics segments must be shorter than 6 minutes and have a touch of humour. The ratio between education and informative entertainment is approx. 75 per cent to 25 per cent. Visuality plays an important role in the educational part (computer animation, easily readable figures, mirrorboard etc.), since the youngsters will zap to other channels if the figures do not move fast enough.

The young spirit of *Repeta* is ensured by the age of the producers, ranging from 22 to 30. The eight years' difference can sometimes cause serious conflicts, since a 30-year-old producer's attitude to the younger generation is different. Sometimes even their pre-recorded material shows this difference.

Rhythm and young spirit are assisted by some other factors, too: the programme is live; there is always a maths problem for the viewers; they can call the studio live with their solutions or send them via Internet. The first to solve the problem correctly receives a valuable gift. Each week we give our viewers five exercises. They send in their solutions by mail or E-mail. On request, we send them back their solutions corrected, the best contribution receiving a prize every week.

In June at the end of the school year, the best 40 kids are invited to the studio. There they solve a test and the winner receives a multimedia computer. The success of our project is shown by the fact that every week we receive 200 to 300 letters with the solutions; there are many classes among the applicants.

The programme has a Home Page where previous examples can be found as well as background information on the programmes and their producers, on weekly topics, planned videoclips etc..

Next year we would like to make *Repeta* even easier to watch: instead of a programme made more digestible, we want to provide a daily 80 to 90-minute magazine for young people. 30 minutes would remain for educational content, the other 50–60 minutes consisting of music charts, scientific news, a lifestyle magazine, news on coming events, sport and anything that is informative, entertaining and of interest for young people.

The third project was launched 6 months ago: *Xenia Fever* was originally aimed at kids from 10 to 15, and as the 25th episode was broadcast in April 1996, it is now clear that people from 6 to 60 watch it. *Xenia Fever* is superficially a science-fiction soap opera, with spaceships, aliens, space wolves, containing all the requisites for such a programme. The episodes of *Xenia Fever* are broadcast every Friday in early prime time and repeated on Sunday mornings at 9 a.m.

The novelty of the project lies a little deeper. The kids, who in Episode 2 were kidnapped by the aliens, can only help themselves if they are able to use what they have learnt at school from Maths, Biology, Physics and Chemistry. Throughout the whole series the different subjects are embedded in the science fiction story, thus kids learn without even noticing. The educational aim of the series is to cover the whole range of subject matter kids should learn at school, taken from the previously mentioned subjects taught at junior high school. But looking at the audience ratings, I would not be surprised if this generation grew up with *Xenia Fever* for years and if the producers soon started writing stories based on the senior high school curriculum.

To sum up our experiences, scientific, educative and educational programmes in Hungarian Television underwent great changes between 1994 and 1996. On the one hand, the producers had to face up to the facts: they had to find the topics and subject matter the audience really wanted to watch, producing and presenting them in a visually high-quality form. They also had to learn that it is necessary to fight for the suitable time slots, as so many conflicting views and interests influence programming nowadays. They have also had to bear in mind that most people like to learn in an indirect way: with the help of scientific and educative documentaries to wrap up your message in.

Pál Sipos, *Ph.D., graduated in 1982 at the University of Budapest, where he studied Hungarian and English language and literature. In 1990 he obtained a Fulbright fellowship to study at Syracuse University, Newhouse School for Public Communications. From 1982 to 1989 he was Assistant Professor at the Department of Hungarian Historical Linguistics at the University of Budapest. Since 1989 he has worked as producer, reporter and political journalist for Hungarian Television, where he was appointed Head of the Department of Cultural, Scientific and Educational Programmes in 1994.*

Péter Stodulka, *Ph.D., is a close collaborator of Dr. Sipos and senior producer of Hungarian Television where he has been responsible for the development and realisation of Repeta.*

The challenge of
making engineering popular

Robert Thirkell
Science Department, BBC Television, London

Introduction

I work for the BBC Television Science Department, which is the largest producer of science programmes in the world, making more than 100 hours of
science programmes a year. We make regular and long-running series – e.g.
Horizon, QED, Tomorrow's World – as well as many special series and seasons
in science and technology. Many of our programmes are used in schools
and for educational purposes, however, we are not part of BBC Education.
Our remit is to make very popular television that lots of people will watch
but that is also instructional and informative. We are trying to compete with
mainstream television programmes at the same time as being educative.

I want to talk to you this morning about the BBC engineering season.
This was a unique season of programmes aimed at popularising engineering with a broad general public. It was called *Grand Designs*, had its own
identifying sting and advertising campaign, and was transmitted in
autumn 1995. It was made up of many programmes and series from different BBC departments, and even included special items from children's
programmes and current affairs.

Our hope was to appeal to both engineers and a more general public
with a mixture of history and the human drama in contemporary engineering stories – to find a chocolate coating for some real engineering detail.

There has long been a strong and vociferous engineering lobby that has
complained about a lack of popular engineering programmes on BBC television. There have of course always been single documentaries in our
major BBC science strands such as *Horizon* and *QED*.

Tomorrow's World, our very popular science magazine, often includes
engineering items, and there have been occasional series such as *White Heat*
on the culture and history of technology. But it has been felt by many that
this is not enough. There had never been a major engineering season before.

The engineering bodies were particularly worried about the poor
esteem in which engineers are held in Britain, and about the frequently low
numbers and quality of students who choose engineering at the universities. In fact, engineering had a very poor press, and there was a very poor
level, or even lack, of understanding of the subject.

There really was a demand that we do something to create a higher image for engineering. Our Science Department took up the challenge, but it proved surprisingly difficult to answer the need and make a series, which would fulfil the dual desire of so many educational programme makers today – the desire for *both* popularity and explanation. We first began by devising a new six-part series format called *The Limit*, which became the inspiration for the whole season to be commissioned.

As to the structure of my paper, I want to talk first about *The Limit*, then I shall say more about the whole season *Grand Designs*, and conclude with some findings of our audience research department on how it was received.

The Limit

The aim of *The Limit* was to make six films, each of which would follow an engineering project that was pushing at the technical limits of what can be achieved today. It was about making the deepest tunnel, the longest bridge, the highest tower, and so on.

We used a combination of our own BBC Science Department's skills and experience in making popular programmes, combined with money, educational expertise and editorial input from the BBC Education directorate, as we set out to beat conventional engineering programme-making limits in trying to make this sort of material interesting to a mass audience.

The idea behind this series was to understand engineering principles by looking at the constraints that hold engineers back, and to reflect on the excitement of engineering at the frontiers. The first programme in the series, titled *Tallest Tower*, starts at the top and scrapes the sky with a building

called Millennium Tower, a 900-metre structure planned by engineers Obayashi in Japan and Britain's most famous architect Sir Norman Foster.

The series continued with *Fastship,* which is about a cargo ship which is designed to travel twice as fast across the Atlantic and to revolutionise cargo trade, as the ship model tests proved that cargo could be carried at high speed on a regular basis. Others in the series included the construction of a new underground train line right under the heart of London with a great host of engineering problems in its construction, and the world's largest plane to be, a 1000-seater super jumbo planned by Airbus Industries (see information in box on p. 171). I now want to continue by explaining some of the problems we had in making the series.

Problems in making *The Limit*

Today major engineering projects are often a very complex multidisciplinary effort. Much of the work is done on computer, by huge teams. Like all branches of science and technology these days, it is also becoming ever more complex. The issues become increasingly difficult to unravel and explain, especially to a non-specialised audience.

How in these circumstances can television tell the world about engineering? As a production team, we often told ourselves how different it would have been if we could have made programmes in the 19th century.

Engineering has always changed lives, but today its rate of progress is faster than ever. The temptation is for viewers to take new breakthroughs for granted. The gasps of amazement now are fewer than they were in the glorious nineteenth century era of record-breaking bridges, trains and ships that made national celebrities out of engineers. Somehow the great achievements of the past seemed all the more romantic because they were often the work of one dedicated individual, led by a vision and fired by a passion. And in a way, television programmes are all about conveying the vision and the passion of a character in order to excite the viewers about a subject.

Solutions in creating *The Limit*

For *The Limit* we wanted to find six stories that would regain this romance for engineers. We had a large number of questions on how best to do this, and sometimes it seemed that we too were pushing the limits.

Our first key initial decision was that we would not just follow the projects, but try to find one key dedicated individual associated in running the project – it might be the project manager, the key designer or the leader of the team – at any rate an individual who could summon up this romance for us.

Our second key decision was that we would not tell stories in the past, but focus on projects where the limits are being challenged now. The problem with this is that the building, the bridge or the plane often does not yet exist. We would often have to create it, or the audience could not see it.

And finally, we decided that we needed the traditional dramatic narrative drive that makes lots of viewers watch. So we would follow the key engineer through the ups, downs and excitement of a year. In some projects this was easier than in others, but if you take something like a bridge, all that happens in a year is that the pillar holding it up goes a few meters higher, and this is not very dramatic.

The problem though with creating this narrative drive lay also in getting our engineers to perform to camera. Another problem was that engineers are used to minimising the challenges and difficulties to their fellow professionals.

Modern engineers are often project managers, more than ever stimulating the creative synergy between many different disciplines. Often it was politically diffcult to follow one key designer or project leader. Even more difficult was that there was a limited number of limit-busting projects, and we were dependent on whichever character might be leading them.

In best scientific tradition we decided to make a single pilot film to see how the concept worked. We chose the longest bridge currently under construction, linking Copenhagen to mainland Denmark. It is part of an audacious scheme that will eventually link Sweden via Denmark to Germany. Danish Engineer Nils Gimsing has been fighting for its construction, and continuously redesigning it for nearly thirty years.

The *Limit* Pilot

We came back to England and made a roughcut of what we had filmed. On review we were not satisfied for three reasons:

Nils Gimsing, our Danish bridgebuilder, was failing to convey his ideas in simple terms, with enthusiasm and real drama; he was afraid of his peer group. He was not keen to convey excitement, and he was not coming over as the engineering star.

Our second problem was that the construction of the bridge was not advancing in any way. It looked just like two pillars standing in the water, and not like a dramatic world-first in bridge building. Bridge construction is very, very slow, and although the towers would be twice as high as any British building, right out in the middle of the sea, it was hard to convey this.

We showed the pilot to people; they said that this was just like the construction of another new car: it is a little better than the previous model, the designer is not very excited – why should we want to watch this?

Which brings me to the third problem: We could not give the viewer a concept of what the finished bridge would actually look like; we needed to show something – in this case the bridge – which did not yet exist, and we needed to understand the challenges of its construction. How could we film this?

Our first solution to these problems was to try to create drama, by putting a 30-seconds sequence on the beginning of each film that would show what could go wrong, to show the stakes our engineers were up against. We tried to use the drama of previous failures.

THE LIMIT

Bridges – buildings – aeroplanes – ships: there are constraints on how tall, long, large and fast they can go, but engineers are out to beat the limits. Robbie Coltrane, actor and engineering enthusiast, tells the stories of six different projects around the world as engineers try to overcome the physical and human challenges.

| 1 | *Tallest Tower* | *Tuesday, 14th November, 8 pm* |

Conventional tower blocks have hit the limits. In the world's highest apartment crockery slides around the table in the wind. Cable strength limits lifts to 100 floors. Earthquakes threaten plans to build tall in the Far East. Now British architect Sir Norman Foster, and Japanese engineer Dr. Keizo Shimizu are planning a tower block twice as high as ever before – nearly a kilometre tall. They'll need to make the shape immune to wind, and design radical new lifts to navigate a city in the sky: Millennium Tower.

| 2 | *Fastest Ship* | *Thursday 16th November, 7 pm* |

Across the Atlantic, waves can slow cargo ships to the speed of a running man. British ship designer, David Giles, wants to break the limit of the waves and transform world trade with a new cargo carrier called FastShip. Never before have naval architects conceived of a high-speed ship of such size. Its hull must withstand angry seas at up to 40 knots and gas turbines will deliver 300 Megawatts of power to massive waterjets.

| 3 | *Trickiest Tunnel* | *Tuesday 28th November, 8 pm* |

The hardest tunnels are the ones under cities because of what's above. Any collapse could be disastrous. Hugh Doherty, in charge of London's new Jubilee Line extension, has hit his biggest challenge yet. At one end he must tunnel under the Thames through the treacherous Thanet sands and at the other the line must pass beneath some of London's most famous landmarks without causing so much as a crack

| 4 | *Largest Plane* | *Tuesday 5th December, 8 pm* |

To cope with the explosion in air traffic, the airlines want a super-jumbo plane, but can Jean-Jacques Huber at Airbus Industries provide it? A 1,000 seater aircraft, weighing 500 tons would be a challenge just to get into the air. Its noise would push limits at the airports – and handling the passengers and baggage could be a nightmare.

| 5 | *Longest Bridge* | *Tuesday 12th December, 8 pm* |

The world's first mile-long suspension bridge is taking shape above the busy channel that separates Copenhagen from the rest of Denmark. Designer Niels Gimsing must decide how to spin cables nearly a metre thick, and how to make the deck sections stand up to the loading of traffic and wind. Getting it wrong could lead to spectacular failure – the Tay Bridge in Scotland, the Tacoma Narrows Bridge in the USA.

| 6 | *Remotest Robot* | *Tuesday 19th December, 8 pm* |

In five years time a robot drill will head off on a ten-year journey to the farthest reaches of space. Its mission? To burrow into a comets icy nucleus, transfer the cometary crumb to instruments for analysis, and relay the results back to earth. Engineers Stephen Gorevan in New York and Mauro Fenzi in Milan are competing to design a robotic drill that can work without gravity, and uses less power than any other used in space before.

Taken from a Press Release

By using a dramatic opening, we hoped to hook in a broad audience. We also persuaded with great difficulties an actor called Robby Coltrane who was staring in Britain´s most popular drama at that time, to narrate the series. He actually loved engineering, and that helped tremendously.

As I have said, our bridge-building engineer was not keen to convey excitement. To address this problem we returned to Denmark with the intention to persuade Nils Gimsing to be more excited and honest about the project, and to do more filming. In fact we used his daughter as our ally. At university dances she told us that if a boy said he was an engineer she guessed he must be boring. 'Tell your dad', we said, 'that he must be more exciting for the sake of all engineers. We and you know that he is really excited by the project. It is up to your dad to show how exciting the subject really is.' With much discussion between Gimsing, us and the family, he decided to show himself as he really was, the romantic engineer.

We came up with the same problem in each of the programmes, as we tried to persuade the engineers to tell us about the downs as well as the ups, and to give us access to dramatic situations. For instance in our programme on the new London Underground Line, the tunnel was going just 20 metres under one of London's poshest swimming pools, in a famous London Pall Mall club, and there was a lot of fear that it would crack it. It became a very serious issue hitting the front page of British newspapers, as Big Ben too was threatend. There was a real fear that it might topple over, and indeed it did begin to move.

But having gained access we continued to keep it. This was to prove true in other stories, though some companies such as Airbus Industries proved particularly hard work. It was all a question of building relationships.

We had solved two of our problems: we had put drama on the front of the films to get a narrative and hook people to it, we had secondly persuaded our characters that they should either give us access or convey the excitement in interview, but we still had a third problem.

As already mentioned, with many of the projects we had the difficulty of showing things that did not yet exist. We could either work with a model, as in the case of the Millennium Tower, or we could make a 3D-computer animation to create the things we could not see. These could show at least the shape and size. This technique was also used to explain technical functioning

All the computer designs were based on a drawing board and a blueprint. In essence we would make a black-and-white 3D line drawing and align it with the existing filmed picture, which took days. Finally we used copious archive material to emphasise the drama through the films.

By mixing the drawing board idea to link everything together, and by mixing the graphics with life action, we hoped to explain in a very dynamic way how things worked and also how things would look if we had not seen them, such as the Jumbo jet and such as the comet and that little spacecraft travelling to it. We also created the whole landing on the comet, the robot drilling in to it, and so on.

Having achieved to finish the six half-hour programmes with a combination of personality, computer graphics and drama, we were ready to transmit them in mid-evening, 8 p.m. on BBC2. But we also needed to sell them to the audience. This was mainly done through a heavy on-screen promotion, broadcast about 20 times in the week preceding the first programme transmitted before all sorts of programmes, really trying to create an impact for the series. But this was not all. A few months before we also decided to go for a whole engineering week to kick *The Limit* series off. This season was called *Grand Designs*; it included programmes from many different BBC departments and was broadcast the week before *The Limit* started.

Grand Designs

The Unseen Hand explored further the theme of engineering and architecture – the tricky relationship between those that do all the work, and those that get all the credit. It was broadcast on the same night as *Tallest Tower*, the first programme from the *Limit* series, and built on ideas that appeared in that part.

There was a special programme in the history series *One Foot in the Past*, which revisited some of the creations of Isambard Kingdom Brunel, one of Britain's great engineering heroes. There were more contributions from very different parts of the BBC; from *Blue Peter*, a children's magazine programme to *The Money Programme*, an economics magazine programme produced by the Current Affairs department.

There was also a collection of 15 short films littered around the schedules called *Working Principles* and made by the departments of BBC Education. Each of these short films was designed to unravel one engineering principle: How wings fly, how ships float, how radar works, or the principles of gears or a suspension bridge. They were all made in a very glossy and imaginative way, but they also had to explain the principle in just 90 seconds.

Again I believe that the secret of their appeal was that they used just one character who functioned as a narrator und appeared at the end of the films. For instance, a falconer tells us about wings, a contortionist explains elasticity, a speed skier talks about streamlining and a hypnotist discusses oscillation. The thinking here was to show that engineering does not just matter to engineers.

Finally it was time to promote the whole *Grand Designs* season with its large collection of programmes on BBC2.

Not only were there television programmes and promotions, but we consulted for months with the many engineering institutes and organisations. BBC's Education Department was extremely helpful in this. With the British government's Department of Trade and Industry, a whole *Action for*

GRAND DESIGNS

A special season celebrating engineers and their remarkable achievements begins on BBC2 (November 1995)

Working Principles   15 short programmes starting *Monday, 6th November; 1995*

From the simplicity of a nutcracker and acoustic guitar, to the complexity of a suspension bridge or aeroplane, the built world depends on elementary machines – gears, levers, wheels, springs, screws, arches, wings, lenses and cantilevers. This stylish series of 90-second film shorts reveals the beauty and natural order of basic engineering principles.

Horizon: Nanotopia   *Monday, 13th November; 8 pm*

When microchips can get no smaller, is the end of technology in sight? Many believe that computer science and molecular engineering could yield the ultimate technology nanotechnology. This would allow us to take control of the physical world at the fundamental level of atoms and heralds a future generation of people for whom every possible wish can be granted – Nanotopia.

This film reveals advances in areas such as computing, microelectronics, optics and microscopy, that are bringing the dream of ultimate technology nearer to reality. Using specialist filming and stylish graphic creations, *Horizon* enters the world of the future where the molecular computer has evolved; a computer literally part of our world, linked to our very thoughts.

The Unseen Hand   *Tuesday, 14th November; 11.15 pm*

As one engineer put it: 'When an architect makes a mistake you can end up with a puddle on the floor. If the engineer makes a mistake, you might not have a floor.' Engineering affects all our lives, yet most of us are startlingly ignorant of the principles which underlie our material world. From the 19th century engineer entrepreneurs, through the heroes of the machine age, to the engineering aesthetic of the 1970s and 80s, this programme examines the relationship between the architect and engineer, exploring the myths which have grown up around each profession. It includes a history of Ove Arup and Partners – an engineering company responsible for some of the landmark buildings of the post-war period.

One Foot In The Past Special: Brunel   *Friday, 17th November; 8.30 pm*

Isambard Kingdom Brunel is famed for building the biggest, the strongest and the most daring structures of the 19th century. In this *One Foot In The Past* Special, Kirsty Wark, Gavin Stamp, Lucinda Lambton and Dan Cruickshank examine Brunel as engineer, visionary, and innovator, visiting his Box tunnel in Wiltshire, the Royal Albert Bridge linking Devon and Cornwall, and Paddington and Temple Meads railway stations.

Engineering Week was created with events around the country and lectures everywhere. This included back-up material, including booklets that were advertised on the television, which more than 10,000 people rang up and asked for. There was a booklet describing many carreer opportunities, and there was also a book on the subjects of *The Limit*.

In conjunction with this there were lectures around the country, and the engineering institutes created a major poster campaign on the London Underground, with huge advertisements in train stations. Altogether it amounted to an unprecedented campaign to raise public awareness of the engineering professions and the opportunities they offer.

The results of audience research[1]

As a follow-up, in-depth audience research was done for both our series *The Limit* and the entire season *Grand Designs*. As to *The Limit*, the key findings were:

- 5.8 million viewers saw at least one of the programmes, i.e. over 10 per cent of the population.
- Over 69 per cent of the viewing audience chose specially to watch the programme, which is far higher than normal, and far fewer watched just because the TV happened to be on.
- The series received a very positive reaction from viewers, in that:
  - 96 per cent thought it was a good idea for a series,
  - 94 per cent said that the programmes were well made, and
  - 88 per cent that the ideas were clearly explained – all far above average for an educational series
- The number of viewers who said that they had learnt something from the series was higher than usual: 71 per cent against 51 per cent for educational programmes as a whole.
- Many viewers also commented that the series had made them aware of the complexities and difficulties of engineering and their relevance to their everyday lives.

However, against all this positive appreciation of our achievements in popularising engineering with *The Limit*, we did have one big disappointment. Unfortunately, it seemed that we were preaching to the converted and the series had a particularly high proportion of male viewers. Although we had tried hard to find a big engineering project for *The Limit* run by a woman, we failed, and the whole series had a particularly masculine feel.

Of those who did not watch:

- 25 per cent said they did not have any idea that it was on, despite the heavy on-screen promotion.

1 A report of findings from a survey conducted with members of the IEE was compiled by Sarah Raven and Gill Hind, February 1996

- 22 per cent said they preferred watching something else on another channel.

Both are average figures for educational programming, but it was disappointing that we did not beat them. I believe that we did not partly because we lost the female audience, but also because despite the heavy on-screen promotion, newspaper coverage, which is all important with newspaper features in today´s competitive market, was very difficult to achieve with the engineers not being as popular as stars. You need famous names to hit front pages of the newspapers.

Finally, there is a proportion of viewers that just does not like engineering, especially in Britain. Of our sample who watched none of the programmes, 30 per cent said they were not interested in engineering, or it was not for them.

In fact, the audience research for the whole *Grand Designs* season engendered a similar response. For the whole season a large number of viewers said they did not watch either because they did not know about the season, or they did not like engineering. There was also a strong bias as to gender – 63 per cent were male viewers. In fact, twice as many female viewers gave their reason for not watching as 'I'm not interested in engineering'.

As well as our own BBC research, the Institute of Electrical Engineers also conducted a survey amongst its members. Unsurprisingly, 94 per cent of the respondents were male; more interestingly nearly half the professionals said they were unaware of the season, despite this massive collection of trails and promotional activities.

Conclusion

So in conclusion, we still need to find ways of achieving larger audiences for engineering, although these were the largest audiences we have ever gotten for the subject. We would like them to be larger still, perhaps by providing star engineering presenters, and so achieving the publicity which is so vital in today's competitive TV market. For we still need to attract a large audience that is not initially interested in engineering, and particularly to appeal to more women.

However, we believe that *The Limit* did manage to overcome some of the traditional problems in making series on engineering by:

- focusing on a key character and developing his or her personality at home as well as at work;
- providing narrative drive by following a particular project and emphasising what could go wrong;
- using novel computer graphics to generate objects that did not exist.

With the whole *Grand Designs* we were able to capitalise on *The Limit* with a major season, which achieved high audience and appreciation for engineering. Ultimately, this is what we call non-targeted educative programme making, and this is what we do in the Science Department, whilst BBC Education makes programmes themselves which are more targeted for specific audiences such as schools.

We found that our non-targeted programmes are actually used very much in educational institutes as well as by the people at home because they excite, they are good points to start off a debate, and they are entertaining at the same time.

And there is the important point: If you do not entertain your audiences, if you do not attract them using all your skill and the tricks of your trade, you lose them. Particularly in that multi-channel environment which we are hitting now, we have to make entertaining programmes that people want to watch. The difference between the Science Department and the General Documentary Department is that we – the Science Department – have an analytic, even a didactic approach as entertainers. We want to put some detail and some fact in, because we believe the audience finds that more entertaining, that is to say, they feel they are getting something extra from our programmes, they feel they are both entertained and informed.

Historically, the Education Department has sometimes been accused of being over-didactic, so not sufficiently entertaining. Now the Education Department's own programmes are changing, and it gets other, general, departments to make educational programmes, too; education on television is becoming more entertaining and achieving great success. We have all to compete for big audiences if we are to survive.

We believe that we can make information and learning entertaining, and this can encourage people to go off and find other information, stimulated by the programmes. Frequently programmes on business and on science from our Science Department, that were not made from an educational perspective, have been used in educational institutions just because they were entertaining and stimulating, because the teachers know that what people want from television is fun and then they can have a debate about it.

I believe that entertainment nowadays is terribly important for another reason. The audience is becoming more sophisticated, and children in particular are seeing and using an increasing amount of visually stimulating and entertaining material. The audience needs to be entertained by television if it is to be educated and informed.

Robert Thirkell *is currently Head of the BBC Science Department's Business and Technology Unit. He was executive producer of the BBC engineering season, with the series* Grand Designs *and* The Limit. *Previously he had been a producer on* Tomorrow's World, Horizon *and* QED *and produced business programmes, including* Troubleshooter *with Sir John Harvey Jones for which he won an award of the British Association for Film and Television for originality.*

With Socrates into Internet

or: How do humanistic traditions survive in the age of the new media?

Markus Nikel

Videosapere, *RAI, Rome*

Short introduction

Cultural television in Italy – what do the people get, what do they want? *Videosapere*, the department responsible for cultural and educational programmes at Italian state television, the RAI, produces a considerable number of short programmes broadcast almost daily, presented under the same general umbrella. Medical counselling programmes, art historical excursions to the most beautiful places in the country, literary criticism, a cultural talk show, and several other items, i.e. a wide range of programmes. The time slots – not exactly favourable for cultural programmes, but hardly unusual – are Monday to Friday from 10.30 a.m. to 1.30 p.m. on RAI 3 and after midnight for approximately half an hour on RAI 1.

I would like to introduce you to two programme sections in a little more detail: the *Enciclopedia multimediale delle scienze filosofiche* (Multimedia Encyclopædia of Philosophical Sciences) and the series *Media/Mente*. At first glance the two productions have little to do with each other with regard to contents and style. The *Enciclopedia* presents lectures by and interviews with eminent philosophers; *Media/Mente*, on the other hand, deals with issues concerning communication and new media. And yet the first impression is misleading.

The link between the two projects is the common fundamental idea that gave birth to them: solidly bridging the gap between our tradition of philosophy-cum-history of human thought and the post-modern world with its increasingly complex media structure. This relationship is known to be anything but straightforward. Critics reproach television, particularly the new media of course, for having little depth, basing their objections on matters of principle.

By contrast, the philological standards that are frequently the subject of academic discussion are generally of little use to programme-makers. Is it therefore impossible to indulge in profound philosophical thought on the screen?

We believe that philosophical thought and digitised forms of communication cannot be dismissed as being irreconcilable, that television and the new media can and must in fact be utilised to render philosophical reflection in its manifold forms also accessible to people who would not normally pick up a book of philosophy. If such a symbiosis should prove successful, humanistic tradition would be guaranteed a place of its own in television and in the new media as well as a general audience. That is precisely what we are aiming for.

The Multimedia Encyclopædia of Philosophical Sciences

The 'Multimedia Encyclopædia of Philosophical Sciences' was developed – and is still in the process of being developed – as a joint production of the RAI, the *Istituto Italiano per gli Studi Filosofici* and the *Istituto della Enciclopedia Italiana*. A number of important institutions – the General Assembly of the United Nations, the Council of Europe, the European Parliament, the President of Italy and, last but not least, the World Congress of Philosophers – have accepted to be patrons or have sponsored the project in other ways.[1]

Since 1986 over 400 of the most significant philosophers and scientists from all over the world have organised combinations of lectures and interviews for the *Enciclopedia*. To date, over 1,000 lectures on a vast variety of topics have been recorded in this way.

The concept – as indicated in the complicated title of the project – is 'multimedial'. In addition to television broadcasts the lectures constitute the basis for radio transmissions, video cassettes, books and computer programmes. Presently the editorial staff are working on a CD-ROM that will contain approximately 700 of the lectures in three different languages as well as an anthology of selected original texts, a wealth of pictorial material and a dictionary of philosophy. As from 1997 the whole of the *Enciclopedia*, if everything goes according to plan, will be accessible in Internet.

What is special about the form of multimedia approach we have adopted? Specific types of media are frequently referred to in the usual discussion on multimedia forms of communication, which combine texts, images, music etc., as in the case of the CD-ROM. Closer inspection, however, reveals that they bear only the characteristics of 'mono'-mediality: various elements are combined to form one product – in one medium. This does not really represent anything new: traditional television, even a book are multimedial in this sense.

What we want, however, is a movement in the opposite direction. Renato Parascandolo, who developed the basic concept of the project a good ten years ago and who has been the dynamic, dedicated director of

---

1 In December 1996 UNESCO became a patron of the Multimedial Encyclopædia of Philosophical Sciences. In connection with this exceptional honour it was agreed that the organisation will ensure that the encyclopædia be distributed throughout all its member countries. This will be carried out in Kooperation with the respective broadcasting stations. So far a coproduction contract has been concluded with Korean Television. Negotiations are also being conducted with the Japanese Broadcasting Corporation.

the Encyclopædia project ever since, prefers to use metaphors from the field of physics. He sets his 'centrifugal' concept of 'multimediality' against conventional 'centripetal forces'. What does this mean in concrete terms? We have a basic component – namely the interview-lectures: we want to propagate their contents in as many forms as possible. Anyone who has seen Popper on television can read further literature on the topics he discusses; soon he or she will be able to consult a CD-ROM. In the foreseeable future he or she will also be able to pursue a possibly newly-discovered interest in philosophy in Internet. Without any exaggeration, in my opinion, this is the only genuine form of multimedia technology. In any event, this is the way we wish to achieve our aim of giving as many people as possible an understanding of classical philosophical ideas.[2]

This concept does of course come to bear on the style and structure of the interviews. The intention to distribute simultaneously the results of the recording visually, in purely audial form and as text must be taken into account in the planning stages – in the script and the directing. (See Appendix to this chapter on pp. 185–86.)

Media/Mente

How is it possible to create space in the post-modern media structure for philosophical reflection, for humanistic traditions, for transmitting so-called refined culture via the mass media? *Media/Mente* approaches the problem from the other end: the series was originally based on the idea that the new media opportunities must be analysed and didactically presented if they are to be made optimal use of by the audience.

The editorship of *Media/Mente* looks like this:

- '*Media/Mente* tackles the problems of modern communication. The programme is broadcast from a studio equipped with the latest technology. The programme series analyses the effects of new technological achievements on our social, economic, political, cultural and linguistic order.
- The world of communication has to grapple with two forms of prejudice: on the one hand, the advocates of apocalyptic visions tend to demonise appliances and technologies, on the other, the effects of the new media are played down on the pretence that people can compensate for the loss of intelligent, person-to-person communication by way of purchasing new communication devices. The aim of the series is to reveal the complexity of the communication world with all its hues, forgoing the black-and-white division of good and bad.

2 Since January 1997 the Department for Culture and Educational Television at RAI - it is also in charge of the encyclopædia project - has been called *RAI Educational multimecliale*. *Educational multimediale* will place emphasis on producing high-quality programmes in the area of culture and education which from the beginning are conceived not only for television but other media as well. This is in keeping with the term developed by Renato Parascandolo of a 'centrifugal multimediality'.

- *Media/Mente* is a telematic programme. It is equipped with a digital library at the disposal of the Internet user, constantly fed with the latest data. Over a hundred interviews featuring mass-communication experts, managers, scientists, computer scientists and telecommunications experts are accessible – both in the original language and in Italian.
- The 'home page' of *Media/Mente* (http://www.uni.net/mediamente) also contains the broadcasting sequence, the scripts and the most significant shots in the TV programmes, creating the opportunity for lively interaction between TV programmes and the telematic edition.
- *Media/Mente* can provide other RAI editorial staff teams with immediate access to its on-line services.
- The RAI *Videosapere* 'laboratory' offers the facility of high-speed surfing in Internet cyberspace. The catalogues of internationally significant libraries and important scientific publications are extremely easy to be accessed. The video-telephones and computer-video conference equipment enable communication with various parts of the globe. So-called multimedia workstations give a wide range of user groups the opportunity to utilise the same data, documents, photos and television images simultaneously. 120 satellite channels from five continents can be received, and of course the important international press agencies are subscribed to. A wide selection of CD-ROMs and CD-Is are also available in the laboratory.'

Here it is possible to observe work in progress: the directing, the editorship and the cutting tables, the whole studio installations are 'visible' even during programme broadcasting, showing how a television programme comes to life.

The studio also boasts quite a few 'antiques', which can also be admired at the RAI Museum in Turin: television cameras from the 1950s in perfect working order; the first experimental television sets from the 1930s; wirelesses designed by G. Marconi as well as telefax appliances from the last century.

A real novelty is View Points, i.e. television cameras mounted in various places all over the world, functioning roughly like the telescope on the Pincio. When the owner of a video-telephone dials a certain number, he can operate these cameras by remote-control. He can produce a long shot of Chicago and watch what is happening at the same time in a certain street in Tokyo. He can get a close-up of a balloon seller at work in Oslo and simultaneously admire the summit of the Cortina. By means of this technology it is possible to show on our studio screens what is going on in several parts of the globe at one and the same time.

Soundly researched data and analyses, exact descriptions of the actual state of things and philosophers', scholars' and scientists' well-founded opinions constitute the basis of *Media/Mente*.

The viewers are not expected to adopt a passive stance in a debate. The aim is to encourage them to reflect and draw their own conclusions from the data submitted. In any case *Media/Mente* requires critical and attentive viewers. The intention is to ask questions, to raise doubts, to destroy clichés and not to propagate pre-coded answers. The aim is a new culture of communication in such decisive issues as the economic equilibrium of the world, national identity, mother tongue, private life, forms of democracy, our way of thinking, leisure time activities, our culture as well as our children's needs and behaviour. The opportunities offered by the new media must be used in this process.

To enable the viewers to participate the appliances installed in the studio are activated. At the end of the broadcast the viewers can transmit via Internet, fax or automatic answering machine their opinions to our editor-

---

Topics for *Media/Mente*

- Interaction. How does it come about and with whom? (Limits of interaction)
- Kill a game? (Violence and creativity in video games)
- Every dream into the Net? (Perspectives and problems of Internet)
- Friends and yet strangers? (E-mail and electronic conversation)
- Easier learning? (Hypertext, CD-ROM, CD-I, data banks)
- Will we talk to the television?
  (Video-on-Demand – other forms of interaction with television)
- Never again outside the home? (Teleshopping, telebanking and other services)
- Money in the Net? (Trade and Marketing)
- Are technologies sexless? (Sex differences between computer science and telematics)
- Are there any secrets left? (Private life and access facilities)
- Anarchists or criminals? (Hackers and cyberpunks)
- Is there ever any end to learning? (Lifelong learning)
- Does democracy come from the screen?
  (The distribution of power in the information society)
- Who controls the media?
  (The structure of the system and the programme makers' responsibility)
- Excuse me, where's the teacher?
  (Modern technologies and their relationship with the teacher)
- At home – at work (Thoughts on 'Teleworking')
- What do the polls really tell us? (The inaccuracy of distance polls)
- Consuming wears you out. (Media consumption seen as 'hard work')
- Is 'faster' the same as 'better'? (Speed – Quality)
- Has reality ceased to exist? (The new scenarios of virtual reality)
- Aren't they all the same – thanks to satellite?
  (The problem of world-wide information distribution)
- Listening is fine – watching is better? (Words-images)
- In search of a lost memory? (Wear-and-tear of data carriers and ageing of hardware)
- Where is my mother country? (The loss of national identity)
- Will the computer think of it? (The borders of artificial intelligence)

ial staff who will go on to evaluate their response. Should a programme have aroused the viewers' interest, the Internet users among them can continue to discuss it. The box on page 182 contains examples of issues *Media/Mente* deals with.

Prejudice and false expectations that are rampant everywhere at the moment and wreak havoc in the discussions on the issues concerned must be unearthed and removed. But the great opportunities inherent in the new media must be interpreted as such and conveyed to a wide audience. *Media/Mente* endeavours to make an active contribution – with its five-minute broadcasts every day and twenty-minute evening edition on Wednesday. The facts are presented in an easily comprehensible form. Experts are asked questions in the interviews. Via Internet all the texts of the interviews, the scripts of the individual episodes can be consulted and background information also obtained.

Concluding remarks

What do the Italians get? What do they want? I have already said a number of things about the first question but nothing at all about the second? Our viewing figures are not exactly fantastic, also due to extremely unfortunate time slots, of course. In the morning we have a market segment averaging 2 to 3 per cent, in the evening we have about 10 per cent, which has been known to rise to as high as 18 per cent.

But the *Enciclopedia* also reaches people outside the television broadcasting framework as a result of the multimedia concept. Italian school classes watch Gadamer's lectures in their philosophy lessons and use our computer programme. The *Enciclopedia* is even used in seminars at Italian universities. The *Media/Mente* editorial staff, who organise a weekly quiz titled 'Treasure Hunt' – the participants being required to research a given topic in Internet – have reported a high number of E-mails from their viewers.

But can viewing figures really be a criterion to judge successful culture work on television? This congress has two questions in its title: the viewers' wishes and what is actually offered. Interestingly enough, a third question is missing, which seems to me to be the most important: What *are* the people *supposed* to see?

Ever since people have thought about education, it has been precisely this question, namely which educational approach should be adopted and which values should be instilled, that has been the main problem. I do not believe that viewing figures help us today to answer this question. The answers, fortunately, can of course take on many different colours. Allow me to introduce one opportunity we have envisaged ourselves.

At the RAI we are in the process of realising new projects in this direction. I myself work on the editorial staff of *Mondo 3* (World 3); the choice of the name was influenced by Karl Popper's designation for the ontological field of cultural products. We wish to create a large virtual museum in Internet containing the most significant works of the culture of mankind and have asked 40 writers, philosophers, scientists and artists from all over the world – including several Nobel Prize winners – to select these works for us, which may be written text, pictures, films, music or something completely different. I think that the leitmotif connecting this new project with my presentation is clear.

Markus Nikel, *M.A., born in Schwäbisch Hall, studied Philosophy, General Linguistics, Romance Studies and Old Indic Philology in Freiburg, Hamburg, Naples and Rome; in 1993/4 he was on the staff of the dpa archives in Hamburg; since early 1995 he has been a scientific advisor to the Enciclopedia multimediale delle scienze filosofiche and on the editorial staff of the project Mondo 3 in the culture department (editorial office Videosapere) of Italian state television, the RAI in Rome. He is also co-editor of the 'Journal for European Psychoanalysis', Rome/New York; reader and translator of the cultural journal 'Lettera internazionale' and contributor to the weekly journal 'In rete', Rome.*

Appendix: Multi-Media Encyclopædia of the Philosophical Sciences[3]

The structure of the Opus

This Opus has been structured in a multimedia fashion and produced in differing versions, each corresponding to the specific characteristics of the relative diffusion media (e.g. TV, radio, videotapes, videodisks, cassettes, computer software, books). This inter-media synergism opens the way to new modalities of knowledge acquisition. If people had made full use of the early potential in movie technology fifty years ago and visually recorded lectures by Einstein, Freud, Husserl, Heidegger, Croce, and Wittengenstein, they would have rendered a priceless service for future generations. However, perhaps the time was not ripe back then. Today it is possible to preserve the teaching of the great living masters for future listening and learning. In addition, the multimedia nature of communication and the wealth of available means of expression nowadays ensure active end-user involvement.

Together with textbooks and anthologies of the works of philosophy, precious tools are now available to anyone wishing to study philosophy. Their range begins with the videotapes of lectures delivered by renowned scholars from all over the world, and goes all the way to a computer-based interactive version of the Opus with the complete and multilingual texts of the original lectures, a computerized dictionary of philosophy, an analytical concept index for guided visits into the history of thought, and an iconographical file of portraits and places where such thought blossomed; and all of this in one and the same multimedia unit. In addition, there are the programmes for radio and TV (air wave, satellite, cable broadcasting).

---

3 Excerpt from: Multi-Media Encyclopædia of the Philosophical Sciences. Rom: RAI Dipartimento Scuola Educazione et al. 1992; pp. 13–14.

In order to set the indispensable bases that render the Opus as complete as possible, an international committee of experts drew up a topic map which is divided into two parts: the History of Philosophy and the Problem of Philosophy. This map serves as a guide to the contents and to the transversal itineraries.

The constituent units of the Opus (one thousand upon completion) are the lecture-interviews with eminent international scholars. The lecture-interview format with the interviewer off stage but in line with the camera creates an immediate visual relationship between the scholar and the individual viewer. In this way the philosophers become the true protagonists of the Opus.

The Multi-Media Encyclopædia of the Philosophical Sciences was begun in 1988 and will be completed in 1997.

The Opus on Videotapes and Videodisks

These are editions with features which also differ in formal terms and correspond to diversified levels of indepth study and to distinct itineraries: for those approaching the history of philosophical thought for the first time; for those who have studied philosophy in school; for university students and scholars.

At present the titles are:
- The Roots of European Philosophy
- Philosophy and Current Issues
- The Masters of Thought
- The Origins of Thought in the World
- The Universe of Knowledge

They are available on videotapes and, in the future, will be available on videodisks. Each videotape is produced in an international edition suited for dubbing or subtitles into other languages as required.

The Series for TV broadcasting by RAIDSE

The TV version of the Opus takes into consideration the special features of the diffusion medium and seeks to affirm the presence of high level culture and philosophy in the mass media which are looked upon as essential tools for civic growth and development. In an effort to experiment a model of TV use implying an active or thinking participation on the part of viewers, a series of episodes are broadcast which cover the entire range of the Department for School and Education's regular programming. The purpose of the episodes is not merely didactic in nature; they serve as an introduction to the problems inherent in every quest undertaken in the realm of human thought.

The TV series via RAISAT Satellite

The prerogative of satellite TV is its international, planetary nature. Satellites constitute the most developed manifestation of the integration underway between nations. As a result of its resolutely international character the Multi-Media Encyclopædia of the Philosophical Sciences is in perfect harmony with this new means of communication. The RAISAT Educational programmes first began regular broadcasts in November 1990 and they offer full-length, original language versions of the interview-lectures delivered by the great protagonists of philosophy and the contemporary sciences. As a result of satellite technology, the outstanding feature of these programmes is the fact that they can be broadcast in three languages at the same time.

Radio

This version is quite similar to the one for TV, but will be broadcast daily and provides for a systematic and indepth presentation of the subjects. In addition to the interview-lectures, the radio programmes will also include the reading of philosophical works, discussions among philosophers of different schools, and direct dialogue between the editors of the Multi-Media Encyclopædia and listeners.

Audiocassettes

The Opus on cassettes is based on the same principle behind the videotape version and offers an analogous programme which, however, is more directly didactic-oriented. It is especially intended to be used as a learning tool for secondary school and university students, but does not exclude the general public from the learning process. A series of this version is devoted to the reading of the most important philosophical texts of all times. Based on the sound medium so widespread among young people, this series is also easily accessible due to the low cost.

The interactive version of the Opus for computers

This interactive version of the Opus employs leading edge computer technology so the material can be consulted in a dynamic and effective way. Equipped with a personal computer, the 'reader' can consult the list of themes, the single items, and the videotapes of each series in the Multi-Media Encyclopædia, follow the suggested itineraries (guided visits) according to his own interests, use an analytical index to explore a complex network of correlations between the various subjects, and query the system to find out where the Opus deals with topics of interest to him. In addition, by using texts, sounds, stills, and images in motion, all blended with a single hypermedia application, the «reader» can construct his own version of the Multi-Media Encyclopædia.

Books and manuels

With its vast programme the Multi-Media Encyclopædia of the Philosophical Sciences in no way seeks to demean the importance of the printed word, and neither claims nor tries to replace it. Books and the printed page retain their full and complete value, and will always be the privileged medium for the transmission of knowledge, especially in the world of philosophy. Hence the linkage with the Italian Encyclopædia Institute; for the series The Roots of European Philosophy, Treccani is publishing monographic volumes on philosophers which are coupled with each videotape in the programme.

6: The Relevance of Educational Broadcasting

Educational television?
Let's change the subject
Statements of the members
of a discussion panel

Karen Brown
Channel 4, UK

In a multi-media world, educational broadcasters have to ask themselves 'Are we becoming dinosaurs?' Are there now more effective ways of communicating insight and understanding to people? In my view the answer is a very emphatic NO, providing we adopt certain principles.

The viewer at home will come to the television screen out of choice, and the first question for educators should be 'What do viewers want to watch?' Television producers have to win their audiences through well made, bold, imaginative and appealing programmes. It is not a sin for an educational programme to be popular. If the subject matter is important, all the more reason for people to see it. But as the Roman philosopher Seneca said two thousand years ago: 'What we say should be of use, not just entertaining.'

To survive, educational broadcasters must make the best use of the unique qualities of television rather than trying to compete with other media which may be more appropriate for certain educational purposes.

Television's best attributes are that it is up to the minute and can keep people informed; it offers a window on the world; it can bring an element of surprise into people's homes; and it gives pleasure. It is a brillant source of inspiration, not so good at instruction. Detailed information is better served up through another supporting medium. Television can also reach out to all sections of society – it has the potential to be inclusive.

Programme makers need to search out and nourish certain human appetites – curiosity, a sense of fun and play, and the power to reason. The best educational television leaves a space for the viewer to think, to be provoked, to answer back, to argue with the television set and to discuss matters with other viewers.

Educators should not ignore opportunities to extend the educational potential of television programmes through the theming of programmes, working with other agencies, written and audio support, CD-ROMs, sell through videos and so on.

In the densely packed media world, new strategies for achieving visibility and impact for educational programmes have to be developed.

Working with other media – newspapers, specialist magazines, or radio – can help. Picking on themes raised by feature films and soaps and commissioning supporting programmes around them can achieve a much greater level of attention.

In the UK educational programmes are going through a bright period. More programmes are being watched by more viewers across a more varied range of topics, and more of these programmes are transmitted in peak time. The audience repays the broadcaster with an ever more developed sense of curiosity and an expectation that television can and should teach them things they do not know. As broadcasters we should not betray that trust.

So, returning to the topic of our discussion with its initial question 'Educational Television? Let's Change the Subject', I say 'Let's Not'.

Karen Brown *joined Channel 4 in 1987 to work in the News and Current Affairs Department. In 1992 she became Commissioning Editor for Education, responsible for developing Channel 4's educational strategy including its programme support, and for commissioning campaigns. The output ranged from philosophy to health, and from food to archaeology, including the Basel Prize winning Time Team. She recently became Controller of Factual Programmes with overall responsibility for approximately 35 per cent of Channel 4's output.*

Ulla Martikainen-Florath
YLE, Helsinki

Here are five theses about educational television from a Finnish point of view:

1. *The national situation defines the challenges posed to educational television.*

The public service television stations throughout Europe face more or less the same challenge: the loss of their monopoly, the ever-increasing supply of commercial, entertainment-oriented programming, the evolvement of a multichannel environment and the segmentation of their audiences. However, the situation of educational television varies from country to country.

My vision of educational television arises from the situation in Finland. The public service duties of the Finnish Broadcasting Company are defined in a law that came into force in 1994. This law demands among other things that television and radio programming in Finland should 'support the people's studies'. This requires a very pragmatic basis for educational programming.

The framework of our activities is also influenced by the high unemployment rate Finland has to face these days. One of the many attempts to solve the problem has been to increase the supply of adult education. Finland is a country with rather long distances and low population density.

Therefore, offering the people distance training and learning possibilities is seen as one way of meeting the growing demand for adult education. Television is still the information highway that reaches everybody and can be reached by everybody. So there is a social need for new ideas about television as a medium for distance education in Finland.

In terms of population, Finland is a small country that has opted for a high level of education and the swift development of an information society as her strategy for survival. Finland has the highest density of mobile phones and Internet connections per capita in the world. A public service broadcasting system also has to face these challenges.

2. Public service broadcasting companies need educational programmes to justify their existence, but only satisfied customers can secure their future.

It is my belief that public service broadcasting companies will have a stronger and stronger need for educational programmes in order to legitimise themselves. With the audiences splitting up into smaller and smaller segments, the importance of programmes that serve special target groups with specific needs is increasing. The future of educational television can not be secured by mechanically reiterating their legal legitimacy. Real success can only be based on the dialogue with the audience, the viewer-friendliness of the programmes and a customer-oriented overall approach.

Educational programmes do not necessarily need to find a broad mass audience, but they have to be of crucial importance for their own target groups. They have to become proprietary products creating a real demand. Of course efficient marketing plays an important role here, too. We cannot just produce good programmes. We also have to know how to promote them.

3. The digitalisation of television and the multimedia-networks offer more opportunities than threats to educational television .

Both the quality of our programmes and their availability create satisfied customers. For the time being educational programmes are broadcast mostly at periods that are difficult for the viewers. The digital thematic channels offer educational television the opportunity to provide our audiences with programming at the best possible times.

The biggest shortcomings of broadcast educational television with regard to the use of programmes in educational institutions are the dependancy on fixed broadcasting times and the lack of interactivity. In this respect broadband digital information networks are a lot more powerful than the traditional broadcast supply. For the future of school television, for example, it would be very important to find new interactive programme types and create means of distribution such as Video-on-Demand.

Within the European Union there is a strong interest in developing distance learning via information networks, but the experiments being made right now still lack truly multimedial content. As producers of such content the public service broadcasting companies are unsurpassable – for the time being, that is. In the future the programmes produced by us can be tailor-made for use with distribution channels, and the user interface can be a digital television set or a personal computer. Educational television should be developing interactive multimedia production know-how regardless of the fact that traditional television programmes are our main product.

4. National and international networking are prerequisites for survival.

It is really surprising that over the years so few large-scale and high-quality international educational coproductions have been produced. While many other businesses have to search for cooperation partners, the European Broadcasting Union has been providing a cooperative framework for educational broadcasting for many years. Now is about the last chance to use this platform in order to bring television series of high educational value to Europe's television screens.

Also, on a national level educational television needs a network of cooperation. We have just started to broadcast programmes for our TV Open University. These programmes are planned in close cooperation with our country's universities and they are a part of their curriculum. However, we always emphasise the fact that the Open University programmes have to be 'good television' rather than simply teaching videos or videotaped lectures.

We are a producer of interactive on- and off-line multimedia, and our partners can be commercial publishers, telecommunication operators, software producers as well as educational and training institutions. This interaction furthers the rise of new skills and know-how for all partners involved.

5. Riding three horses at the same time requires very special skills.

Our own educational television department's survival strategy these days is riding three horses at the same time:

- We want to offer 'edutainment' programmes that attract a larger audience on our main television channel at an evening viewing time. These programmes have to provide the viewers with in-depth information, life-management skills and positive learning experiences. Also, in this field there is a need for high quality international co-production series.
- A part of our educational broadcasting activities offers an open, diversified distance learning channel to the learners. The programmes and the 'learning entities' they follow are planned and implemented in close cooperation with the educational field.
- We are involved in the development of the digital age as producers of interactive multimedia, creating new service concepts and products.

191

Riding three horses at the same time requires the skills of a circus artist. Whether Finland's educational television will manage this feat remains to be seen. Maybe we shall fall off, maybe we shall have to change riders, maybe we shall have to change horses, maybe we shall have to change the arena – the future will show.

Ulla Martikainen-Florath, *MA, is Head of Educational Programmes/ Television 1 at the Finnish Broadcasting Company YLE since 1994, a department with 40 collaborators. Previous to her appointment, she was Head of Educational Services for YLE. From 1981-1991 she worked as Managing Editor at Otava Publishing Company. Before this she worked in different teaching occupations at high schools and universities. She has published various books for German language training.*

Ingo Hermann
Zweites Deutsches Fernsehen (ZDF), Mainz

Anyone wanting to reach an audience with television programmes needs a *concept* with regard to form and content. And he needs a *strategy* for the complicated process of offering the audience something that it accepts. So let us talk about the concept and the strategy. Part of both of these, of the concept as well, is the *image*. And part of both is the *overall situation* which the programme suppliers tend to reduce to the market situation.

On the *overall situation* of television: Television in Europe is in the process of making its programmes infantile (following the example of America?) to an ever greater extent, especially in the prime time. Above all, the programme presentation and the trailers follow a trend towards speculatively humouring the audience, which then continues even into the arrangement of the news broadcasts. This trend (which I can only point out here, but not describe or prove) cannot be stopped with cultural niches in the main programme, with cultural programmes or thematic channels. Anyone still preferring to understand television basically as a cultural organisation rather than a market event must be worried about the whole phenomenon of television as soon as there is talk of television's cultural or educational remit.

Part of the overall situation of television is the upheaval in the system which can be indicated by the key word digitalisation. This upheaval calls for changeovers and alterations in almost all areas of television operations. Digitalisation cannot simply be added to the others as a new technology. But, rather, it radically changes everything we have known up to now. When Martin Heidegger or Walter Benjamin thought about what changes the invention of the typewriter would bring about for creativity and communication, one can begin to realise what considerations we are forced to undertake in view of the new electronic media: the new media are revolutionising not only technology, but the entire conditions of possible life schemes for the next few generations.

On the *concept*: The concept of education and upbringing – generally and in the medium of television – is also part of what has to be disposed of in our thinking. I shall here attempt a partial approach by means of subjective comments. I am convinced that the term education, especially in adult education, is less and less useful and can only be retained in the strictly pedagogical sense, in the true sense of the word. The interactive possibilities of use within a worldwide network integrating different media rule out any pedagogising of the learning and education process. The borders between childhood, adolescence and adulthood are breaking down. Guidance in the individual's life is initially only carried out by 'pedagogues', but is then soon replaced by complex interactive autonomy. (I am disregarding here the problem of external guidance by computer programmes.)

The term 'lifelong learning' is also turning into a banality in the face of media reality. What used to be understood as learning or as learning for life will tomorrow be the daily and hourly business of informing. Then, during the so-called training, a set of cultural techniques or educational material will not be learnt and made available for the whole of one's life. The networking and constant change in everything will force people, in every case anew, to make sure of the particular state of information and not to understand this as a learning process but as an utterance of life. The idea that a person is born, brought up, taught, trained and then released into life in which all he has to do is to make do and function with what he has learnt has long been abandoned. However, the substitute term of lifelong learning or of adult education has replaced it. This perpetuation of the pedagogical approach is obsolete.

A decline in educational programmes on television corresponds to the 'end of education'. That there are still successful school television broadcasts or course programmes in quite a few European countries is not a counter argument, because these endeavours will, in the long term, be unable to escape the changes. The combination of television and the interactive media, from the CD-ROM to the Internet, will almost automatically change the attitude and the 'user surface' of the medium of television.

On the *strategy* of cultural television: If the leading forces of cultural television fail to join in making the changes in the communication society they will sink into a niche existence and become ineffective. Talking in metaphors: We must not cling to oil, while solar energy can already be used; we must not hold up the flag of nostalgia, while the ship is sinking; we should not knit by hand, while millions of pullovers are needed; we should not plant flowers in the ghetto front garden of educational television; we should stop calling for educational remits and instead culturally challenge television as a whole. I would therefore prefer to talk of communication culture instead of education, because this term replaces the passive viewer with the user's active opportunities.

Considerations of educational policies (like Peter von Rüden's) quite rightly point out the problem of the 'education divide' and ask whether television only makes the educated more educated with its efforts to educate, but provides the uneducated with mindless entertainment and thus only stultifies them even further. The question is important and decisive for the future of our society. The answer of the educational concept on the ZDF is unequivocal: after educational and cultural programmes did not seem to stand a chance, in spite of the fairly convenient transmission times, as a result of a development I do not want to comment on here, which resulted in a steady decline in the quantitative acceptance, the study programmes (chemistry and the like) and the educational programmes were discontinued as programme forms. They were replaced by new programme forms at the best transmission time (7:30 on Sunday evenings) and were no longer designated as educational programmes, but they nevertheless met the requirement for cultural communication: broadcasts on archaeological and historical material, reports from the natural sciences, information from research and technology (e.g. *Terra X, Sphinx, Wunderbare Welt, Knoff-hoff-Show*). These programmes, by their time and their lavish presentation alone, reach an audience which extends far beyond the circle of those formally interested in education. In this way more is being done in my opinion to solve the problem of the education divide than by efforts in the wrong place, however ingenious they may be.

The demand for high audience ratings is being abused if it is believed that what the programme offers has to become increasingly shallow. Certainly, a station, a broadcast, has to seek its audience. But this does not involve opening a discount shop and trying out every way of toadying to the viewers. With self-respect and self-confidence we should only give the public a choice of what we ourselves consider good. It is cynical to offer something which you yourself despise. That the wishes and needs of the public provide a feedback for the image of yourself must be considered as obvious as it is professional.

The future perspectives associated with these thoughts are not complete without a self-critical look at our readiness to think over anew the situation of the programme-makers and those in positions of responsibility. Are we prepared to accept digitalisation and to translate the new opportunities into the programme work? Are we in a position to adapt ourselves to the digitalised – and that means interactive – user? Are we capable of also opening up new subjects with the new ways? Can we develop new definitions of aims and success without taking leave of the old ideals of journalistic ethics?

Ingo Hermann, *Doctor of Theology, has been ZDF Departmental Head 1969-1989. Among many others, he has been in charge of the ZDF series* Zeugen des Jahrhunderts *(Witnesses of the Century) and has collaborated on the series* Sphinx *since 1994. For his work he obtained a German Journalists' Prize and various Adolf Grimme Prizes. He has published numerous books, contributions to radio and television, newspapers and magazine articles on matters relating to theology, education and broadcasting policies. He also teaches at the Universities of Frankfurt and Mainz.*

Hans Paukens

Adolf Grimme Institut, Marl

To talk about educational television these days seems to strike one as rather anachronistic in view of the debate about telecommunications and multimedia. If one considers the situation of the media or broadcasting in 1996 one cannot help noticing that the development has progressed so far – concerning both the programme and economics – that education with a place of its own in the programme now has only marginal significance or none at all. In fierce polemical debates, the educational institutions and their representatives repeatedly refer to broadcasting legislation, which requires not only the public service broadcasting corporations but also the private broadcasting companies to place in their programmes 'considerable proportions of information, education, counselling and entertainment'. Even if the German Federal Constitutional Court no longer explicitly resorted to the term education in its ruling in November 1989, in which it undertook to determine the duties and position of public service and private broadcasting, but preferred to speak about 'cultural responsibility', the requirement to safeguard education as a programme remit remains intact in broadcasting law.

When we now additionally discover that the public apparently has only little interest in broadcasts which programme-makers label educationally relevant, we have to start considering educational programmes from other angles. Apparently the viewers refuse to be told what education is, when and where they have to educate themselves or there is something to be learnt. But at the same time we also notice that the public is very interested in well-made documentaries, in interesting feature films. Do programmes of this kind have anything to do with education, with learning? Yes, I think they do.

Not only the interest in strands or series like *Terra X, Universum* etc, but also the print runs of non-fiction books and the number of people going to museums and concerts indicate cultural interest and a need for education and learning. There is little interest in 'pedagogised'[1] events to administer education paternalistically.

On the other hand, educational programmes on television are certainly some of the services still expected by many people from broadcasting. Mixing the terms culture and education indicates, however, a problem, namely the problem of categorising. Even though it is still relatively simple to formally allocate school broadcasts and language teaching programmes to a programme category called 'Education', these programmes occasionally – I restrict this, however – have a connection to sectors of the institutionalised education system. When taking a look at the programme previews or listening and looking at the programmes, it is difficult to draw

---

1   This word is coined to describe an educational broadcast in a formal teaching environment, e.g. a classroom with a teacher facing the class, or television audience. (Translator)

the dividing line. The distinction between education and information very quickly disappears, and even differentiating between them and the programme remit Entertainment can, in some cases, no longer be upheld. But if, according to the media researcher Müller-Sachse, no clear distinction is made between the educational function and the other functions of television, then there is a danger that the demand 'education for all' turns into a statement of principle 'everything is education'. One may regret this development, but the decision as to whether something offered by the media is useful for education or not, isn't this up to the listener and viewer or reader? Concepts of education on television are, as a rule, clearly and emphatically related to a user interested in education, to viewers who arrange and organise their learning opportunities and media mix themselves according to their individual requirements in each case. Viewers, by the way, who are highly motivated and interested.

While one position laments the disappearance of education from the programme, voices have been heard in the last few years which go hand in hand with and support the withdrawal of the broadcasting stations from the 'educational sector' by an attack and which see wirepullers for popular education at work in television and in the demands for educational policies which are made on the mass media. Barbara Sichtermann wrote in *Die Zeit* in November 1993 about the 'mania of the old elites for education'. It seems as if scientists, cultural critics and journalists are taking their leave of considerations of and demands for educational policies and want to participate in the attraction and prosperity of the media branch. Criticism of television as a 'teaching authority', as an institution, which functions according to the 'pedagogic principle' or to the perception of an 'extensive 'pedagogisation' of public service television', is aimed at popularisation, ties television entirely to the taste of the masses, tries to reconcile media criticism with a medium that in recent years has got back on even keel – got back to entertainment. In the meantime there are also representatives, especially in educational science, – who is surprised by that? – who are trying to establish a fresh approach to the subject of education and television and who confirm the thesis of media criticism presented above.

And so television as a 'pedagogic organisation' is – from the point of view of educational science – turned into something positive. Jochen Kade, an educational scientist at Frankfurt University, also states that television, like other mass media as well, is pedagogised to a high degree – adding that this is, however, not how educationalists and politicians responsible for education see this. In crime series like *Tatort* or *Polizeiruf 110*, in talkshows like *Boulevard Bio*, *Talk im Turm* or *Schreinemakers live* the educationalist finds pedagogical endeavours and pedagogical situations. And television critics agree with the science of education, by stating, like, for example, Werner Burkhard, on Monday, 9th April 1996, on the media page of the *Süddeutsche Zeitung* at the conclusion of his commentary on *Pretty Woman*: 'Note: whoever wants to learn, will always learn something'. But what conclusion must be drawn from this? Apparently it is a matter of learning and not of education here, in other words television for learning and not television for education.

However one may assess the description of the 'pedagogisation' of television, it remains for me to state: Classic educational television, which conceived education according to didactic premises, has had its day. The audience is not reached by imputing situations of educational teaching or communication to the conceiving and planning of television productions. Classic educational television or, rather, course or teaching programmes, was – unlike pure information programmes – distinguished by imparting information or even knowledge in a pedagogically structured form and wanting to produce connections to serve educational purposes. When we talk about educational television today, it seems appropriate to me to change the angle from which we look at it.

It is a question of beginning with the audience, the viewers, and thinking about when, where and also how educational processes take place on television, with which strategies educational processes are carried out, and how, for example, the viewer creates a relationship between the subjects dealt with and content and his environment and plans for life. It follows from the concept of the learning processes that it is every individual's decision whether he chooses to accept a programme, with how much concentration and continuity he relates to it and what he actually learns in the end. Such a concept supposes a learning ability of the human being which calls for methodical competence, otherwise every casual offer of education would disappear in the disordered plethora of programmes.

In the last few years television has also undergone a change in function or has been forced to accept a loss of function in the ensemble of the mass media. Ever more programmes offering information, guidance, culture and education in all programme genres, and particularly in the genre channels that are to be expected, are as a rule used by an audience interested in education and culture, in the same way as computers, CDs, audio and video cassettes, theatres, museums, libraries and adult education centres. That education and learning are becoming more individual and flexible – as part of the tendencies towards individualisation and partitioning in society – is expressed in, among other things, the fact that a selection from the large ensemble of institutionalised and non-institutionalised educational offers can be made and an individual learning programme can be put together depending on interests, budgets, methodical competence, involvement and the degree of commitment and that this is apparently being done when knowledge is acquired in about 700 hours a year individually and flexibly with regard to time. The television programme is used in the same way as literature, books, magazines or newspapers, films and theatre. It seems as if the viewers no longer require 'didacticised'[2] television any more, just as they no longer need the school textbook after leaving school.

2   Similar to 'pedagogised' above. (Translator)

If one considers the interests of the audience in its use of television, it can be noted that very few people watch television to educate themselves. At any rate, 88 per cent of the viewers – according to a viewer survey – do not connect the term education with television as far as its function is concerned. Television does not possess – at least in the minds of the viewers – the image of an institution associated with education and culture. In 1991 ARD and ZDF published the cultural study which counts 13 per cent to the 'core public of the cultural scene'. This group has medium to high educational qualifications and a medium to upper professional position. The time these people spend in front of the television set is all in all below average. On the other hand, however, they devote relatively more time to watching cultural and educational television programmes.

Most of what the media offer seems to result in learning being changed, as it moves away from institutionalised, formal learning and educational processes in the direction of informal and non-institutionalised learning processes. As a consequence, there is at the same time a growth in the responsibility for each individual to cultivate and evolve the skills necessary to participate in social life. During the development of these skills the institutions (school, adult education, educational organisations etc) have new duties to take over. In this context they have to manifest a new identity of themselves. This also applies to television, especially educational television. The never-say-die policy with its slogan 'Carry on as before!' gets us nowhere. Self-assured restructuring and opening up the educational rooms must be the strategy, so that television can be accepted by the public at the height of its efficiency, namely as a mass medium that can also impart education and culture. The whole spectrum of structuring form and content has to be the distinguishing feature of modern-day educational television. Only in this way will the public find it attractive.

Another prerequisite for modern and competitive educational television is the necessary funding and staffing resources. Co-production and cooperation relationships should be established which thus contribute the substance which educational television requires. This also includes relationships which extend beyond the system limits in public service and private television. The private educational market is expanding, especially in the area of on-line but also off-line services. The public service stations have a large reservoir of programmes which could bring them into cooperation arrangements of this kind. They should use it. Educational programmes must relate to the so-called 'individual learning projects', and they must find and offer points of contact which allow and enable the public to share in the programmes.

But educational programmes also have an importance at present for producing an educational climate, for creating an image, the aim of which is to open up social participation. This socio-political intention then distinguishes educational programmes from good television programmes and virtually frees them from the strictly pedagogical impetus.

Hans Paukens, *Ph.D., following his studies in Educational Science, Sociology, Psychology and Media Science, became Departmental Head at an Adult Education Institute. Since 1977 he has worked at the Adolf Grimme Institute, where he was of recent date known as a specialist for radio, media, education, and culture. In 1996 he was appointed Head of the Institute. He is the author of several specialist works and essays on media development, media education, radio, and audience participation.*

Robin Moss

Independent Television Commission, London

My friends in Britain would say that regulatory agencies have a poor image generally, which is why they spend large sums of money on publicity campaigns that do not work very well. So perhaps, coming as I do from a regulatory body, I am not the best person to ask about 'image'. Nevertheless, I do feel that we have had plenty of evidence at this meeting that the educational force of broadcasting is still potent.

Some people have said to me that the optimistic reports from Britain are based on our understandable pleasure in the excellent educational work of Channel 4. It is said that Channel 4 is unique, that it could only be established in Britain. Not so. If the political will is there, to ensure that broadcasting has at least some public service purpose, that will can be translated into law. And it is the law, first, that established and maintains Channel 4, and indeed the BBC or any other powerful public service broadcaster, whether maintained by licence fees or commercial revenue. Pál and Péter reminded us of the fundamental importance of the law, in describing change in Hungarian broadcasting.

Laws are made by man, they can be unmade if they are wrong. When the walls came down in Eastern Europe, the new freedoms meant that businessmen saw some wonderful opportunities. I even heard a story of one country in which a group offered to set up a commercial television service, in return for a fee from the government, and expected to run the service, free of restrictions, and pocket the revenue.

My first point, then, is that educational broadcasting is healthy where the law is healthy. The Hungarian media law of 1997 will draw on German experience and on the BBC Charter: the shape of that law will determine the nature of the programmes, and their scheduling and funding. The law, by the way, is much more signifikant than the source of funding in determining the nature of the service, as you can see, for example, in Africa where the World Bank will no longer fund new radio stations unless they are backed by commercial rather than state funds.

My second and last point is that once the law has established the basis of a proper service, the high quality of educational programmes has to be ensured. How does one ensure the continuing supply of superb programmes such as Robert Thirkell's engineering series *The Limit* that we saw? The money is crucial.

And there is one area in which education has an advantage over many other programme genres: such programming has a very long life. We are now seeing not just impressive new international coproductions that ensure many long-term showings for the programmes themselves, but also valuable contributions from television to new technologies.

In Britain, CD-ROM publishers are competing fiercely for the home/school market. It is no accident that the most successful competitors have been able to draw on large libraries of educational television programmes and the skills of former educational television producers. There is a rich new market here for educational television, which should contribute powerfully to sustaining the supply of quality programmes. The determination and ingenuity of dedicated producers must supply the rest – and it can.

All I can say is that I have seen in Munich examples from Finland, from Hungary, from Britain, from elsewhere, which show two key competitive qualities. The best educational programmes do compete well: they have excellent production quality and they meet a felt need in society. They are therefore appropriate to the place they have in the schedule and they deliver educational material to which the audience respond. It is true that some material (the BBC's *Learning Zone*, for example) is shown at dead of night, but other material is competing in the main marketplace, in peak or close to peak parts of the schedule. People are not couch potatoes and they welcome programmes that aim to satisfy their natural curiosity. The trick is to design effectively and compete aggressively.

Robin Moss, *Ph.D., is Head of Educational Broadcasting at the Independent Television Commission, London. He studied Classical Literature and History, London and Oxford University. His doctorate was awarded by London University for a thesis on* The Fall of the West Roman Empire. *Robin has worked in educational television since 1966, both in Britain and abroad. He is the author of two books and numerous articles on broadcasting. For over a decade he was a Director of the National Health Education Authority, a member of the Board of the Health Education Council and actively involved in the Educational Television Association.*

Peter von Rüden

Norddeutscher Rundfunk/ARTE, Hamburg

I do not think that we should cease to use the term. Educational television is every presentation by this medium which sets out to treat a subject not just superficially but which refers to its background and context, consciously tuning into an educational need. This is the difference between educational and informational programmes. It is, however, arduous to link educational television to only the formal criteria of the medium. The magazine *Markt im Dritten* on Norddeutsches Fernsehen is formally not an educational programme but a current affairs magazine on economic issues. The way it is made, however, reveals a significant consumer information role and indisputably an advisory service.

Many educational programmes draw on the abundance of television forms. It is possible to observe the crossing of the borders between education, information, play and culture in the everyday programme reality of the 3rd television channels of the ARD. Furthermore, from a functional standpoint any channel may contain educational elements, particularly in the realm of fiction. Nowadays it is certain that more historical information is conveyed via television plays or good feature films than by history programmes in the narrow sense of the term.

The constantly proclaimed shortage of educational facilities on the German television screen does not exist, in my opinion. The endeavours undertaken by the ARD institutions in the field of education are still quite respectable. The forms adopted are different, possibly the contents, too, to those adopted during the foundation phase of the 3rd channels but the educational remit is still upheld. It is debatable whether the current range of programmes is adequate or whether it should be extended. But this would be tantamount to a social debate, which does not take place or not frequently enough, in my opinion. The educational programmes of a public broadcasting corporation are always only as good or extensive as a society demands or permits. This is the well-known correlation: the medium is never much better than the society to which it broadcasts.

There have been changes in the educational claims raised by television, however. Initially, the 3rd channels of the ARD claimed to be a promoter of education in their own right, on an equal footing with schools, universities and further education centres. Meanwhile, we have come to the straightforward but apt conclusion that television is a useful but at the same time an extraordinarily precarious educational medium, that in fact the services provided by the established educational agencies in society (school, university and adult education institutions) can hardly ever or rarely be supplied by television, and in most cases not as proficiently. Television is not dialogic. Despite all our efforts television remains a mass medium, and is therefore unable to cater for individual educational needs satisfactorily.

The thesis, however, that education is totally unsuited to the television screen has definitely been proven wrong. The question as to television's potential in the field of education is as old as the medium itself and the discussion engaged in by the media didactic clan. The attempts by media didactics to develop media taxonomies – i.e. systematic classifications of which contents should be offered to which target group in which form – have failed. The issue has nothing to do with the medium television in the first place. It is an ancient discussion we also know from the days of the school radio debate or from the early discussion on educational film.

Today we know every form possible in television can be used for specific educational purposes. The effect of fictional forms, even the popular ones, with regard to educational motivation was for a long time underrated. Using a film story we are able to reach more people than with documentaries. Theme evenings on the European culture channel ARTE are undoubtedly an exceptional educationally significant event for many viewers, as they illustrate a theme from various perspectives and via an impressive array of television forms.

Educational television should also play a role in the discussion on the future of television. The question is not whether we can imagine a thematic channel for education. I am convinced that such a thematic channel for education will come about in the foreseeable future. Irrespective of the question as to whether we will be able to receive digitally 100 or 200 television channels in five to ten years, it is certain that technical distribution facilities will multiply. I no longer exclude the possibility of commercial suppliers offering thematic channels for education, culture and science. Certain products are not advertised at present on television, as the losses incurred by non-selective advertising are too great for the industry wishing to promote them. Established book publishers advertise in the newspaper ZEIT, not on the ARD.

If a channel existed that was directly targeted at the upper segment of culture and education devotees, new advertising clients could doubtless be acquired for television. Besides, it is not merely a question of additional distribution opportunities for educational channels on the German market: the international media giants are sure to develop strategies for channel distribution in Europe, even world-wide. An average market coverage of just 0.1 per cent in the whole of Europe means a considerable number of viewers in absolute figures. Even the inherent language problems can be technically solved within the channel, as is illustrated by the example of ARTE.

I believe we should continue to use the term 'educational television'. If we dismiss it from our vocabulary, the danger arises of our dismissing it altogether. Presently, no one would wish to abandon the programme remit to provide 'culture' on television, but it soon becomes clear that the term 'culture' is neither better nor more clearly defined than that of 'education'.

We should, however, eliminate one other term from our discussion, which is 'life-long learning'. This term almost sounds like a court sentence: 'You are sentenced to life-long learning!' Are we really condemned to educating ourselves from kindergarten to the grave? Personally, I prefer the term 'life-accompanying learning'. Striving for education will not be equally intense in every phase of life.

One problem in educational television will remain and become even more acute. We know this problem of the knowledge gap from sociological research. In sum, those who are broadly less educated find it increasingly difficult to extract specifically any new information they may require from the growing flood of offers and to assimilate the process of life-accompanying learning. Those who are broadly more educated, on the other hand, select according to specific criteria and their own educational needs from the whole range of offers. The group having a higher level of education and income may not even need public educational television programmes. The others, the less educated, frequently lack the ability of select learning. The problem for the future, in my opinion, is the following: the groups in society presumed to be dependent on a public free-of-charge range of educational programmes, which objectively they may even need, do not use it to the extent we hoped. Those that do make use of it are not really dependent on it. We must find ways out of this dilemma. Ingo Hermann, using the ZDF as an example, talked about several programme strategies, which in this context I very much support.

Peter von Rüden, *Ph.D., studied the History of the Theatre, History and German Language and Literature. He obtained his doctorate with a thesis on the early German workers' theatre. He was Director of the* Adolf-Grimme-Institut *in Marl from 1974 to 1983 and acquired a post-doctoral qualification* (Habilitation) *at the University of Osnabrück in 1979 as a university teacher for Media Science. Since 1983 he is employed as Head of the Education Department at the* Norddeutscher Rundfunk (NDR), *where he is now representative for ARTE. His publications are on television drama, television entertainment, the cultural history of the workers' movement and multimedia systems. Since 1985 he has been honorary professor of media studies.*

7: Television and Continuing Education:
A Look into the Future

What is public service broadcasting doing on the information superhighway?

Herbert Kubicek

Professor of Applied Computer Science, University of Bremen

Introduction

The conference was held to deal with the important question of how educational programmes on television can be made more attractive for the viewers. In the conference draft it was pointed out that in recent years a number of measures to this end had been developed and tested, for example,

- promotional and marketing activities;
- developing programme formats to attract mass audiences;
- ascertaining the educational and informational requirements of certain target groups;
- opening up new groups of viewers by concealing explicit educational intentions.

These efforts are said to have already achieved successes. I welcome this very much and am as pleased about it as the innovative programme-makers. But is it sufficient to continue the successful strategies of yesterday, today and tomorrow? How far into the future will the effects of these efforts still be felt? Are they not based on a fundamental basic understanding of television which, in the opinion of many observers, only partly concerns the present and could fail in the future?

The catchwords slogans for the media future already exist: multimedia, information information superhighway, cyberspace. And well-known reputed experts were already writing about 'Life after Television' (Gilder, 1990) five years ago. The present-day computer kids and network surfers, according to what has become a common thesis, are perhaps no longer satisfied with the passive role of a television consumer and may not buy another television but only a PC.

I do not understand much about educational television. What is understood by that here I find extremely important today and for the future:

- instructional programmes such as science magazines or broadcasts about animals and foreign countries;
- programmes to meet the needs for information and guidance (advice programmes);
- programmes to impart basic knowledge about important societal connections.

Programmes of that kind do already exist to some extent on CD-ROM and on computer networks. Educational and informational programmes have been promised there for 20 years. But by no means everything that was promised actually materialised.

I should like to present you with some assumptions about the foreseeable development of the media and then put up for discussion some theses on positioning this (educational) television in this development.

Treat forecasts with caution

The future of the media is characterised by various terms, which, however, mean largely the same, namely a merger what were the separate technologies of data processing (computers), of telecommunications (telephones) and broadcasting (television). In the U.S.A. the term Information Superhighway has been coined for what is emerging. The German translation Datenautobahn has, however, not caught on. Here *Multimedia* became the word of the year 1995. Business consultancy companies are forecasting for the year 2000 a market volume of DM 30 billions in Germany (Booz, Allen & Hamilton, 1995). The main obstacles on the way to these new markets are seen as Telekom's network monopoly and broadcasting law. The Federal German Government is therefore preparing not only the reform of telecommunications but also a multimedia law to remove these obstacles. But how realistic are such forecasts?

1. Wrong forecasts are the rule.

Whether in the case of the first television transmission in the 1920s or of the introduction of the new media cable television and *Bildschirmtext* (Btx, similar to viewdata), not only the speed and extent of the spread but also the later contents and forms of use were for the most part wrongly forecast. The respective models (e.g. the electronic newspaper for the *Bildschirmtext*) misled those who assess the consequences of technology, politicians who call for regulation and also those who take investment decisions in industry. Thus it is unlikely that any product development that backed television for use with *Btx* turned in a profit.

2. Differentiating between media of the first and second order can help to straighten things out.

The discussions on the new media were always tied down to technical innovations. This is generally nothing new for the development of the media. The 'old' media press and broadcasting got their present names from technical innovations. You can talk of technical cores, of technical media or media of the first order, because in each case they are characterised by their technology. It opens up options and also determines restrictions on the contents and on the processes of production, distribution and reception, and influences the culture of these media.

This influence, however, is not deterministic. Complex production and distribution organisations have been developed around the technical cores. When we talk of press and broadcasting today, we mean these socio-technical complexes with their organisational structures and cultural conditions. Technical media are institutionalised and cultivated in an evolutionary process and thus become a socio-economic complex, a medium of the second order. This also includes an integration of the use into everyday life and a similarity between the expectations of the makers and the users. Only when this succeeds will a technical medium turn into mass medium. Since the Second World War only television has managed to do this. All other attempts have not extended beyond the use by early adopters. In the area of multimedia we are still at the very beginning of the institutionalisation process.

3. The current multimedia discussion suffers from a double shortcoming.

With multimedia it is, as it was earlier as well, not only quite an open question what the later contents offered and their production and use will look like. Added to that is the fact that this time the technical core either remains very nebulous or that on a concrete level so many technical options and variants are described that one cannot know for sure which technology can and is meant to be institutionalised and cultivated. This has something to do with the enormous momentum and competition in the field of information and communication technologies and – to a certain extent – also with a certain convergence of developments in the previously separate areas of data processing, telecommunications and broadcasting/electronic home entertainments.

4. Structural analyses are needed instead of forecasts.

Nobody can resolve the complexity arising from this momentum and large number of players and achieve his objectives promptly. Nor can anyone forecast the development in detail. On the other hand, we are not completely helpless either and can certainly try to distinguish between advertising and analysis.

Thus the debate on the PC or the television set as the terminal in private households does not seem to be dampened by either the experience with *Bildschirmtext* or by simple considerations of everyday psychology. And the conclusion that on account of the digitalisation of sound radio and television these markets are now growing together with those of data processing is really only viable because hardly anyone inquires what is meant by 'market' and 'growing together'. Nor does a merger of two companies from different sectors say anything about future products, production processes and ways of use.

Forecasts of what will be offered and/or used and to what extent can only be regarded as expressions of opinions formulated on the basis of certain interests or conjectures. But structural analyses are possible and necessary, analyses which open corridors of development and identify factors which might have a certain influence on the further development.

The confusion in the multimedia sky and the inertia on the ground of everyday media production and use

5. Multimedia is a terminological jungle.

On an abstract technical level there is a large measure of agreement on the contents of terms. On the basis of digital data processing, with the aid of data compression procedures, static media (data, texts, pictures) and dynamic media (audio and video) can be combined and jointly stored, processed, transmitted and used interactively.

As soon as one wants to be one step more concrete and wants to define transmission networks, terminals, technical features or even content, the consensus ends, however. This complexity makes it difficult to find one's bearings. But many can live quite well with this – and from this – because there one does not have to commit oneself and can leave various options open, make political demands without any detailed explanation or even produce studies and expert opinions.

Figure 1: Sectional markets for multimedia components

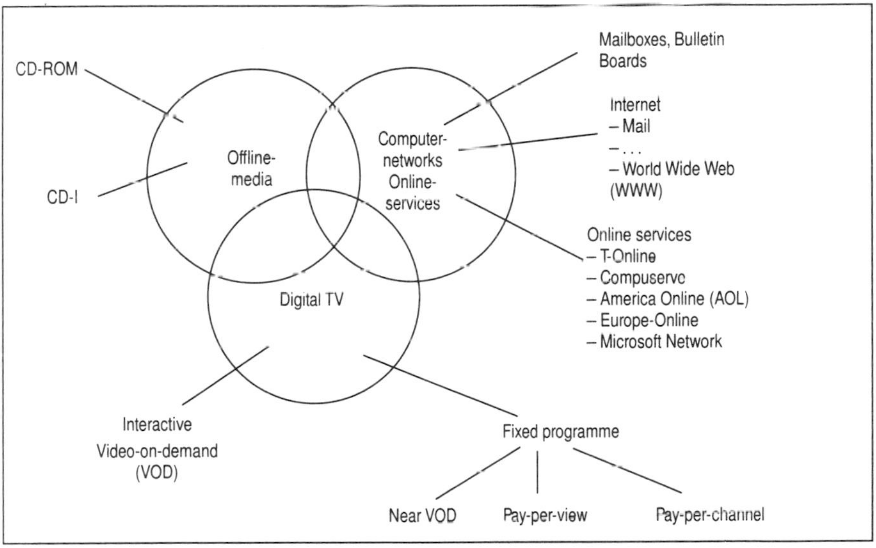

6. Currently there are in particular three sectional sub-markets.

If a market is understood as an area of exchange between supply and demand, there are at least three sectional markets among consumers each of which, however, satisfies the general definition of multimedia only more or less:

- The market for offline multimedia applications in the form of CD-ROMs is developed furthest.
- The market for online services in telecommunications (from the former *Btx* or Datex-J to CompuServe, AOL and Europe Online and the World Wide Web in the Internet) is in process of integrating the dynamic elements (audio and video).
- In the market for television, which traditionally builds on the dynamic elements, digitalisation is being introduced, and an attempt is being made to implement interactive forms of programmes and use (pay-per-view, near-video-on-demand, interactive television).

7. Media have not just one but two value-added chains.

Some applications can be clearly assigned to one or the other market. With others, for example home shopping, experiments are being carried out in all three sectional markets at the same time. These applications are dependent on certain telecommunication services and networks. These are often at the forefront of the debate. A value-added chain is frequently drawn in which there is one single stage with the catchword 'Content' between five and seven technical stages (network infrastructure, network management, server, providing service, terminal, software, consulting).

This way of looking at things does not by any means do justice to the production structures that in the meantime have been achieved in the case of the 'old' media. Apart from the technical chain there is also a multi-stage value-added one for content. In the area of the press and topical broadcast items the content value-added chain extends from the correspondents, agencies and editorial offices to the radio and TV guides and other kinds of guidance.

Figure 2: The two value-added chains

INFORMATIONAL VALUE ADDED		TECHNICAL MEANS
Information production	⟷	Data entry equipment (text, audio, video, etc.)
Information preparation (editing, etc.)	⟷	Workstation and Software
Providing Information	⟷	Servers and databases
Information distribution	⟷	Telecommunication networks and services
Information use	⟷	Terminals and software

8. Digitalisation does not lead to a merger of production and use:
  The value-added cup as a guide.

Just because data, texts, pictures and audio and video elements can be digitally stored and transmitted does not mean that for the time being anything grows together. The same servers and telecommunication networks may be used. This has just as little influence on the media content as the fact that a literature database and the financial accounting run in the same computer network of a company. If the idea of the value-added chain is taken seriously it has to be considered from the content sources right up to the use. Then, from the economics of the organisation and the everyday and media-psychological point of view, there is every reason to continue as hitherto with television existing side by side with computer-aided information systems with only slight modifications.

Figure 3: The value-added cup

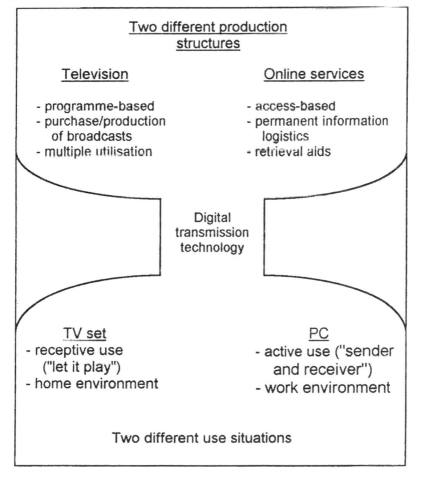

9. The majority of households still have a long way to go to dual use.

So that the market potential for multimedia that is often painted in the sky by wishful thinking can be realised, the private households would have to acquire separate technical equipment and connections for digital TV and multimedia online services in the foreseeable future. For the vast majority of private households this is a long way away – both in an economic and behaviour-related respect. The cable and satellite infrastructure is being put into place for digital television. The set-top boxes are about to go into serial production.

The suppliers have not yet really got very far with the 'pay' in pay-per-view services, and interactivity as well as video-on-demand is still encountering a number of problems. But a selection from 500 channels does seem feasible in the medium term, and demand can also be expected for that.

This is much more difficult for the area of multimedia online services. The growth figures in the Internet or the online services in the U.S.A. are hardly relevant for assessing the development in Germany. It is true that statements on the current distribution of PCs with and without modems in private households fluctuate. The upper estimates are around 30 per cent for PCs and 5 per cent for modem connections. These figures include the Datex-J subscribers and the entire mailbox scene. Neither is representative of the whole population; and neither possesses technical equipment with multimedia-capability.

The share of households with multimedia-capable PCs is estimated at 2–3 per cent. The growth forecasts for the multimedia market assume an increase of 20 per cent by the year 2000 and 60 per cent by 2010. Not only financial obstacles but also established behaviour patterns and a lack of ability stand in the way of this.

According to estimates made by a German consumer research company the media behaviour of the Germans can be divided into three segments:

- one quarter uses television only;
- two quarters use television and press;
- one quarter makes intensive use of several press products and of television only occasionally.

It is only this last quarter which displays an active media behaviour and is most likely to be interested in interactive online services.

So far there is a lack of representative surveys on the users of online services. The studies available point to a dominance of a young, male audience with higher educational qualifications. Two different sectional cultures, which clearly differ from the majority of the population, have formed around the Internet and the mailboxes. For nowadays to use online services you need both technical know-how and also the abilities to apply search strategies, to structure information, to evaluate sources as well as an ability to articulate oneself in the case of communication services. These have not increased in the overall population in the last few years despite all the talk about the information society.

What can be expected from a deregulated telecommunication market?

10. The forthcoming deregulation of telecommunications reduces the possibility of major outlays for the infrastructure.

In the past the technical network infrastructures for the new media have been funded out of monopoly profits from the telephone network and services. The broadband cable networks and the *Btx* infrastructure are still not turning in a profit. The Teletel system in France, often described as a success, has not yet covered its initial investments. In expanding a broadband transmission network the principle of the infrastructure outlays has not been realised because of a scarcity of funds and uncertain demand. Under the conditions of competition for all networks and services as well as an asymmetrical competition for the telephone service, outlays such as those for the cable and satellite television will no longer be possible unless a great effort is made. The regulation of the so-called universal service is to be regarded as a critical element.

11. The market mechanism will result in a broad supply in the case of cable and satellite broadcasting networks and a strictly demand-orientated supply with broadband exchange connections.

The market mechanism will guarantee (relatively) low-priced access to digitalised cable and satellite broadcasting networks . Thus the access to at least 500 television channels, pay-per-view and near-video-on-demand is likely on the scale of the current proportion of television households.

Connections to a broadband network which will expand the functioning of the present television and data networks by means of broadband subscriber connection lines for video-on-demand will, on the other hand, still involve high costs. Today connections to the broadband transmission network of the *Telekom* cost a monthly establishing charge of about DM 2,500 a month and transmission fees up to DM 200 per hour. That is why, for example, video conferences for companies are in many cases too expensive. In this way, however, competition will lead to a certain price reduction in the area of business customers. But in the foreseeable future prices will not come anywhere near those of the current or even future telephone rates. Video-on-demand as a mass application has therefore been taken off the agenda for the time being.

Even in the narrowband range (digital telephone connections, ISDN) increases and not reductions in the local area are to be expected, as the changes in the *Telekom*'s rates at the beginning of 1996 show. When future competition is concentrated on business customers in particular, further price increases for private customers in local traffic are certainly to be reckoned with.

12. The vision of the information society as an informed society presupposes multimedial online services which the market will make rapidly and widely available.

The above-mentioned comparison of online services and television can be expanded even further in view of the societal significance of both complexes. It is likely to be undisputed that the claim of the information society to be an informed society as well calls for the widest possible access to networks such as the Internet.

A modern PC and a fast modem is sufficient technical equipment for the present-day qualified user population. If, however, the number of users is to be increased it must be possible to transport and use multimedia applications. Within data processing multimedia in the sense of the integration of audio and video elements means a considerable lowering of the use threshold. Just as it was the graphic surface which first made the PC the everyday tool in the office, so video introductions and audio explanations can make the use of the computer something that can be learnt by anyone in a few hours.

This leads to a revision of the thesis that was previously supported – by me as well earlier on – that the bandwidth requirement rises as the application becomes more professional. Now the reverse is the case: the lower the technical and content know-how of the potential users of online services, the more bandwidth is necessary. But if the price for this equipment and connections is much dearer than current telephone connections, the degree of active participation in the information society will then depend directly on income.

The idea of a dual information order

13. All media require the support of public institutions.

When nowadays deregulation, liberalisation and privatisation are recommended or applied as the strategies to open up and develop the multimedia markets, there is a tendency to explain this by the success of the existing competitive markets. Examples range from the book market to broadcasting and the mobile radio telephone service. The effect of competition, in principle encouraging innovation and reducing prices, certainly also has to be recognised. But in none of these cases was it possible for competition to bring about the degree of supply achieved without complementary public institutions. The printing press and all other technical innovations in the area of the press are a necessary but not adequate condition for the market for print media. There are many countries in the world in which this technology exists, but neither a comparable market nor a comparable effect were achieved as far as education and political participation are concerned. What is needed, however, is a highly developed school system and also public libraries.

Figure 4: Television vs. online services

	Cable and satellite television	Internet
Structure	Distribution	Switching
Topology	Tree:	Star:
	'Data water pipe' or 'Data railway'	'Data Highway'
Capacity	Broadband; full-size videos	Text, photos, small videos
Content	Programmes with fixed patterns	Individually accessible information,
		communication functions, transactions
Technical	Depending on network access and the	Technically on an equal basis,
role division	necessary technical equipment a	anyone can be
	distinction must be made between	– user and supplier,
	– suppliers	but here, too,
	– providers	– service providers are emerging.
	– viewers	
Suppliers	500-1000 programme suppliers, mainly	unlimited,
	media groups, heavy investments	low costs
Providers	large companies make package offers	some large and many small ones,
	and send their bills	as with the press
User	selects and receives (let it play),	selects from a universe
	hardly any chance to intervene,	reacts,
	none to transmit	interacts
Culture	department store model:	
	everything is arranged and	community model (up to now):
	accounted for contractually	sharing, freeware, 'netikette'
Super-vision	legal supervision by	'netikette'
of content	regional control bodies	
Legal	broadcasting law:	international: national law relating to
questions	bureaucratised, ritualised,	telecommunications, data protection
	party-politically charged	and copyright only partially effective

In the field of broadcasting the term dual broadcasting order was created for this coexistence of private and public suppliers. This principle of complementariness can, with some limitations, be transferred to all media and be developed into a dual information order. Apart from the developing multimedia market the mainstays for an expanded basic provision with information, in telecommunications called universal service, would have to be put into place.

14. With regard to an expanded universal service the European states can learn a lot from the current development in the U.S.A.

According to conventional stereotypes the European states have a developed tradition of a cultural state based on social justice with a high priority for the public interest and general education, while the U.S.A. is far more individualistic and gives more backing to private capitalist mechanisms. This may have been the case and in many areas perhaps still is.

With regard to the basic provision with information and politics on the way into the information society, however, the precise opposite can be noticed. Where the EU Commission and the German Government completely back privatisation and deregulation, the Clinton/Gore Administration sees the main point of emphasis of its task in promoting general access to networks and services in addition to initiating private investments, and in the public interest supplementing the commercial applications whose markets are growing by applications which require State promotion.

15. There are cornerstones of a universal service.

A comprehensive concept for a basic provision with information should be built up on a number of cornerstones which concern both access to the networks and relevant information content. In the following diagram several cornerstones are listed which would have to be appropriately regulated for general information access and which have been explained in more detail elsewhere. (cf. Kubicek, 1995)

In the U.S.A. an understanding which seems to be much more common than in Germany is that corresponding regulatory intervention is necessary to give as many citizens as possible access to the new media and thereby to create mass markets, also in the fairly long term.

However, the U.S.A. is not a model example of how to handle public service broadcasting. Germany and the rest of Europe has to further develop its own way of doing this.

The role of television in a dual multimedia order

16. There are tendencies to uncouple content production and technical distribution.

The fusion often noticed of television/electronic home entertainments, data processing and telecommunications was judged above to be misleading in view of the media development with regard to the organisation of content production. Contrasting television and information systems was offered as a help in finding our bearings. More refined distinctions, however, have to be made to avoid producing any new misunderstandings.

It looks very much as if television broadcasts such as cinema films or live transmissions will also become accessible over the Internet. The television stations have even created the first systems with videotext. In the case of home shopping, combinations made up of broadcasting and backward channel via telephone are emerging. At the moment certain technical distribution paths are allocated to the content applications. Digitalisation will, however, allow a certain uncoupling in the future.

Figure 5: Cornerstones for a general access

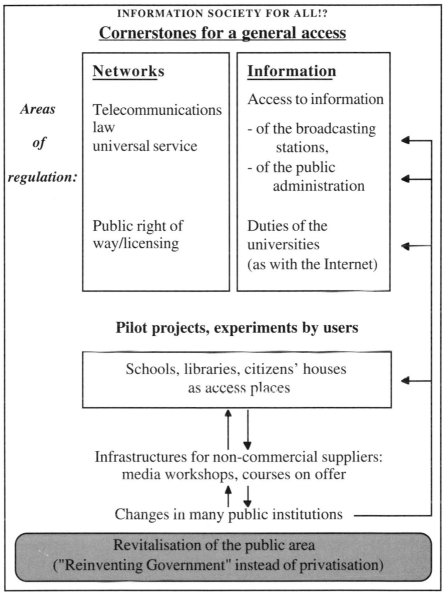

17. *Multimedia online access in the Internet also means in the future distribution of certain contents via several technical media.*

Even today feature films are shown at cinemas, broadcast on television and offered for sale on cassettes. Added to these are the Internet and CD-ROMs.

Videotext can be called over the TV set, but also with a PC. Apple supplies a corresponding programme with the video card. In Bremen the

Telecommunication Research Group which I run is building up a City Information Network on which not only local city information but also information from *Nordtext* can be called up over the Internet and public kiosks and, in the near future, Datex-J or T-Online.[1] Negotiations are being conducted with Radio Bremen to include traffic information, news and selected manuscripts to sound radio programmes.

The content programmes, as already mentioned, account for a large share in the value-added chain. For this reason the obvious thing to do is to make multiple use of these contents over all suitable distribution channels. This, however, is not a growing together by something old is assimilated by something new, but an enhancement of the sectional markets that exist at present and will continue to exist in the future as well.

18. For the discussion on what multimedia offers it seems more important to make distinctions between content genres than according to technical criteria.

Multimedia applications range from calling up video films and games and information to video conferences, teleshopping, and teleticketing. When you examine the production structures, the content logistical chain and the use situations great differences between these areas emerge. The comparison between calling up films and calling up information is then not identical to comparing television and online providers. The line that separates them runs inside the broadcasting station or television transmitter somewhere between the areas of entertainment and current events. The requirements concerning content, organisation and technology vary very greatly between these four application areas.

These have still not been researched and worked out in depth. Nevertheless, the thesis is to be advanced here that this differentiation is more relevant for strategic orientation than emphasising technical convergence. It is connected with dividing television up into genres. But it also means changing foregone conclusions, because up to now the image the content-makers had of themselves was strongly influenced by the technical cores. Anyone who works on current events in television often feels closer to his colleagues in other television departments than his colleagues in the print media or future online services.

Figure 6: Differentiation of broadcast services

Entertainment	Information retrieval	Transactions	Communication
One-off production	Information sources	Services	
Broadcasting/ dissemination	Editorial selection, processing, arranging, updating if appropriate	Data processing	Presentation
Viewing	Access	Input/output	Broadcasting/receiving

1 See 'http://infothek.uni-bremen.de'.

218

But this is going to change in the future because the common interests in contents are becoming more important and the technical differences less important. I expect a development similar to the one that took place in many industrial companies in the 1970s as a change from a functional to a divisional or genre organisation, because it was noticed that for various products the procurement and sales paths are so different in each case that combining them into separate buying and sales divisions does not create synergy, and instead procurement, production and sales for one product group (division) were integrated organisationally.

Accordingly, you could expect, for example, one genre current events and one genre entertainment which make their products accessible by television broadcasting, online demand and perhaps CD-ROM as well. This multiple utilisation option does not mean, however, that the same contents can always be disseminated without any modification to the contents by all technical media. Here special features and limits first have to be ascertained and established.

What chances does the development outlined offer to educational programmes?

19. The further development of a tradition: educational programmes in the integrated media?

The word 'multimedia' is already fairly old and used to refer, among other things, to instructional material consisting of books and audio cassettes. Particularly in the field of education, public service broadcasting, too, has traditions of the integration of broadcasting and print media, from back-up booklets for school broadcasts and the university of the air to the book, the video cassette and television programme.

In keeping with the uncoupling of content and technical medium that I have outlined the main points of emphasis in the contents could be analysed to find out which other media are especially suitable for multiple use and complementary support.

As was pointed out at the beginning, I am not very familiar with the usual distinctions made in this area. However, a division into two would seem sensible to me as an initial approach.

On the one side are the classic educational programmes, which try to impart basic knowledge in fairly long, connected broadcast instalments. Their contents are valid and relevant for a certain length of time. In addition, they can be marketed on video cassettes and after being edited (list of contents, index) can also be distributed on CD-ROM as illustrated electronic books.

When broadband networks are available at reasonable prices, programmes of this kind could also be stored on servers and be accessed by educational institutions. Trials along these lines even seem feasible in the short term as part of multimedia pilot projects, where the school textbook publishers are interested in gaining experience.

On the other side are programmes which are intended to satisfy the needs for information and guidance. Advice and magazine broadcasts of this kind are predestined for individual online access. Their usually short contents, often only valid for a limited time, would have to be more intensively prepared, developed and cultivated. When, however, editorial competence has been acquired in certain areas the individual programmes can be offered over all online services. This would enable part of the production costs to be covered. Then hosted forums can also be set up to promote the dialogue between makers and users.

20. Regulation should strengthen the educational remit.

The valid provisions of broadcasting law do not stand in the way of this kind of multiple use and support for broadcast programmes. There are, however, problems with contractual rights pertaining to intellectual property, as there are no tested arrangements for paying for contractual access. But nor does broadcasting law encourage the developments I have outlined. Especially at a time of increasing commercialisation of knowledge and the increasing substitution of knowledge by opinions, an expansion of the broadcasting remit to include the interactive media is particularly important. For this reason the politicians should explicitly extend the broadcasting remit to cover interactive media. By doing so the television fees can also be better justified.

The politicians do not, however, seem to be doing this of their own accord. The broadcasting stations must make appropriate proposals and set examples. At the moment this appears to be a matter for individual pioneers. In order to arrive at solutions that would be viable in the longer term not only does a better integration within the broadcasting stations seem necessary but also a binding cooperation with other institutions involved in education.

Bibliography

A broad spectrum of the subjects treated here are covered by the articles in the annual *Jahrbuch Telekommunikation und Gesellschaft* (Yearbook Telecommunications and Society), for example:

Kubicek/Müller/Neumann/Raubold/Roßnagel (Eds.): *Jahrbuch Telekommunikation und Gesellschaft*. Bd. 3: Multimedia – Technik sucht Anwendung. Heidelberg: von Decker 1995

Kubicek/Klumpp/Müller/Neumann/Raubold/Roßnagel (Eds.): *Jahrbuch Telekommunikation und Gesellschaft* Bd. 4: Öffnung der Telekommunikation: Neue Spieler – Neue Regeln. Heidelberg: von Decker 1996.

Other sources used or referred to are:

Booz, Allen & Hamilton: *Zukunft Multimedia. Grundlagen, Märkte und Perspektiven in Deutschland*. Frankfurt/Main: Institut für Medienentwicklung und Kommunikation (IMK) 1995.

Gilder, George: *Life after Television*. New York and London 1994 (1st edition 1990).

Riehm, U.; Wingert, B.: *Multimedia. Mythen, Chancen und Herausforderungen.* Mannheim 1995.

Kubicek, H.: 'Duale Informationsordnung als Sicherung des öffentlichen Zugangs zu Informationen'. In: *Computer und Recht*, 6/1995, pp. 370-379.

An up-to-date comparison of developments in the U.S.A. and Europe is possible on the WWW in an online reader about an international conference 'The Social Shaping of Information Highways' (http://infosoc.informatik.uni-bremen.de/nii/). Contains references to a large number of other relevant servers.

Herbert Kubicek, *studied Business Economics at the University of Cologne, where he gained his doctor's degree in 1974. From 1977 to 1987 he was Professor of Business Studies at the University of Trier, since 1988 he has been Professor of Applied Computer Science at the University of Bremen, specialising in Office and Administration Automation. He is the editor of the yearbook 'Telekommunikation und Gesellschaft' (Telecommunications and Society) published since 1994. Moreover, he is a member of the enquiry commission 'Future of the Media in the Economy and Society' of the German Bundestag.*

Interactive television:
How far does it go?

Gerhard Eitz
Institut für Rundfunktechnik (IRT), Munich

Introduction

Many experts in America, Japan and Europe are at present working on the effects of digitalisation. Some of the slogans that could be mentioned here are the terms 'multimedia', 'set-top box', 'Video-on-Demand' and 'interactive television'. It is generally assumed that the viewers are becoming increasingly 'interactive' and in future will put their ideal programme together from a large number of channels (300–500), will access additional information and shape the programme according to their wishes.

This change in the use behaviour will be made possible by new digital technologies. It is established on the broadcaster side by digital signal compression and if needed encryption of the video, audio and text information and by a space-saving transmission of data packets on the new digital, terrestrial and satellite channels. Thus predictions assume, for example, that the number of available transmission channels and with them the number of possible services and programmes will double in the next two or three years.

An attempt is made at many meetings and conferences to answer the following key questions on the new interactive services:

- When: 1997, 1998 or 2000?
- Using which medium: television or PC?
- Which households and how many?
- Which programmes and services?

In my paper I should like to explain the various forms and types of interactivity and address the principal differences between television sets and PCs as well as the user interface for television sets. After that, I shall present existing interactive services which are already at the viewer's disposal and new interactive services. In conclusion I shall take a closer look at the potential and limitations of the so-called set-top box.

Types of interactivity

Some decades ago there were only a few television programmes. To choose a particular programme you had to switch over to another channel directly at the set. The (first) interactivity with television was already possible in the 1960s, when remote control was introduced. With it you could select the programme you wanted from your television chair. As more and more programmes became available you could jump from one programme to another in a simple and convenient way (so-called 'zapping').

In the last few years the number of functions and the complexity of remote controls have steadily increased. Thus today, for example, different picture formats (4:3, 16:9, Cinemascope) or stereo and dual channel sound can be selected, and subtitles can be called up.

Table 1: Types of Interactivity

Type of interactivity	Communication	Examples
Local Interactivity	parallel services, no feedback channel)	Teletext
		School TV Bulletin, *NexTView*
		Near-Video-on-Demand (NVOD)
Simple Interactivity	feedback channel to sender	Interactive teletext, online services
		Games, Homeshopping
		Pay per Channel, Pay per View, Pay per Time
Full Interactivity	bi-directional channel	Video-on-Demand (VOD)
		Homeshopping

Nor should teletext be forgotten, the additional service which is transmitted together with the television signal. It would be impossible to imagine choosing a page with the desired information without remote control. Nowadays satellite receivers and video cassette recorders can also be programmed and operated by using the remote control.

All this kind of interactivity is, however, to be looked upon as *local interactivity* with the particular television set, with which the viewer uses information and functions which are stored in the television set or transmitted with the television signal and are repeatedly renewed. That means that all accessible information and programmes are supplied to all television sets at the same time; the user has no chance of influencing them or receiving feedback and can only select what is on offer at the moment.

Local interactivity also occurs when teletext information, a school television newspaper or an electronic programme guide (*NexTView*) are accessed. In the course of my paper I shall introduce these services, which are to be regarded as developments of teletext.

In future digital services 'Near-Video-on-Demand' (NVOD)[1] will also gain in importance. Here, too, the viewer can be locally interactive when he selects the programme which is about to begin from an NVOD programme packet.

In contrast to local interactivity with the television set, there is the so-called *simple interactivity* with a television station with which the viewer is

---

1   In the case of NVOD a certain programme is transmitted in several channels. Thus, for example, nine channels are needed to transmit a 90-minute film with a time offset of 10 minutes in each case. The viewer only has to wait 10 minutes at the most until it is possible for the film to begin.

linked by a telephone line for his replies. The user can request participation in further services over this telephone line and select the information desired (e.g. interactive teletext, online services such as Internet) or place orders for goods from a so-called electronic catalogue (teleshopping).

In future digital systems the acquisition of rights also takes place via the return line. Thus telephone rights can be acquired for a channel (Pay-per-Channel), for a particular programme or a programme packet (Pay-per-View) or tokens for 'Pay-per-Time' programmes.

Also, the viewer can, as has been possible for years, influence the course of a programme by means of simple interactivity over the telephone by, for example,

- voting for or against an opinion by entering a special number, as in the broadcast *Pro and Contra*;
- transmitting his own questions and contributions to the discussion on a programme which are then dealt with in the course of the broadcast, for example *Monitor*; or
- intervening in a broadcast himself, for example, to take aim with a crossbow mounted on a television camera (*Der Goldene Schuß*).

But really new interactive services, like Video-on-Demand (VOD), are only possible with so-called *full interactivity*. Here a bi-directional channel with an individual line (made of fibre optic glass, for example) to the subscriber and a return line are necessary.

The viewer can select his ideal programme as at a news stand from a large number of films and other programmes, usually for a fee, and has the same possibility of control as in the case of a video recorder. Thus he can start the programme selected at a certain time (play), interrupt it as he wishes (pause), see it in slow motion or skip parts that do not interest him (fast forward).

Moreover, so-called 'fully interactive' films are possible in which the plot can be influenced and shaped by the viewer. Here the film consists of pre-produced film scenes which can be pieced together by the viewer, much in the same way as nowadays with computer games on CD-ROM, according to his own ideas and wishes.

One of the main applications for this is likely to be homeshopping: you leaf through an electronic catalogue of goods and access further information and films on certain products direct from the server.

Technically such services are only possible with considerable investments both on the server-side and in the transmission (network infrastructure with broadband cable or fibre optic cable).[2] Therefore it is unlikely that VOD services will be suitable for the mass market either in the short or mid-term. At present only field trials are being carried out for these inter-

---

2 A simple calculation shows that to supply a town of 100,000 inhabitants and 10 per cent simultaneous use and a programme of 1,000 90-minute films in VHS quality (2MBits/s MPEG-II) with TV-on-demand a capacity of the digital videobank of 1,350 GBytes (= 1,000 * 90 * 60s * 2 MBits/s) and a broadcasting transmission capacity of at least 20,000 MBits/s (= 100,000 * 0.1 * 2 MBits/s) are necessary.

active services to study the technology, the costs and the viewers' acceptance for these new media before they are commercially introduced.

Television set vs. PC

Consideration of interactive television should, however, not remain restricted to television sets alone. The PCs with rapidly growing online services must also be taken into account, in particular the Internet with its 25 million users worldwide and, for example, the Telekom 'online' with 0.9 million. For many PC users interactive services such as homebanking, teleshopping, interactive games and calling up information from databanks throughout the world are a matter of course. That is why for many experts the online services offered are a test field for interactive television of the future.

The use environments of PCs and television sets are quite different (see Table 2). The PC is usually to be found in the work room. The user is a short distance away from the screen or display and he enters his input by means of a keyboard or mouse. By comparison a television set has a screen which diagonally measures twice as much, the viewer usually sits with other people in the room at a considerably greater distance from the screen and the input is effected by using the remote control.

Table 2: Use environment of television set and PC

	Television set	PC
Environment	Living room (many interruptions and disturbances)	Work room (few interruptions and disturbances)
Use (main emphasis)	Entertainment	Work
Size of the screen	35cm	72cm
Viewing distance	Far	Near
Control	Remote control	Keyboard and mouse
User interface	Menus (eg choice of channel)	Windows
Users	The whole family	Professionals
Use	Intuitive	After some training

The emphasis of use is here on entertainment and (occasionally) information, while with the PC attention is focused on work with text programmes, table calculations etc. and now to a growing extent information and entertainment. Thus in addition to the modem connections for communicating with the online services, more and more television and teletext plug-in boards for installing in the PC are being bought.

It is thus emerging that the PC is becoming increasingly video-capable, while television sets are being equipped with ever more computer performance in order to be able to cope with the new (interactive) services. Examples that could be given of this are the decoding of High Level

Teletext, Electronic Programme Guides transmitted via DataBroadcasting services and Palplus as well as the decompression and deciphering of future digital television signals.

The graphical user interface

A great problem is designing the user interface, with which the user operates the device, calls up the services offered and selects the desired information. For interactive services which are meant to appeal to the broad mass of the public simple, reliable and absolutely error-free operation is necessary.

In the PC world the Windows surface has become the recognised standard. In the television world, however, there is still no generally recognised operation philosophy, although it is urgently necessary, not only for the traditional services television and teletext but also, more than ever, for the new interactive services. Thus today almost every television viewer has problems operating his video cassette recorder or picking information out of the teletext.

It is true that appropriate operating aids have been developed in cooperation with industry. For example, there is 'Videorecorder Programmed by Teletext' (VPT) to simplify the programming of video recorders using the programme pages from teletext, or 'Table of Pages' (TOP) to make it easier to find teletext pages by the use of coloured keys on the remote control. But there is here no general operating philosophy and surface – there are many different ones depending on the manufacturer.

The user interfaces for interactive television should be adapted to the medium of television, easy to understand and intuitively operable. Special importance in this connection is attached to a navigation system which guides the user through the services offered.

Existing interactive services

Below I should like to give a closer description of the opportunities for interactions with teletext in the light of some examples. Nowadays not only the PC user can access information from online services, but also the viewer with a television set and built-in teletext decoder is in a position to interactively call up information from databases (see Table 3). About 70 per cent of the 21 million television sets sold in Europe each year are fitted with a teletext decoder.

Teletext

Many broadcasting stations offer teletext as an additional service to the normal television programme. The viewer can choose between information from the areas of news, sport, stock exchange, service and programme preview ('TV-Guide'). A typical teletext service consists of 200 to 300 pages which in Germany, for example, are transmitted with the television signal in 7 to 10 television lines of the blanking interval at a cycle time of about 20 seconds.

Teletext offers the chance to broadcast additional information hidden in a page. The user can uncover this information by pressing a certain key on his remote control.

Interactive teletext

For some years several station operators have been offering 'interactive teletext' to a greater extent. It is possible with this procedure to give the viewer direct access to additional information which is not contained in the normal teletext programme. To do this the viewer calls up the computer of a databank and selects the information desired with the aid of a telephone keypad. The information is output in coded form according to the teletext standard together with operating instructions on reserved teletext pages, which are transmitted together with the normal teletext pages in the teletext cycle. The advantage of this system is that the waiting period for other users of the normal teletext is not increased.

Figure 1: Interactive teletext

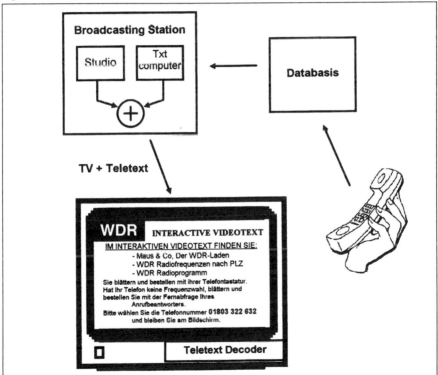

Source: G. Eitz, IRT

New interactive services

In the following section further examples are given of interaction for the television viewer or the PC user which will soon be possible (*NexTView* and school television newspaper) or which could be realised in the future in the way described or some other way. ('YES', 'TeleTip Info Dialer' and 'CD-Online', see also Tables 3 and 4).

Table 3: Interactive services for an analogue television set

	Local Interaction	Interaction with broadcasting centre
Teletext decoder	Teletext	Interactive Teletext
DataBroadcast decoder	NexTView + Database applications	YES system

The 'YES' system

The 'YES' system is a simple interactive system which allows the television viewer to react to broadcast information by pressing an additional key on his remote control – the so-called 'YES' key (see Figure 2: Basic principles of YES). The Yes-information is transmitted in a specially coded teletext page similar to subtitles together with the normal teletext pages. The user's answer is automatically transmitted via a telephone line to the evaluation point, e.g. a credit card organisation, which in turn informs the station operator concerned or passes the order on to a trading company.

The 'YES' system can be used not only for transmitting orders for certain products as easily and fast as possible, but also for providing a simple, universal way of conducting a dialogue between viewer and broadcasting station. In addition to interactive games, it can handle, for example, orders for study companion material, TED polls and answers to questions accompanying the programme.

The 'YES' system was developed by Philips and the IRT at the request of an Austrian group. Implementing 'YES' requires only a slight increase in the software of the teletext decoder on the part of the manufacturers and, of course, a telephone connection between the television set and telephone socket.

'Teletext Shopping' is another possible use of the 'YES' system. Thus not only texts but also references to other teletext pages can be transmitted as YES-information. This enables the viewer, guided by the programme, to use the 'YES' key to skip to certain teletext pages that can be specified by the programme. Thus, for example, the relevant order page for CDs can be directly chosen during a commercial for CDs and the order page for PCs during one for PCs.

TeleTip Info Dialer

The 'TeleTip Info Dialer', developed by Landmark Design & Technology, is a special remote control for interactive (television) applications. It has an alphanumeric keypad and an LCD display, and it can be connected to the telephone socket.

Figure 2: Basic principles of *YES*

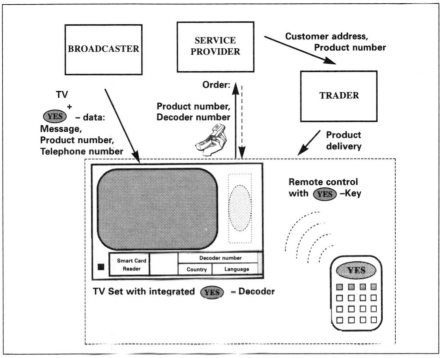

Source: G. Eltz, IRT

The viewer, while sitting in front of the television, can enter and store a piece of information (e.g. the solution to a competition). As soon as the device is connected to the telephone socket a telephone connection is established automatically with the evaluating computer and the information entered is transmitted together with the user's identification.

DataBroadcast

DataBroadcast can be regarded as a further development of the present-day teletext. In addition to information accompanying the programme, a school television newspaper, weather information or an electronic TV programme guide are possible new applications of DataBroadcast services. These new services are transmitted in analogue systems under fixed (hex) page numbers together with the normal teletext in one or several television lines of the blanking interval.

If, for example, only one television line is made available for the data service, it can transmit 2 KBytes/sec or 120 KBytes/min. If several lines are used for transmission the transmission time is correspondingly shortened, or correspondingly more data can be transmitted in the same time. In the data channel of digital systems, on the other hand, there is no restriction of this kind. Here far higher transmission rates are possible, for example between 400 KBits/s (= 50 KBytes/s) and 4 MBits/s (= 500 KBytes/s).

The future DataBroadcast decoder will be programmed in a similar way to a present-day video recorder. The user selects the desired data programme from the data offered; the data decoder switches itself on at the broadcasting time, receives what was selected and records it.

Possible users of such future broadcasting data services can be not only PC users with a special DataBroadcast reception card but also television viewers with a data decoder in the television set and, if necessary, restricted possibilities of operation.

Such a DataBroadcast service was already transmitted as an experiment to the Berlin Broadcasting Exhibition in 1995 in the television signal of the Bavarian Broadcasting Corporation via satellite, was received by data decoders in Berlin, decoded and displayed.

A TV guide could be built up in much the same way. Such a TV guide allows, for example, the individual programme announcements to be filtered according to station, section and time as well as further detailed information with text and picture elements to be called up.

It is possible with this type of TV guide to inform the viewers comprehensively about the ever growing programme.

School Television Bulletin

At present the Bavarian Broadcasting Corporation (BR) is testing transmission of a school television bulletin for PCs as a DataBrodcast application. Figure 3 shows one of the first versions of a user interface for selecting a desired data programme.

Figure 3: Page from the School Television Multimedia

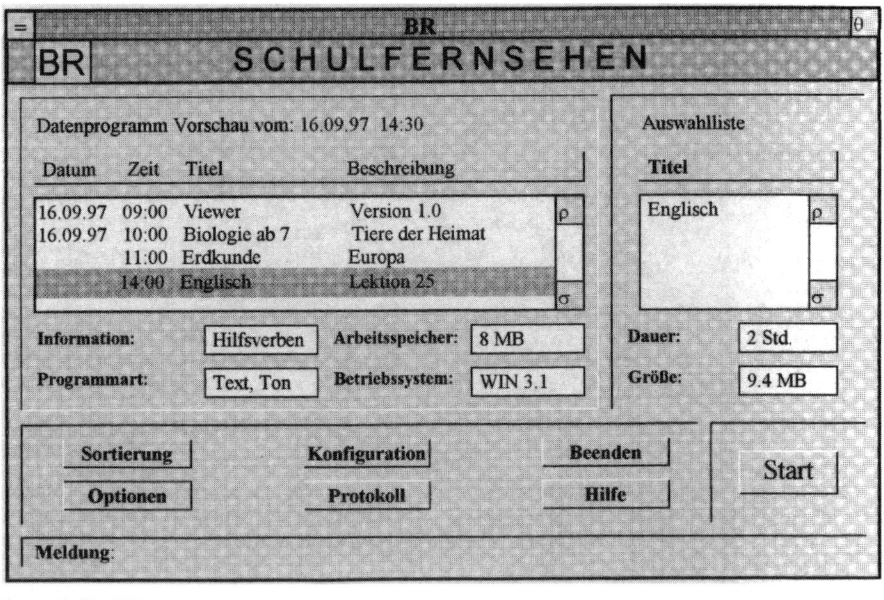

Source: G. Eitz, IRT

In this example the teacher chooses between the data programmes 'Biology – animals in our home country', 'Geography – Europe' and English – Lesson 25'. Additionally information about the content of the programme, the kind of programme ('Text, sound') and on the size of the data programme ('9.4 MB') is given.

The advantage of the electronic transmission of the school television newspaper is that the information transmitted can be edited by the teacher on his PC as he wishes.

NexTView

The first DataBroadcast decoders in television sets for the electronic programme guide *NexTView* are supposed to come onto the market on the occasion of the Broadcasting Exhibition 1997 in Berlin. The specification for it was developed in co-operation with the European broadcasting bodies and industry, EBU and EACEM. *NexTView* contains not only the title of the broadcasts and the transmission times but also further information on the editorial rating, the recommended age of the viewers (parental rating), the genre (according to DVB specification) and a short index of contents. About 10 per cent of the teletext capacity is necessary to transmit this data service.

The viewer can display titles of programmes arranged according to genre (e.g. sport – tennis) or broadcasting station from a databank which the decoder builds up and manages on its own. Titles of broadcasts can also be shown for certain periods of time, for example all the broadcasts being shown at the moment and those that follow on next.

CD-Online

Mention must also be made of the new development 'CD-Online' from Philips, which can be used to connect the television set to the Internet world. CD-Online is intended to supplement Philips' well-known 'CD-i' system (Compact Disc interactive). CD-i offers not only interactive games and the playback of feature films, photos and music in digital picture and sound quality but also makes it possible to interactively handle themes from the areas of culture, art, music, health and sport.

Combining CD-i and CD-Online results in further new interactive services, for example games with other partners on the Internet or ordering from a catalogue, storing the text with pictures and video sequences on the CD, while the current prices can be requested and orders placed over the online connection.

The set-top box

The interactive systems described above have been developed for the analogue world. For the new digital world they have to be adapted accordingly. The set-top box will stand at the centre of the new digital services as an auxiliary decoder in the viewer's home.

The television set, on the other hand, will only be used to show pictures and to reproduce the sound. The set-top box converts the digital signals which are received by cable, satellite or telephone connections into analogue signals and passes them on to the television set, the video recorder or the stereo set. In addition, a CD-ROM drive and a PC can be connected.

Figure 4: Set Top Box (Media Box)

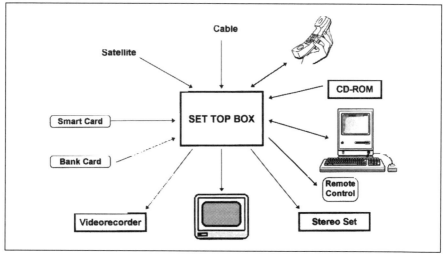

Source: G. Eitz, IRT

A scanner for bank cards and a so-called 'Smart Card' are also integrated into the set-top box.

It is thus possible to pay for subscriber programmes directly or by means of so-called tokens or to store access rights already acquired. The set-top box is controlled by the user's own remote control.

The development of the television set for the set-top box is certainly a quantum leap as far as the extent and functionality of the hard- and software are concerned. The processor controls the satellite or cable tuner, the demultiplex procedure and the decoding of the different video, audio and data packets. Additionally, the processor queries the remote control and manages further processes for operating the telephone modem, the scanners and the external equipment that is connected (CD-ROM drive and PC).

The set-top box can be used for receiving and decoding not only 'Near-Video-on-Demand' but also 'Pay-per-Channel', 'Pay-per-View' and 'Pay-per-Time' services. Table 4 gives an overview of the possible interactive services of the set-top box.

Much in the same way as with a PC, programme and data modules can, automatically or at the instigation of the user, also be loaded out of the digital data stream or over the telephone modem and executed. With these programmes (applications), loadable by remote control, the set-top box first becomes interactive. The bandwidth of the various applications ranges from user-controlled graphics, the electronic TV guide, the applications for booking pay-TV programmes to interactive games, calling up other programme modules on CD-ROM or the Internet and decoding teletext and DataBroadcast services.

Table 4: Future interactive services

	Local	Interaction with
	interaction	broadcasting centre
		Pay-per-Channel TV
	Near-Video-on-Demand TV	Pay-per-View TV
		Pay-per-Time TV
Set-top box	Applications:	
(Media box)	TV guide	Homeshopping
	Teletext (incl. Subtitles)	Viewers' queries
	Data services	Return channel
	Games	applications
	Teleteaching	

The set-top box was introduced on the market in Germany at the end of 1996. The predominant use of the set-top box will be for digital Pay-TV, which will gradually be expanded by the inclusion of other interactive services.

The outlook
With the introduction of digital interactive television the supply and competitive situation will undergo radical changes resulting from large numbers of new commercial genres and specialised channels. By means of the return channel the viewer will have a chance to express his opinion in a simple way and to take part in polls.

It is not to be expected, however, that the viewer in the near future will advance from a zapper to a film director. Instead, he will be given the chance to subscribe to cinema films, to take part in games and to order from mail order catalogues. But there will also be an opportunity for the viewer to be introduced into a new world of learning for culture and education and to supplement the programme he has chosen with further information from teletext, online and DataBroadcasting services and CD-ROM according to his ideas and requirements.

Gerhard Eitz *studied Communication Engineering at the Technische Universität München from 1968 to 1972. In 1973 he completed his diploma dissertation at the Institut für Rundfunktechnik in Munich, where he has been a scientific collaborator since 1974. He has worked on various new technical developments such as extensions to teletext, data broadcast, procedures for rectifying errors and for compressing data, etc. He has also worked on national and international committees for radio (EBU) and European industry (EACEM) on the standardisation of teletext, data broadcast and DVB.*

A Brief Introduction to the IRT

The *Institut für Rundfunktechnik* (IRT) is the research and development body of the public broadcasting authorities in Germany (ARD and ZDF), the Austrian Broadcasting Corporation (ORF) and the Swiss Radio and Television Corporation (SRG).

The IRT co-operates in national and international Projects with R&D bodies of broadcasters of other countries as well as with industry and universities, and thus contributes to an efficient exploitation of available R&D resources. The IRT sees its role as that of a technical adviser to broadcasters as well as a body for industry to contact with technical problems related to broadcasting.

The R&D activities of the IRT focus mainly on the improvement of existing analogue systems and on the development of new systems for radio and television, which will be all digital.

Examples where IRT has played a major role in system development and succesful introduction into practical operation are:

- the PAL colour television system
- electronic slow motion
- dual channel sound in television
- the teletext system 'Videotext'
- the Radio Data System (RDS)
- Digital Satellite Radio (DSR)
- the Video Programme System (VPS)
- the digital sound coding system MUSICAM.

The intense involvement over the past years in the fields of frequency planning and room and building acoustics as well as the support in all matters related to sound and television studio planning have led to a high level of competence. Experts from IRT represent German broadcasters in all major national and international standardisation bodies.

Address: Institut für Rundfundtechnik, Floriansmühlstr. 60, D-80939, Munich.

Has international cooperation a future?

Chris Jelley
Chairman, EBU Education Group

In recent years education has been high on the European Broadcasting Union's agenda. In May 1995 at an important meeting of the Administrative Council its members were asked to support a radical new initiative designed to boost the production and distribution of educational television.

The Educational Television Clearing Unit
Arising out of the activities of the EBU's Education Programme Group, 14 Broadcasting Organisations, some with the support of their Ministries of Education, have made a commitment to support the creation by the EBU of an Educational Television Clearing Unit designed to promote the broadcasting and use of educational television programmes, both nationally and internationally.

In May other EBU broadcasters were asked to approve the Unit's creation – the appointment of a permanent staff of 3 and a business plan for the first four years of its operation – planned to start in September 1996.

The Clearing Unit will be based in Geneva, it will have a budget of over 600,000 Swiss Francs a year, and most importantly under the new terms of the EBU it is to be self-financing after two years. It represents a major commitment for all concerned, and a measure of their commitment to and belief in the future of Educational Television and International Cooperation.

In this paper I want to explain:

- why we think the time is right to create an Educational Television Clearing Unit;
- what the Clearing Unit will do; and
- why we think it can be successful.

First, then, why do we think that now is a good time to seek to promote educational television?

A Chance for educational television
We are currently witnessing developments along a number of paths each of which provides a reason to believe that educational television will prosper.

In the field of technology, the combination of developments in satellite and cable transmission plus a shift from analogue to digital technology is resulting in a rapid growth in the number of television channels that viewers can watch. What I think is particularly interesting and heartening for those involved in educational television is that many of these new channels are niche factual and educational channels.

Joyce Taylor has already talked about the Discovery and Learning Channels, and we have heard from *ARTE* and *La Cinquième*. The United States is perhaps the area where there is most evidence of success: not just the Discovery Networks but Arts and Entertainment, the History Channel and Jones Cable are very prominent. In Asia, BBC Worldwide Learning are developing plans for educational channels along with many others, and educational channels are emerging in South America, South Africa, and of course here in Europe other educational channels are being planned.

These channels represent an emerging opportunity for educational producers and owners of educational television programmes as each channel has an enormous demand for programming, not all of which they can afford to originate themselves.

Secondly, a technological development which we sometimes ignore, the video recorder. Mass ownership of video recorders is most developed in western countries and now allows broadcasters to transmit programmes which appeal to minorities during the night hours, so that minority audiences who want to use the programmes can record them for later use.

At first this use of the night time hours was limited to schools broadcasts but now in the U.K. the BBC transmits *The Learning Zone* between midnight and 4.00 a.m. – this provides a range of educational programmes, some linked to Open University courses, others at a lower level, including language and business programmes. These television programmes may reach small audiences but their impact can be considerable and taken in conjunction with their associated educational courses and publications, can provide an important educational service, and earn revenue for the provider.

The third technological development which we have already heard about today is in interactive television services. Many broadcasters now have their own Netsite on the Internet. Which they use to advertise programmes and sell videos and associated educational courses and materials. At present the Internet cannot deliver television programmes or moving video fast enough for acceptable reception so the Internet relevance to educational television is limited to promotion. But online delivery of television using fibre optic cable is probably only a couple of years away in many countries.

As many of you know, in the United Kingdom British Telecom is currently running an online trial, offering over 5,000 homes a range of television services on demand. Each home has a set top box and remote control which is simple to use enabling users to call up for almost instantaneous transmission to their home a range of services. The services include movies, music, games and children's TV, a 'What's On in Your Local Area' service, with local news, schools providing promotional videos and local authorities giving information about services they offer. They are also offering a service of educational programmes, some schools documentaries, health education, cookery and various 'How To ...' programmes. This educational service, far from being ignored, is the third next popular service after movies and local news. So online services present another new secondary market for the owners of educational television programmes.

Interactive technologies

But perhaps the most exciting technological development for the owners of educational television programmes is currently CD-ROM and CD-I. CD-ROM offers a new and educationally important secondary use of television moving pictures and sound. The broadcaster now has the opportunity to excite and motivate the viewer with an entertaining but educational television programme which then can refer the interested viewer on to pursue his or her interest in the subject by acquiring a CD-ROM or CD-I. This will allow the viewer to go into more depth than the TV programme, study the information, pictures, text, archive film at his or her leisure and re-read or watch key passages from a TV sequence or text. I believe that CD-ROM and CD-I will enhance the broadcasters ability to meet viewers' demand for knowledge.

Educationally, the new interactive technologies are immeasurably satisfying, combining many of the motivational benefits of television with the ability to read detailed text and go at your own pace – and as such they complement educational television, providing the detailed back-up and support to a viewer's interest which has been aroused by broadcast television. And, what is important, the market for educational CD-Rom is expanding very rapidly.

In the UK at the end of 1995, there were 2.9 million personal computers – that is 12 per cent of all homes possessed a PC. All secondary schools and over half of the primary schools possessed a PC but, more significantly, 1995 had seen a 45 per cent growth in PC sales and 95 per cent of all those PC sales included a CD-ROM drive.

But, one may be asking, do people use personal computers for education? Well, education is given as one of the five main reasons for buying PCs and the level of sales of educational CD-ROM indicates that, yes, people are interested in interactive educational software, they do buy it and in increasing quantities.

Education matters

The truth is that education does matter to people. Many ordinary people are passionately concerned to improve their own understanding and skills and of course they are concerned for their children's education. This is an international phenomenon: education is high on many people's priorities.

Politically, here in Europe the significance of education is recognised. The ratification of the Maastricht treaty has set the European Community the task of becoming more active in the field of education. As a response two major new education programmes have been launched:

- *Leonardo* for vocational training;
- *Socrates* for general education including distance learning.

These two programmes provide political support and financial means for those who become involved in them, and of course 1996 has been designated *European Year of Lifelong Learning*.

The progressive integration of Western Europe and radical changes in Eastern Europe have made us all aware of the need for measures to help ensure the harmonious development of Europe – a development in which people learn to understand each other's cultural identity, for each country has its own identity, whilst at the same time being able to work alongside and with others.

Integration and economic mobility demand an understanding of other people's language, culture and ways of doing business, from simple questions of etiquette, to the legal and tax questions also associated with international trade. There is a role for educational television in facilitating this process and meeting this need, and television programmes which address these European and international needs will have a significant audience.

It is against this background of confidence that there is an expanding demand for educational programmes from viewers and broadcasters alike and a real need for educational programmes that cross political and cultural frontiers, that speak to people from different cultures, that 14 European Broadcasters are proposing to establish an Educational Television Clearing Unit. But what will the Unit do?

The tasks of the Clearing Unit

The Educational Television Clearing Unit will provide its subscribing members with a range of services – classified under four broad headings:

1. *Programme Production* – generating new television programmes.
2. *Funding* – raising funds from European, national and international institutions and commercial enterprises.
3. *Educational Publishing* – the development of educational materials, distance learning courses, books, CD-ROM and CD-I associated with its members' programmes.
4. *Distribution* – the marketing and distribution of educational programmes throughout Europe and the rest of the world.

In practice, what does this mean? Firstly, Programme Production: The Unit will initiate or assist with the development of educational programmes, often coproductions. It will gather partners together, a group of broadcasters who will each contribute to the financing of the programmes

238

in return for the right to transmit in their own territory. It will coordinate the agreement of programme content, which production company or combination of companies will make the programme. It will, with the assistance of the EBU's legal and financial departments, draw up the legal coproduction contracts and administer any necessary financing. It will use its experience to advise on the acquisition of rights and the opportunities for exploitation.

Educational broadcasters in the EBU already have considerable experience of mounting successful coproductions – programmes which meet the needs and requirements of a range of broadcasters from different countries. These coproductions often have to be devised so that different versions can be produced for different countries – a different language sound track is one obvious requirement – and in this case the producer has to be experienced enough to recognise that some languages require more time to articulate information than others.

We foresee the Unit developing a wide range of programming, from popular documentaries featuring human interest stories, historical dramas, travel and holiday programmes, music and arts programmes to programmes about health and family relationships – programmes which can appeal to the general public in a range of countries.

Then there will be programmes which inform and educate viewers about political, economic and social life within Europe, then more specialised programmes which inform and update people about business and management practice and give information about working conditions and job opportunities in Europe all these backed up by language programmes. And finally but not least because these have historically been some of the most successful – there will be programmes for children at home and school to supplement their education.

The importance of international coproductions

In case this sounds rather idealistic, which of course it is, let me tell you that such international coproductions are already in production – as we speak, a second series of *Kontakt Deutsch*, a language course for people who need to be able to speak and understand German at work, is being planned.

This will accompany the first series which was produced as a European coproduction by the Finnish Broadcasting Company for *Deutsche Welle* and *TransTel*, the Swedish Broadcasting Company, the Danish, the Norwegian, the Irish and Czech Television.

Work in Progress, a seven-part series about the future of work and how the working environment and work practice is changing as we move towards the millennium – is being produced by an independent television production company for Westdeutscher Rundfunk, RTE Ireland, Swiss Broadcasting and Finland.

The *History of Arts*, coproduced by CNDP for ARD, Switzerland, Belgium, the Czech Republic, Portugal and Catalonia, is another copro-

239

duction in progress, and one which crosses national frontiers, speaking to the peoples of Europe. The organisation of this coproduction is, however, different from the former two examples. In *Kontakt Deutsch* and *Work in Progress* all the programmes are made by one company working to an executive producer who co-ordinates the views of the coproduction partners. This method of working ensures a common style and production values on all programmes.

The *History of Arts* coproduction, however, is an exchange of programmes each produced by the coproducers themselves using their own facilities with a central coordinator. The advantage of this structure is that it allows Eastern European countries who cannot easily obtain hard currency to pay for a foreign producer to make an entire series, to nevertheless participate in an exchange of programming enabling them to get a series of 6, 8 or 10 programmes depending on the number of participating coproducers for the price of a single programme. Exchanges like these are often the only way that broadcasters without access to hard currency can obtain high quality programming featuring international subject matter.

The importance of such educational programming, and particularly programming which is of benefit to Eastern European countries, is well recognised by European political institutions. So it will not be a surprise to hear that the European Union's Commission has made available a considerable tranche of funding to support the establishment of the Educational Television Clearing Unit, within the context of 1996 being the *European Year of Lifelong Learning*, and that the EBU has made an application for further funding from Directorate General XXII.

National governments too have been most receptive of our plans and the German Federal Ministry of Science and Technology has earmarked a significant sum in its 1996 budget to support the activities of the Clearing Unit. The truth is that the many of the television programmes which the Unit will be developing are precisely those which will be most likely to further those European Educational Needs that I have referred to earlier.

Programmes which will support continuing education and training, school education and initial vocational training. These television programmes will often promote amongst viewers internationally a mutual understanding of our diverse European cultures, help the workforce to be more mobile and raise understanding of the activities of the European Union. Such programmes will do much to raise public awareness of the many opportunities that exist for people to study or undergo training. Either through distance learning courses or by attending study classes locally near their homes or of course using the new technologies CD-ROM, CD-I and Online Services.

Raising funds for individual projects from European and national institutions to help fund international educational coproductions will be a second and important role for the Educational Clearing Unit. Fund raising is never easy but we are confident from our experience to date that, for the right projects, it will be possible to raise funds, at least for individual programmes, and that this is much more easily achieved when programmes will be broadcast in several countries, especially including those in Eastern Europe, than when they are aimed at a single, more limited national market.

A third task for the Unit will be to establish the links with national and international educational institutions to publicise, and where appropriate, develop educational and training courses which link to the television programmes. Of course in many cases television programmes are devised to be used alongside an existing course. The EBU's television series on technology, for example, is used throughout Europe in schools as a resource which enhances the science and technology curriculum. Another example, a coproduction on import/export management is used in Portugal, Belgium and the Netherlands alongside existing courses.

But an important new dimension for the Clearing Unit will be in recasting educational television programmes into other forms of media – CD-ROM, CD-I or Online Services. In this they will need to seek out new parties from the world of publishing – the new multimedia corporations as well as the broadcasters. The fact is that there are few public service broadcasters who can find the funds themselves to develop these new resources. If you are a broadcaster funded by a general licence fee levied on all viewers it is difficult to justify using that money to develop services that will not be freely available to all your licence fee payers but for which they will have to pay.

No, the Unit will need to form new partnerships, with the international media groups the Philips, the Pearsons, the Bertelsmanns and others to help its subscribing members exploit their educational programme resources. My own company, Yorkshire Television, for example, has formed a joint venture with the Thomson Corporation to develop multimedia educational materials, taking advantage of Thomson's funding capacity, its knowledge of educational publications and its ability to distribute internationally, to convert and develop our own television library of educational programmes. In the same way, we anticipate that the Clearing Unit will help its subscribing members to enter into similar relationships designed to get the maximum use of their educational resources. And that brings me to the fourth function of the Unit.

The Educational Clearing Unit will assist its members in the marketing and distribution of their educational programmes throughout Europe and the rest of the world. In most broadcasting organisations certainly the Public Service ones, educational programmes are often sold by a sales team who are also selling drama, current affairs and entertainment. So when the sales person visits a buyer he naturally want to sell the most popular, the most profitable TV series. So the first programme to be shown will be the drama, the top rating entertainment show – not the educational programme. Inevitably with this organisation, educational programmes have not been marketed very vigorously.

We believe that the Unit will have an important role to play as a specialist distributor of Educational Programmes. It will, on request, evaluate programmes selecting those with international potential. It will compile a catalogue detailing members' programmes, selecting those with international potential and providing the names and addresses of its members' sales agents.

So for any channel wishing to acquire educational material, the Clearing Unit will become an essential first call – a single place where a buyer can go to find what is available – and incidentally to say what they are looking for and hence sow the seeds of possible production opportunities.

In this context one of the first actions of the Unit will be to organise and administer a new Educational Programme Market. Detailed planning of this is already being undertaken by the EBU's Educational Group and the first market will take place in April 1997 in Rotterdam. It will be open to all buyers and sellers of educational television programmes, and will have the advantage over other markets of being tightly focused on education and of assembling all new educational programming with international potential under a single roof.

Clearly these are ambitious plans for the Educational Clearing Unit, encompassing, generating new production, fund raising, educational publishing and distribution, and the EBU will make its final decision in May whether to go ahead. Will it succeed, can such a unit provide a valuable service for its members? Can it be self-financing?

We believe that it can, and the reason? Well quite simply, the EBU's Educational Group has been quite successful in the past few years – and this has been on the basis of a few individuals in interested European educational broadcasting organisations working on a voluntary part-time basis, whilst at the same time running Educational Programme Departments or producing television series. The Unit will be staffed three full-time professionals recruited over the next three months from the very best educational broadcasters and publishers and working in the most well equipped of working environments with the enthusiastic support of all the experience and knowledge of the EBU's permanent staff – for whom this is an important first international broadcasting project – one by which they can prove that international cooperation in educational broadcasting can bring significant benefits for its members.

PS: Since this talk was given, the EBU´s Educational Administrative Council has approved the establishment of the Educational Television Clearing Unit, and Robert Winter, formerly Commercial and Business Development Manager for BBC News and Current Affairs, has been appointed Project Leader to spearhead the Unit´s work.

Chris Jelley, *after 15 years as Yorkshire Television's Controller of Education, Religion and, since 1986, Children's Programmes, was appointed Director of Television and Video for Yorkshire International Thomson Multimedia Ltd. (YITM), a joint venture between Yorkshire Television and Thomas Nelson Ltd. that has been established to develop and market television programmes, CD-ROMs and video products for educational use. At Yorkshire Television, he was responsible for the development of ITV's largest and most successful educational television department. Before joining Yorkshire Television he was a television producer at BBC Television for ten years. Chris Jelley is Chairman of the European Broadcasting Union's Education Group.*

The Educational TV Unit's first steps

1. Two-way communication with all of the subscribers in order to gather their educational material and data, and to build a strategic 'picture' of the strengths of this new educational platform.
2. To communicate the existence of the Unit to all international programme markets and buyers, in order to seek outlets for existing programmes, and to help develop new coproductions and new opportunities for commercial exploitation.
3. To develop strong relationships and joint venture partnerships with commercial organisations and associations who can help fund the development of exciting and new educational learning materials and publishing opportunities.
4. To design and present a new electronic catalogue of all subscribers' material and publish this and other educational resource data on a new web site created for the Educational Unit. This will be linked to the subscribers' own web sites and to the main EBU web site.

In 1997 the Educational TV Unit has appeared and plans to appear at the Rotterdam Education Market, the Milia New Media Market in Cannes, and the MIP TV Market in Cannes.

Appendix
List of Abbreviations

A2 (A2F)   Antenne 2, France
ABC   Australian Broadcasting Corporation
ARD   Arbeitsgemeinschaft der öffentlich-rechtlichen Rundfunkanstalten der Bundesrepublik Deutschland, Germany
BARB   Broadcasters' Audience Research Board, United Kingdom
BBC   British Broadcasting Corporation, United Kingdom
BBC/OUPC   BBC Open University Production Centre, United Kingdom
BR   Bayerischer Rundfunk, Germany
BRF   Belgisches Rundfunk- und Fernsehzentrum der Deutschsprachigen Gemeinschaft, Belgium
BRT   Belgische Radio en Televisie, Belgium
BRTN   Belgische Radio en Televisie, Nederlandse uitzendingen, Belgium
CEN   Central Independent Television, United Kingdom
C4   Channel Four, United Kingdom
CNDP   Centre National de Documentation Pédagogique, France
CPB   Corporation for Public Broadcasting, United States
CT   Ceská Televize, Czech Republic
DR   Danmarks Radio, Denmark
DRS   Radio- und Fernsehgesellschaft der deutschen und der rätoromanischen Schweiz, Switzerland
DW   Deutsche Welle, Germany
EAC   Education Advisory Council, United Kingdom
EBC   Education Broadcasting Councils, United Kingdom
EBS   BBC Educational Broadcasting Services, United Kingdom
EBU   European Broadcasting Union
ERT   Elliniki Radiophonia Tileorassis SA (Greek Radio and Television), Greece
ETC   Educational Television Company, United Kingdom
FR3   France Régions 3, France
GTV   Granada Television, United Kingdom
HR   Hessischer Rundfunk, Germany
IBA   Independent Broadcasting Authority, United Kingdom
IETV   Israel Educational Television, Israel
ILEA   Inner London Education Authority, United Kingdom

ITV	Independent Television, United Kingdom
ITC	Independent Television Commission, United Kingdom
ITN	Independent Television News, United Kingdom
IZI	Internationales Zentralinstitut für das Jugend- und Bildungsfernsehen, Germany
JRT	Jugoslovenska Radiotelevizija, Yugoslavia
MBA	Malta Broadcasting Authority, Malta
MTV	Magyar Rádio és Te;evízío, Hungary
N3	'Nordkette', Norddeutscher Rundfunk (NDR), Germany
NDR	Norddeutscher Rundfunk, Germany
NHK	Nippon Hoso Kyokai, Japan
NOS	Nederlandse Omroep Stichting, Netherlands
NOT	Nederlandse Onderwijs Televisie, Netherlands
NRK	Norsk Rikskringkasting, Norway
OECD	Organisation for Economic Co-operation and Development
OIRT	Organisation Internationale de Radiodiffusion et de Télévision, Czechoslovakia
ORF	Österreichischer Rundfunk, Austria
OFRT	Organismes Français de Radiodiffusion et de Télévision, France
PBS	Public Broadcasting Service, United States
PRT	Polskie Radio i Telewizja, Poland
RAI	Radiotelevisione Italiana, Italy
RB	Radio Bremen, Germany
RTB	Radiotelevizija Beograd, Yugoslavia
RTBF	Radio-Télévision Belge de la Communauté Française, Belgium
RTE	Radio Telefís Éireann, Ireland
RTP	Radiotelevisão Portuguesa, Portugal
RTSR	Radio-Télévision Suisse Romande, Switzerland
RTVE	Radiotelevisión Española, Spain
RUV	Rikisutvarpid-Sjonvarp (Icelandic State Broadcasting Service — Television), Iceland
RVU	Radio Volks Universiteit; Educatieve Omroep, Netherlands
SDR	Süddeutscher Rundfunk, Germany
SFB	Sender Freies Berlin, Germany
SR	Saarländischer Rundfunk, Germany
SR	Sveriges Radio Ab (Swedish Broadcasting Corporation), Sweden
SR/UR	Sveriges Utbildningsradio Ab (Swedish Educational Broadcasting Company), Sweden
SRG	Schweizerische Radio- und Fernsehgesellschaft, Switzerland
SSR	Société Suisse de Radiodiffusion et Télévision, Switzerland
STV	Scottish Television, United Kingdom
S3	Südwest 3, Germany
SWF	Südwestfunk, Germany
TELEAC	Stichting Televisie Academie, Netherlands
TRT	Türkiye Radyo-Televizyon Kurumu, Turkey

TRU	Kommittén för television och radio i utbildningen, Sweden
TSI	Televisione della Svizzera Italiana, Switzerland
TSR	Télévision Suisse Romande, Switzerland
TVE	Televisión Española, Spain
UKIB	United Kingdom Independent Broadcasting, United Kingdom
UER	Union Européenne de Radiodiffusion (EBU)
UTV	Ulster Television, United Kingdom
W3	West 3, Westdeutsches Fernsehen (WDF), Germany
WDF	Westdeutsches Fernsehen, Germany
WDR	Westdeutscher Rundfunk, Germany
YLE	OY Yleisradio Ab, Finland
YTV	Yorkshire Television, United Kingdom
ZDF	Zweites Deutsches Fernsehen, Germany